MASS VIOLENCE IN AMERICA

Advisory editors:

MASS VIOLENCE IN AMERICA

CHICAGO TO-DAY

THE LABOUR WAR IN AMERICA

W. T. Stead

ARNO PRESS & THE NEW YORK TIMES

New York • 1969

Editorial Note

Nations, like men, are sometimes interested in burying the past.

In early 1968, after more than five years marked by political assassinations, racial uprisings, campus disorders, mass demonstrations and the violent suppression of protest, *The New York Times Magazine* asked a group of distinguished scholars to reply to the question, "Is America by nature a violent society?" In answer, University of Chicago anthropologist Clifford Geertz wrote:

> "We do not know very well what kind of society we live in, what kind of history we have had, what kind of people we are. We are just now beginning to find out, the hard way . . ."

The proposition was astonishing but correct: what was least understood about domestic political violence was its role in American history. It was common knowledge that the United States had had a Revolution, a Civil War, some trouble with the Indians and a period of labor-management conflict. But one could search the shelves of the nation's great libraries without discovering more than a handful of works on the subject of violence in American history, and these hopelessly out of date.

Historians had generally ignored or soft-pedaled the history of farmer uprisings, native vigilantism, labor-management struggles, ethnic conflicts and race riots; comparative work in the history of social conflict was particularly weak. Sociologists and political scientists in the grip of "consensus" theory tended to treat episodes of mass violence in America as insignificant or aberrational—temporary exceptions to the norm of peaceful progress. Psychologists and behavioral scientists discussed "mob violence" in terms which suggested that riots, revolts, insurrections and official violence were the products of individual or group pathology. All such interpretations had the effect not only of minimizing group violence in America, but of depriving it of political content—hence, of relevance to the present.

As a result, as late as 1968, the rich, multifarious and often terrifying history of domestic political violence was still largely *terra incognita*. So long as most Americans wished to keep certain skeletons locked away in their closets, few scholars would attempt to open doors. Conversely, once the American people, frightened yet emboldened by the sudden reappearance of intense social conflict, began to ask new questions about the past, so did the scholars.

Our purpose in helping Arno Press and *The New York Times* select and publish significant documents in the history of political violence has not been to compound past errors by overemphasizing the role of conflict in American history. On the contrary, our aim has been to provide materials which will aid in the search for an accurate perspective on the present. MASS VIOLENCE IN AMERICA includes eyewitness reports, government documents and other descriptive and analytic material relating to mass political violence in the United States. These documents not only provide information—they give the "feel" or "flavor" of past eras of civil disorder by evoking the emotional and political context in which revolts took place. Most of them have long been out of print and are obtainable, if at all, only in the nation's largest libraries.

The scope of this series is wide, ranging from accounts of Indian warfare to descriptions of labor-management violence, from narratives of colonial insurrections to reports on modern racial uprisings. It is not, however, limitless, nor were the constituent volumes carelessly selected. The principle of coherence which guided the selections is implicit in the phrase "mass political violence." "Mass" denotes activity engaged in by large groups rather than individuals acting alone; "political" suggests a relationship between such activity and competition among domestic groups for power, property and prestige; and "violence" is narrowly construed as resulting in physical damage to persons or property. In short, the materials reproduced herein are intended to illuminate the resort to violence by American groups seeking to change or to preserve the status quo. Although historical, they are of interest to any who wishes to understand the causes, nature and direction of domestic political violence, whether they be social scientists, historians or just interested Americans.

Of course, we are particularly hopeful that these volumes will prove useful to those now engaged in curriculum-revision and the teaching of high school and college courses in the area of American studies. What Christopher Jencks and David Reisman term "the Academic Revolution" has made difficult demands on all educators, not the least of which is the demand for courses which are both relevant to the condition of modern America and of the highest academic quality. These volumes are meant to provide raw material for such courses— primary source matter which will help both instructors and students to deepen and enrich their views of the American experience.

Most important, the editors and publisher recognize that these volumes appear during a national crisis which is also a crisis of the spirit, a time in which the public response to various manifestations of civil disorder is increasingly governed by anger, fear and hysteria. In such an atmosphere it is important to recognize that one is not alone in time—that such events have taken place before in America and, unless fundamental changes in our social and political life take place, will probably recur in the future. Our fondest hope is that this work, and others like it, will help to keep alive, in a time of growing unreason, the spirit of reasoned inquiry.

RICHARD E. RUBENSTEIN
The Adlai Stevenson Institute
Chicago, Illinois

ROBERT M. FOGELSON
Harvard-MIT Joint Center
for Urban Studies
Cambridge, Massachusetts

CHICAGO TO-DAY

THE LABOUR WAR IN AMERICA

THE WORKING MAN AND HIS VAMPIRE.

(BUT IS THE VAMPIRE RIGHTLY LABELLED?)

(*From a design by Herr Otto Marcus, reproduced from " Der Wahrer Jacob."*)

CHICAGO TO-DAY;

OR,

THE LABOUR WAR IN AMERICA.

BY

W. T. STEAD.

Then I looked back along his path,
  And heard the clash of steel on steel,
Where man faced man in deadly wrath,
  While clanged the tocsin's hurrying peal.
The sky with burning towns flared red,
  Nearer the noise of fighting rolled,
And brothers' blood by brothers shed,
  Crept curdling over pavements cold.
I shouted, but he would not hear,
  Made signs, but these he could not see,
And still without a doubt or fear
  Broadcast he scattered Anarchy.

  The Sower of the Old World in the New.
                                    LOWELL.

LONDON:
"REVIEW OF REVIEWS" OFFICE.
1894.

LONDON:
PRINTED BY WILLIAM CLOWES AND SONS, LIMITED,
STAMFORD STREET AND CHARING CROSS.

PREFACE.

THE recent terrible outburst of industrial war in the United States of America leads me to issue this brief and rapid survey of the events which have occurred this summer at Chicago.

During my sojourn last winter in that great city, I had the opportunity of making the personal acquaintance of most of those who are leading the forces on either side, and since my return to London I have neglected no opportunity of keeping myself informed of the way in which things were going.

In this volume I have endeavoured to piece together several more or less fragmentary studies of the labour movement and the problems which it raises in America to-day. Three of the chapters have appeared respectively in the *Contemporary Review*, the *New Review*, and the *Review of Reviews*, but the bulk of the work is now printed for the first time.

I hope I may be excused for reproducing some passages from my earlier book, "If Christ came to Chicago?" They are very brief, and they are necessary to the due presentation of the case. With that exception this book covers new ground, and may be said to be in some sense as a sequel up to date of the other volume.

All who are interested in the evolution of modern society from the competitive to the co-operative stage in human progress will find the story of this Labour War full of intense interest, both for its cruel pathos and its ominous suggestions. The outbreak, although violent, was by no means unexpected. I wrote on leaving Chicago in March :—

"I have had some little experience of agitation in the Old World, and I must say that I have never seen a condition of things in an English-speaking land where the signs point so unmistakably to change, and it may be to violent change. . . . There is ample need for the advent of a Peter the Hermit if the social crisis in America is not to culminate in bloodshed. The working people without allies have given no hostages to fortune, and have no visible reason for refraining from violence. It is true that violence will injure them in the long run far more than it can help them : but like all men who suffer and who are weak, they think more of the immediate winning of a strike by knocking a few 'scabs' on the head than of the permanent loss which such violence inflicts upon their cause. If they had been within the pale they would long ere this have emerged from the stage of incipient Thuggee in which many of them dwell."

"A stage of incipient Thuggee" seemed rather a hard phrase to apply, but unfortunately subsequent events show that it was only too well justified.

W. T. STEAD.

LONDON, *July* 11*th*, 1894.

CONTENTS.

Contents.

PART III.—WAR.

PART IV.—DEFEAT.

APPENDIX.

MR. J. S. COXEY,

President of the "J. S. Coxey Good Roads Association of United States."

CHICAGO TO-DAY;

OR,

THE LABOUR WAR IN AMERICA.

PART I.

THE RIDDLE OF THE SPHINX.

CHAPTER I.—THE CRY OF THE UNEMPLOYED.

THE First Armoury in Chicago was last year the scene of a fatal fire. It is a massive fortress of brown stone, standing in Michigan Avenue within gunshot of the Millionaire's Row, a grim and burly warder behind whose shadow Messrs. Pullman, Armour, and Field can sleep in peace. When I was in Chicago it was an empty ruin. The interior was heaped with ashes and debris. The fire-scarred ruins which were still standing testified to the fierceness of the flames which had raged as in a furnace within the four walls of the Armoury. When the fire broke out it was at night, after the massive sallyport had been securely locked, and the inmates—two or three coloured men employed as janitors—had gone to sleep. No sooner had the alarm been given than the nre-engines were on the spot, only to discover that all access to the massive Armoury was impossible. The lofty walls, erected of a strength sufficient to defy all attacks by hostile mobs or by an army unprovided with artillery,

B 2

offered no point of ingress for the fireman with his hose. The narrow loopholed windows, which were a safe protection against bullets, were not less efficacious against water. The only means of obtaining access to the building so as to fight the flames, which were every moment gaining ground, was by the door. But the door was locked. The key could not be found ; and from the interior of the great building flames mingled with smoke climbed up into the midnight air.

The firemen were baffled. While they were anxiously deliberating what should be done, their attention was suddenly arrested by a terrible sound. Inside the building, fast becoming a flaming fiery furnace, were heard sounds that told only too plainly that human beings were within, frantic with dread of being burned alive. The firemen tried in vain to burst open the massive door. It defied their utmost efforts. A howitzer would not have burst open the portal of the Armoury. Huge sledge-hammers pounding upon the ironclad gate only served as signals of unavailing hope to the doomed inside. Then re-membering the tremendous pressure of water, they turned jets from all available hose upon the stubborn door. But all these tons of steady pressure failed even to strain the door on its hinges. The knocking within grew fainter and fainter. The cries of agonised despair became weaker and weaker. Eager and stalwart men, with all the resources of the great city at their back, were straining every effort that in-genuity could suggest or human energy could carry out to rescue the doomed prisoners on the other side of the door. All was in vain. The door was locked. The key was lost. And so it came to pass that the feeble knocking ceased. No more cries were heard, and when the fire had burnt itself out three or four calcined corpses were found on the other side of the bolted door.

It was a grim and horrible experience, not to be thought of without a shudder ; but it resembles only too closely the miserable tragedy at which civilisation is now assisting in the city of Chicago. The edifice of our competitive commercialism built four-square to all the winds that blow, massive, imposing, im pregnable, has taken fire. But the door is locked, and neither is there any key forthcoming to unlock the wards of the great gate through which the inmates might go free. The world watches and sickens with horror ; but the fire burns, the flames mount higher and higher, and there seems to be no escape. It is the tragedy of the Armoury fire rehearsed on a thousandfold greater scale.

Chicago has become for the moment only too authentic a reproduction of the Bull of Phalarus, nor can any way of escape be suggested for the victims. The denunciations of the press,. and the invectives which are freely showered on all concerned from one side to the other, are as impotent as the hammers and the water-jets with which the firemen endeavoured to force open the door of the Armoury. Day by day as the Old World and the New keep watching the progress of the blaze, the more hopeless seem to be the efforts to extinguish the conflagration. It all results from one thing. The door is locked, and the key is not to be found. The key in the present instance was at first in the keeping of Mr. Pullman, to whose dogged refusal to permit any reference whatever of the dispute to arbitration is due the whole of the catastrophe ; but its real root lies deeper. It is to be found in the rooted distrust which is the canker of American civilisation. In business, men have forgotten God, they have lost faith in man, and they are reaping the penalty. From of old was it not written, " If ye be willing and obedient, ye shall eat of the fat of the land, but, if ye refuse and rebel, ye shall be devoured by the sword, for the mouth of the Lord hath spoken it."

This is not merely true of the immediate dispute and of the refusal of Mr. Pullman to accept any form of reference to arbitration. In every direction, wherever we turn, we are confronted with the same phenomenon. In place of the co-operation of confidence, there is everywhere the fiercest rivalry of cut-throat competition, eating confidence out of the heart of man. If, as Aristotle said long ago, civilisation can be measured by the extent to which suspicion has been replaced by confidence, then, in the headlong rush after the Almighty Dollar, the attainment of which has almost become the chief end of man, we are face to face with a very real retrogression towards barbarism.

It would seem as if we were witnessing the break-up of the old commercialism, which seems as if it were about to expire amid convulsions possibly as violent as those which marked the disappearance of feudalism from Europe at the close of last century. But he would be a bold man who would assert that even now the labour pains of the new era have begun, they may be but false pains, and the new birth of time may still be many years distant. Mankind is slow to change, and as long as an old system can be made to do, it lasts. Only when things are quite intolerable do the children of men, more frequently in black despair than in gladsome hope, venture to abandon the old for the untried new.

Even the old Feudalism, which was supposed to
have expired in earthquake and crack of doom, contrived to creep back again with indispensable modi-
fications after millions had died in order that it might
not be, and modern Commercialism seems to have no
less firm a grip upon the world which it has ruled
so long. For one reason, its heirs are not ready for
the heritage, and we must, therefore, regard the industrial convulsion which has just taken place in
America as rather a warning than a judgment. But
of the significance of the warning there can be no
doubt. As usual, it is the economic crisis which
shakes the old system to the ground. At the end of
last century, it was the deficit which forced on the
Revolution, and never was a truer word spoken than
that it was a deficit which saved the Republic. But
for the deficit, the old regime might have continued
secure in all the panoply of its power. So now, at
the end of the 19th century, the unemployed are our
industrial deficit which yawns wider and wider, and
refuses to be choked.

All the trouble in Chicago at this moment has
arisen from the presence of the unemployed. As
John Bright long ago remarked, whenever there are
two men trying to get one man's job, wages go down ;
and it is the presence of a mass of unemployed men
in and about Chicago which has at once provoked the
struggle, and led to the outburst of violence which
has attracted the attention of an amazed and indignant world.

One of the Chicago newspapers, commenting
bitterly upon the Mayor's suggestion that in place of
legislation to close shops on Sunday, the shopmen
should secure their one day's rest in seven by a
strike, asked pertinently enough, "How men could

be expected to strike when every man knew that there
were half-a-dozen others who would eagerly compete
to fill his berth the moment he left the shop ? "
When the boycott of the railroads was declared, an
official of the Illinois Central is said to have remarked
that, if all their 2,000 men left them on the spot,
they could fill their places ten times over from a list
of applications by unemployed men which had been
compiled a short time previously.

Whatever may have been the original cause of the
depression which has affected so severely the great
industrial community of the West, there is no doubt
that it has been aggravated and perpetuated by the
unrest and uncertainty as to the tariff which is due
to the dogged refusal of protected monopolists to bow
to the declared will of the majority of the people.
Until the tariff is settled one way or another no man
knows under what conditions he can manufacture.
It is asserted, not apparently without cause, that those
interested in the maintenance of high duties have
deliberately prolonged the stagnation in order to
emphasise their arguments for perpetuating what is, to
all intents and purposes, a subsidy from the general
public for the enriching of a comparatively small but
very powerful fraction of the community. But even
uncertainty of the tariff would not have done so
much mischief if there had been a little more sense
of brotherhood infused into the business relations,
not only between employers and employed, but
between the employers themselves. However that
may be, it can hardly be said that " each for himself, and the devil take the hindmost," is working very
satisfactorily in the great Republic of the West.

In England we have certainly no reason to indulge
in any Pharisaic reflections upon the misfortuncs of

our American kinsfolk. We have too many illustrations at home of the evil consequences of the working of the same spirit, although fortunately with us they are on the smaller scale which corresponds to the comparative dimensions of our respective countries. But on a smaller scale or large, the riddle of the Sphinx confronts us as well as the United States, and it will best be solved by those who have most of the spirit of Him who said, " Blessed are the peacemakers, for theirs is the kingdom of heaven." Sooner or later the race will learn that it is not merely the kingdom of heaven that is the heritage of the peacemaker. Without the spirit of peace and of brotherhood, and a readiness to bear one another's burdens, all the harvest of the world's wealth seem to turn to dead sea fruit in our mouths.

The providing for the unemployed is one which some Americans are very slow to recognise. At Chicago last winter the question of the relief of the unemployed was one which forced itself upon my attention by the barbarity of housing the casuals in the police-stations and in the corridors of the City Hall. At first there was a disposition to resent the maudlin sentimentality of English philanthropy, and to maintain that the American tramp deserved to be kicked by day and housed in the police-stations at night. But after various ministers, professors, and labour leaders had visited the police-cells and the City Hall, sufficient steam was generated to get the whole question of the relief of the distress taken in hand by a representative committee of citizens. For the first time for many winters the unemployed were furnished with work on the streets, by which they at any rate could earn their rations and pay for lodgings in a decent lodging-house. Hitherto, they had always camped in the corridors of the City Hall or been lodged in the police-stations ; this year they were brigaded into street gangs three thousand strong, and set to work at the necessary work of cleaning the streets. The formation of the Relief Association was due to the Civic Federation. The Committee, unorganised as it was, took the initiative, summoned a conference of all the charitable associations and societies in the city, and at that conference formed a central relief committee, which took the whole subject in hand. Mr. Harvey, well known as Mr. Moody's chairman, and founder of the town of Harvey, who had from the outset taken a great interest in the movement, was appointed chairman of the relief association, and for the next three months he devoted the whole of his time to this necessary and indispensable work. A sum of from £40,000 to £50,000 was raised for the relief. Three thousand men were set to work on the streets. Some two thousand women were assisted through the agency of the Woman's Club and its indefatigable president, Mrs. Dr. Stevenson. It was found, contrary to general belief, that seventy-five per cent. of the men out of work had resided in Chicago for more than five years. The unions did a great deal to support their own members, and the saloon-keepers, by their free lunches, fed a larger number of people than the public and private charities provided for ; and so, by one way or another, the distress was tided over. The men employed in the relief work on the streets were paid ten cents an hour for shifts varying from three hours in the case of single men, and of eight hours in the case of married. They were provided with tickets, which were redeemable in goods at certain central stores, where each ten cent ticket was exchangeable for food and clothes, which, if they had been purchased in the stores, would have cost from fifty to a hundred per cent. as much. That is to say, the ten cent ticket had a purchasing value of from fifteen to twenty cents.

That was very good, and nothing could have been more commendable than the zeal and the energy which Mr. Harvey and Dr. Stevenson and their zealous assistants worked in administering to their less fortunate fellow-creatures, but it was a significant fact that the bulk of the contributions for the relief of the unemployed came, not from the wealthy, but the workmen who worked, the shopman, and those who were much nearer the low level of the out-of-work than the millionaires. Still relief work is but a miserable, although necessary palliative of a social disaster, and many a time I recalled Carlyle's eloquent and indignant discourse on a similar state of things in England, as he saw it nearly half a century since :—

England is full of wealth, of multifarious produce, supply for human want in every kind; yet England is dying of inanition. With unabated bounty the land of England blooms and grows; waving with yellow harvests; thick studded with workshops, industrial implements, with fifteen millions of workers, understood to be the strongest, the cunningest, the willingest our Earth ever had; these men are here, the work they have done, the fruit they have realised is here, abundant exuberant on every hand of us: and behold some baneful fiat as of Enchantment has gone forth saying, " Touch it not, ye workers, ye master-workers, ye master-idlers; none of you can touch it, no man of you shall be the better for it; this is the enchanted fruit!" On the poor workers such fiat falls first in its rudest shape; but on the rich master-workers too it falls; neither can the rich master-idlers, nor any richestest or highest man escape, but all are like to be brought low with it, and made poor in the money sense or in a far fataler one. Of these successful skilful workers some two millions, it is now counted, sit in Workhouses, Poor-law Prisons, or have "out-door relief" flung over the wall to them,—the workhouse Bastille being filled to bursting, and the strong Poor-law being broken asunder by a stronger. They sit there these many months now, their hope of deliverance as yet small. In workhouses, pleasantly so named because work cannot be done in them, Twelve-hundred-thousand workers in England alone; their cunning right hand lamed, lying idle in their sorrowful bosom; their hopes, outlooks, shares in this fair world, shut in by narrow walls. They sit there, pent up, as if in a kind of horrid enchantment; glad to be imprisoned, enchanted that they may not perish, starved. The picturesque

Tourist in a sunny Autumn day, through this bounteous England, descries the Union Workhouse on his path. "Passing by the Workhouse in St. Ives, Huntingdonshire, on a bright day last summer," says the picturesque Tourist, "I saw sitting on wooden benches, in front of their Bastille, and within their ring-wall and its railings, some half-hundred or more of these men. Tall robust figures, young mostly or of middle age; of honest countenance, many of them thoughtful and even intelligent-looking men. They sat there near by one another; but in a kind of torpor, especially in a silence which was very striking. In silence: for alas, what word was to be said? An Earth all lying round crying come and till me, come and reap me;—yet we here sit enchanted! In the eyes and brows of these men hung the gloomiest expression, not of anger, but of grief and shame and manifold inarticulate distress and weariness; they returned my glance with a glance which seemed to say, 'Do not look at us. We sit enchanted here we know not why. The Sun shines and the Earth calls and, by the governing Powers and Impotences of this England, we are forbidden to obey. It is impossible, they tell us.' There was something that reminded me of Dante's Hell in the look of all this; and I rode swiftly away."

Dante's Hell indeed is suggested by all such doleful spectacles, of which the United States has this year seen more than enough. Unfortunately, we cannot, like Mr. Carlyle, ride swiftly away from the miserable spectacle.

The question of setting the unemployed to work was much discussed in Chicago last winter, and one evening the Sunset Club made it the subject of a special discussion. Professor Henderson, of the University, opened the discussion with a carefully written paper, in which, after surveying the whole of the situation, he finished by declaring that the appalling suffering of the year might purchase great improvement by compelling the people to study the fundamental laws of social health, and to drop all social antagonism, in order to promote the common welfare. It fell to my lot to follow Dr. Henderson, and I do not think I can do better than reproduce what I said :—

I am very glad to have an opportunity to put before you, who represent much of the youth, of the enterprise, and of the brain of Chicago, some conclusions that have been rather forcibly brought home to my mind during this stay which I have made in your midst—a stay which has been so pleasant and so profitable that I feel as if it was never going to come to an end. But there is one thing about your city which is not pleasant, and that is the re-appearance, in the midst of one of the newest communities of the new world, of that spectre which haunts the older civilisations of Europe. A Danish lady talking to me since I came to this city said, "Is it not dreadful, this civilisation of Chicago? It is like the wizened features of an old man upon the body of a child." That is rather a cruel saying, but unquestionably there are many of the old world features with which we are too painfully familiar, reproducing themselves in your midst this winter, and reproducing themselves as a characteristic of the old world nations transplanted to a new world soil, on a larger scale, and with hideous accompaniments from which we in the older world are happily free.

But in relation to the treatment of the homeless destitute, I have not yet seen any city in Europe which has been so hard driven and so ill provided with what we should consider the ordinary appliances of a civilised community as to use its worst police stations in which to herd unemployed workmen, side by side with the refuse of your criminals; or to convert the stately municipal palace in which you transact the business of your city into a casual ward for homeless workmen. *That* we have not in London; *that* is an aggravation and a refinement which I have not been accustomed to; and to the gentleman who said " No, no," I can only say, mention a city in which it is worse.

Now the first thing that strikes you, as it strikes every other man, is what Carlyle put so forcibly and strongly years ago. He said, "There is not a horse that is sound in wind, limb and sight, which, if it is straggling round without an owner, would not eagerly be led to a stable, housed and fed, but your able-bodied biped, to rear whom it has cost much more in food and thought than it has your horse, who from the cash point of view, if you could put him upon the block and sell him, would probably bring more than the horse, yet wanders round ownerless and masterless, seeking in vain as the greatest of earthly blessings his share of the primeval curse upon mankind."

It is a great line, that of Mrs. Browning's, that " God in cursing gives us better gifts than man in blessing," and it would be a great thing indeed if to our one hundred thousand unemployed in this city we could give their share of that "work" which was in ancient days regarded as a curse, and now is sought for in vain as an unattainable blessing by so many.

Now, think for one moment what it means. One hundred thousand men and women out of work in this city, representing to the community which might profit by their work, five hundred thousand dollars a week. Five hundred thousand dollars a week is the fine which society, thoughtlessly, or at any rate arbitrarily, loads upon one hundred thousand; they bear it, and are bearing it. Five hundred thousand dollars represents their loss; and it is going on. There are in this town some million odd who are employed, who are well fed, more or less, who at any rate have fire in their stoves and a roof over their heads, and something to eat. Do you mean to tell me it is impossible for this million who are employed to provide means, to find employment for those who are unemployed, seeing that one hundred thousand have to bear a fine amounting to five hundred thousand dollars a week in enforced idleness? The unions are supporting skilled labour, so I am told by their leaders, to the best of their ability, and probably on the unionists of this town there is placed a heavier tax *pro rata* than is falling upon any other class in the community except those who are actually out of work. But when we leave the unionists, and those who are absolutely out of work, there remains a great body of more or less well-to-do people, whom I presume you represent, and of whom for the moment I am one. What shall *we* do for the unemployed? The answer is very simple—

employ them! Employ them! Don't pauperise them; but give them work as you would if these people were your own blood relations, brothers and sisters, born of the one father and mother. But as they happen to be more or less remote relations, it does not come home to you. You say, " What can we give them to do?"

I speak with some trepidation, for fear I shall be taken up by the gentleman who resents these passing observations from a stranger, but I will say this, that I realise the compliment paid to the stranger in the extreme sensitiveness shown to his passing remarks, and also that if the gentleman who has intimated his dissent were to come to London and say of us a thousand-fold harder things than any which I have ventured to hint of Chicago, there is not one of us would care a straw what he said.

Now, if there are those who think there is no practical work waiting to be done in Chicago, upon which you can profitably employ the unemployed at this moment, I think that that person must have what we should call in England a very insular and parochial conception of the world and the things that are therein. I do not know how it strikes you, living in the midst of this city, but, coming to it as a stranger, coming to it with an immense admiration from old time for the enterprise and energy and wealth of your city, I must honestly say that I was taken not a little aback to see how very much you still had waiting to be done in order to bring your city up—I won't say to the level of an ideal city, in an impossible world—but to the level of a city in an ordinarily well governed and civilized state in Europe.

I think there are many things in which your city is far and away ahead of any city that I have ever seen in my own country, or in Europe ; but side by side with the things of which you are proud, and justly proud, you have allowed what we should call the pauper class, a poor, forlorn, dirty class, to grow up under conditions where they are without the appliances of civilization which an ordinary German or French or English city would think absolutely indispensable for the living of an ordinary human life. There are multitudes of little things that attract a stranger. I will only mention one as a very small thing, but I do think that to the stranger and wayfaring man your city would be more attractive if you would condescend to follow the ordinary practice of civilized cities and put the names of streets at every street corner, so that we might know where we are going.

I think also it would be a little improvement, both for health and for convenience, especially of the poorer people, if you should provide, as Paris provides, and as London has begun to provide, lavatories and other conveniences, at accessible and easy spots all over your great city. The neglect of the ordinary necessities of human nature in your city is a disgrace to any community, civilized or barbarous, and I have never met any person, who talked straight and plain across the table, who would not admit it. Why is it not done then? And until it is done is there not work waiting to be done?

Take again the question of cleaning your streets. Perhaps some persons may think that your streets are in an ideal condition of cleanliness, but if so, I think that their ideal of cleanliness would not be found very general in Chicago. There are streets that would employ many able-bodied men, and I am glad to think that the Relief Association is going to employ men in that way. There is also something that has been urged by mayor after mayor of your town, better paving on your back streets, where your poor live. To you and to me a badly paved street means little more than the change of boots after we get home ; to the poor man it may mean colds, pneumonia, rheumatism, and it means much to the poor man's children. Of course, if it be thought desirable to keep down your

ntipathy which was far greater than the merely
rface outcry that was raised after my remarks at
e Woman's Club. No doubt I spoke frankly, and
e curious may see in some of the suggestions the
rm of the idea which, working in other minds, led
Coxeyism and the armies of the Commonweal.
oxey, however, was far from being a Napoleon, and
e winter passed without any serious trouble.

The spring brought with it hopes of revival in
ade, and immediately, like a frost, came the fierce
ruggle in the coal trade, of which I give some
count in another chapter. Notwithstanding this,
d the continued uncertainty about the tariff, keen
servers rejoiced to note that the industrial de-
ression showed signs of departing.

Dr. Albert Shaw, writing in the *American Review*
f *Reviews* for July, publishes the following re-
suring report as to the shrinkage of the unem-
loyed. He says :—

We are inclined to accept certain evidences that have come to our
tice which indicate that a turn of the tide of business affairs will soon be
parent in all quarters. We have now received direct and authoritative
formation from nearly all the cities which adopted relief measures early in
e present year, and almost everywhere it was found possible several weeks
o to abandon all special relief measures, and to disband the Citizens' Com-
ttees under which relief was administered in most of the large towns. Our
iladelphia informant gives us the very striking information that the recent
ening of mills, factories, furnaces and manufacturing establishments in
neral, has given employment to more than 80,000 persons, the greater part
whom had been dependent upon the relief committee for help. He declares
at 'the committee's work would have been kept up during the summer
nths had there been any necessity for it; but matters have improved in
most every direction.' From the New England towns, where important
lief measures were necessary, we have received very encouraging reports.
his is particularly true as regards such manufacturing places as Lynn, Cam-
idge, Springfield and Providence. From Boston Mayor Matthews writes:
n reply to your letter I would say that the relief work is all ended, as well
the necessity for it." This short sentence speaks volumes as to the
pacity of American industry to absorb labour temporarily out of employ-
ent.

The greatest relief work of all, in some respects, was that instituted by the
tizens' Committee at Pittsburg. It expended more than a quarter of a

population, there is a good deal to be said in favour of keeping your pavements and alleys in such a state of filth. But considering the economic value of labour, and how much each workman loses every day he is out of work, considering the children's stunted limbs and the maladies from which they will never recover, I think you will find a great deal to do in making the tenement houses and the back streets of Chicago fit for your children to live in, and for mine; and yet other people's children have to live there now. You may go on to enumerate, as the preceding speaker did, the work to be done in your parks; work to be done in putting up laundries and baths as civic institutions in every corner of your densely populated districts, and which we in our retrograde and backward country have learned some years ago to regard as necessities of civilisation, even though we do not quite hold that because a man is dirty therefore he is a tramp and outside the pale of civilization. Yet here you have a town where the only place in which a poor man can get his face washed is a saloon, and when a man does not get his face washed and goes about dirty he is treated by many among you as if he was a dirty tramp who was uncivilized and unworthy the sympathy of any well-disposed citizen. Give a man a chance to get a clean face anyhow.

Then there are many other things. There is the People's Palace which you are going to put up on the lake shore. There is a post-office which you want to have pulled down—and the sooner the better. There are police stations which are not altogether creditable to the civilization and philanthropy of your town. I do not know how long it would last if you would go around Harrison Street Station to-night after leaving this place and see how your fellow-citizens are locked up. I think it would do you good, and I am quite sure it would do you more good if you might be locked up yourself for the night.

There are other works, such as making main drains, and making roads, and especially building what I think ought to be regarded as indispensable if Chicago is to hold up her head among the cities of the world. I think in every ward of this great city you should have at least one People's Institute or Civic Club House, where the poorest of the people would be at home, instead of having no home but the seven thousand five hundred saloons into which they must go in leisure hours after they have done their work. There is the providing of clothing for school children. There is an endless amount of work to be done that needs to be done, and you have an army of a hundred thousand unemployed with which to do it, who want to do it, and yet you say you cannot get it done. You want the money, you say. You want money to bring the two together. Well, you know you are rich in Chicago. You are not laden down and burdened as we are in the old world. But we get many things that you have not, and among other things good roads, which you have not; and how did they get them in France? War, ladies and gentlemen. It wasn't philanthropy; it was not an enlightened interest; it was the dire exigency of war that made it necessary for the Revolutionary armies and for Napoleon to be able to trundle his cannon to the utmost parts of France that made the roads of France at this moment the ideal roads of the world. Are you going to wait for a similar compulsion?

You know your great poet Lowell has said

"Not but wut abstract war is horrid,
  I sign to thet with all my heart;
But civlyzation *does* get forrid
  Sometimes upon a powder cart."

And it certainly has made better roads in France than peace and prosperity have in America. Could you not make roads? Are you to wait for war?

But we have another factor in Europe which I hope you will not have here. Civilization gets a lift upon the powder cart of war, but civilization has also received many a lift from the hand of revolution, in the tumbril of the death cart. It is a habit which human beings have when they don't get enough to eat to go out and kill somebody. That rule, I believe, is the almost universal rule. Let it go long enough, and, gentlemen—and ladies too—if there is no other way in which to get something to eat you and I would go out and kill somebody. It is the fundamental, and so far as we can see, the invariable law of human nature. We have found it in Europe and we have taken lessons thereby, imperfectly, but to some extent. I sincerely hope you may never have to take it to heart here. But I do not think I exaggerate when I say that one single night of wild despair in the streets of Chicago, without the use of dynamite, merely with the use of torch or club, would do your city more harm and shake your credit worse than all the millions that would be needed to give every-one of these people work all through the winter.

Do you think that if among our hundred thousand unemployed men and women there were to rise a Napoleon, a man with the brain of Napoleon, with the power of organisation and the energy of Napoleon, and with that magnetic power over his fellow-men, that these hundred thousand would not try to do something for themselves? I do not mean by violence; I mean by endeavouring so to organise the whole mass of the unemployed into what may be called an industrial co-partnership or army, under strict discipline, ready to work for rations, determined and ready to dedicate themselves, the whole army of one hundred thousand, to supply to Chicago those appliances of civilization for the poor and for those who are down in the world, which at present Chicago lacks—do you think that if such a man were to arise, with the confidence of his fellow-men, and were to get those people together, and they were to parade your streets, a great army, a hundred thousand strong, and were to ask, "Will you who own the money supply us with the tools?" Do you think that you would hesitate? I don't think you would. I think that you would find a way to answer them; because whatever offence I may have committed in speaking of your city, I have a great and boundless faith in Chicago, and the people of Chicago. It is because I have that faith I have lingered here so long; it is because I believe you, more than any people in any city in which I have ever been, respond to a great and noble ideal, that I am still here for some weeks, and because I find in you a faith, and a courage, and a determination, to try things to see what can be done, which older cities have not; and I believe when our unemployed show that they are willing to enter into such an industrial co-partnership or co-operation, in which each man would work according to his might, and receive according to his need, you will raise as much money as is necessary to put the whole army at work. You will say, "How?" Well, Mr. Chairman, I have the misfortune, it may be, to come from an old monarchical country where we have some government of the people by the representatives of the people, and when I look at your city governments, with my English instincts, I say that your mayor and your city council are, according to our English ideas, the natural and proper authorities by whom this thing ought to be done. And we are more and more learning, in England, to look to our municipal authorities as the moderating power. Instead of crowding all the work to be done in the summer time, we keep back as much as possible for the winter time, so as to equalise the demand for labour within the area of the municipality. I know I shall be told, "Your civic government in England is one thing, but civic government in America is another thing." Gentlemen, I believe your civic government in Chicago is very much what you wish it to be. When you wish to have it different it will be different. But, mind you, you must will it, and

will it hard. It will not do to will it in a nice nam go to bed and think it will be changed, for nothing if you make up your minds to use that lever that the City Hall, in order to do whatever is necessa employment for your people, to renovate your city, world as a city in which people live, as she led the which people went to enjoy themselves and admi world, you will find that whoever is mayor and what tion of your city council, they will do your bidding.

Then it may be said, "That is all very well; constitution of the city of Chicago, its charter, and Illinois."

Well, gentlemen, is it not time to stop this fooling it is foolish, just as your regulations about gamblin Stop this opera bouffe government, of which yo respectable and serious citizens of Chicago, althougl

The comptroller goes on to say that you cannot r for the most necessary work, because you have reach charter, which is five per cent. of the assessed valu troller, if the assessment were raised to its proper f difficulty in raising fifty or a hundred millions of doll Then, surely, if you mean business, don't pretend y because for some inscrutable reason you keep your cannot raise the money which you ought to raise you may be compelled to raise by more difficult met have suggested.

There is another thing—and this is the last word your municipality cannot raise the requisite number of you would go to a pawnbroker; I think he would money. I look at your funded debt and I see it amo and for that you have forty-one million of assets in waterworks. In other words, your funded debt is co realized property. Why, there is not a man in Chica shirt if he wants to, and if you tell me Chicago money upon forty-one millions of property, I cannot s ability of the city of Chicago.

Don't delude yourself by pretending that there are in the way. What is the motto of the city of Chicag To think that a city that has the sublime audacity should stand swathed like a babe in swaddling clothes If I had the power of Haroun al Raschid, of the An stand at the door with my janissaries and compel ev you to dress yourselves in the apparel of the poorest o city of Chicago and could take your clothes and unemployed, and then should turn you out into the keep you there all Christmas week, living as they li hungering as they hunger, looking forward into a fu look forward, you would raise all the money neede every cent of it.

The speech attracted a great de was rather bitterly discussed, and le —why I do not know—to regar

million dollars, half of which Mr. Andrew Carnegie contributed. The committee gave total or partial support to more than 14,000 men, representing 47,000 persons dependent upon their labour. The relief operations have been wound up, and while we are informed that there are still a good many men in need of work, the exceptional stress has wholly disappeared. The Cincinnati situation, which, though severe, was admirably met by the rally of business men and municipal authorities around the Associated Charities as a centre, is quite normal again; and one-third of the special municipal relief fund that was appropriated remains unexpended. In Milwaukee and Toledo, in Cleveland and Columbus, greatly improved conditions are visible. Our report from Kansas City begins with this sentence: " All necessity for special relief of the unemployed has disappeared in this community." The adjustment of the strikes and the resumption of mining activity gives Colorado the assurance of a very busy autumn. It can be said for New York City and Brooklyn that most of the men and women who were seeking work in the winter and spring have found employment. There is every reason to believe that if Congress will but pass the tariff bill and adjourn, the quickened wheels of manufacturing industry and the call for men to harvest ripening crops and to supply the demand for coal and lumber and other materials, will at once afford a chance for every able-bodied man in the United States to work. It is reasonable to estimate that fully nine-tenths of the unemployed labour of three or four months ago has already been absorbed, and a very little quickening of the industrial life will provide for those remaining.

This, I am afraid, is a too sanguine estimate, but whether it was so or not will never be ascertained, for once again, just when the cup of prosperity seemed to be returning to the lips of a suffering people, there has broken out an industrial contest, so fierce and so widespread as to compel even the optimist to mutter the terrible word " Civil War." How it all came about, and how it is that this summer's Chicago, the great commercial centre of a peaceful commonwealth, was like a city in a state of siege, will be told in subsequent chapters.

MR. CARL BROWNE, COXEY'S LIEUTENANT.

CHAPTER II.—THE PETITION IN BOOTS.

"THE opening passages of Carlyle's ' Past and Present,'
describing the state of England about 1842, are a
very perfect description of the United States to-day.
Unrest, discontent, and fear are present in all minds
and among all classes of people. We seem to be on
the edge of some great upheaval, but one can never
tell whether it will turn out a tragedy or a farce.
Whatever the end is, the present is full of speculation and wonder, and it is not a time when one can
expect calm reasoning and deliberate unselfish action
on the part of anybody. The determined optimist
will see promise in this state of things, and the pessimist will see the opposite. I being sometimes an
optimist and sometimes a pessimist, feel and think
accordingly. Between times I wonder."

So wrote to me, on the 7th of June, one of the
shrewdest, brightest, and most sympathetic observers
of the course of events from the vantage point of the
city of Chicago. Her observation is just. Over and
over again, when I was in Chicago, I remarked that
what the West most wanted was the widespread circulation of Carlyle's " Latter-Day Pamphlets," his
"Chartism," and his " Past and Present." The gospel
of Carlyle is much needed across the Atlantic, where
hitherto, despite Emerson, the prophet of Chelsea
has been at a pretty considerable discount. As was
England in 1842, so is America to-day. When
Chartism was brewing, hardly thirty years had

elapsed since the battle of Waterloo had settled the
fate of Napoleon. About the same space of time
separates the Americans from the surrender of General
Lee, which marked the final overthrow of the Con-
federacy. Capitalism in America, for the most part,
is where Capitalism was in the Old Country, when
even men as advanced as Bright and Cobden regarded
factory legislation as a monstrous invasion of the
liberty of the subject.

It is like going back to the middle of the century
to visit the American Republic. In most matters
pertaining to social evolution, in things industrial,
and, indeed, in many other things, they are about
fifty years behind us. Their trades unions are still
regarded with the same suspicion, resentment, and
distrust that they were looked upon in the Old Country
before the repeal of the combination laws. Labour,
on its part, relies more upon violence than upon organisation, and when a strike occurs, slaughter, on one
side or the other, is regarded as an ordinary and
unavoidable incident. It is difficult to conceive a
more cruel satire upon the simple faith of the Radical-
ism in which I was brought up than to witness
how little free education and the penny daily paper
have succeeded in helping these millions of English-
speaking men to keep step with the vanguard of their
race.

It seems almost incredible, but let any one who
questions it test the truth of it by one very simple
experiment. The English in their own land, fifty
years ago, by dint of much suffering and sympathy,
succeeded in becoming articulate in the verse of two
poets. Mrs. Browning's " Cry of the Children " remains on record as the imperishable protest of the
mother-heart against the massacre of child life be-

neath the Juggernaut of modern industrialism ; while
Ebenezer Elliott, the Corn Law rhymer, expressed in
ruder, but not less vigorous, verse the sentiments of
the passionate indignation which misery, aggravated
by class legislation, excited in the mind of the British
democrat. Mrs. Browning and Ebenezer Elliott are
somewhat out of date in England. Their verse has the
same kind of historical interest that is possessed by
Longfellow's poems about Slavery. But they are both
up to date in the United States. The waste of child
life and the misery engendered by a fiscal system of
monopoly and plunder, which reproduces in the New
World many of the evils so familiar to the anti-Corn
Law men in the old land, fit only too aptly the
description of the sufferings of the English poor half
a century since.

And now, as if to point the moral and to emphasise
the parallel, we have Coxeyism as a kind of bastard
Chartism of the New World to proclaim to the world
the need for a policy other than that of *laissez-faire,*
and of a religion more helpful than that of the
worship of the almighty dollar. Coxey and his
tatterdemalion followers are laughable enough no
doubt to those who from the stalls of full-fed comfort can only see the ludicrous side of weltering
misery ; but to the masses who suffer it is not surprising that they should appear in another and much
more serious light. For they are the sandwich-men
of Poverty, the peripatetic advertisers of Social
Misery. They may be the *avant-couriers* of Revolution, maleficent or beneficent, as the case may be.
From that point of view they have done their work
with notable success, and in that also they resembled
their predecessors, the much ridiculed Manchester
Insurgents, who killed no one, but merely asserted

their grievances and then went home. Carlyle's vindication of the Manchester Insurrection applies without the alteration of a word to the Coxeyism of to-day.

"An insurrection that can announce the disease, and then retire with no balance account of grim vengeance opened anywhere, has attained the highest success possible for it. And this is what these poor Manchester operatives, with all the darkness that was in them and round them, did manage to perform. They put their huge inarticulate question, ' What do you mean to do with us ? ' in a manner audible to every reflective soul in this kingdom, exciting deep pity in all good men, deep anxiety in all men whatever ; and no conflagration or outburst of madness came to cloud that feeling anywhere, but everywhere it operates unclouded. All England heard the question : it is the first practical form of our Sphinx riddle. . . . And truly this first practical form of the Sphinx question, inarticulately and so audibly put there, is one of the most impressive ever asked in the world. ' Behold us here, so many thousand millions, and increasing at the rate of fifty every hour. We are right willing and able to work, and on the planet Earth is plenty of work and wages for a million times as many. We ask, If you mean to lead us towards work—to try to lead us, by ways new, never yet heard of till this new, unheard-of Time ? If you declare that you cannot lead us ? And expect that we are to remain quietly unled, and in a composed manner perish of starvation ? What is it you expect of us ? What is it you mean to do with us ? ' This question, I say, has been put in the hearing of all Britain, and will be again put, and even again, till some answer be given it."

That is Coxeyism. The description fifty years old fits the circumstances to-day to a nicety. And the world waits and wonders what the flippant dilettanteism of the press and the Midas-eared Mammonism of the market will answer to this riddle of the Sphinx. Certainly there are few portents of our time so well worthy of study as this phenomenon of Coxeyism, of which our British press has hitherto given us but most imperfect and misleading accounts.

There is nothing new in Coxeyism. It is as old as the hills. The only novelty is to find in this respect, as in many others, Russian methods reproduced in the American Republic. Try as we may, we never escape from Muscovy in the Western World. Coxeyism in its methods of organising petitions in boots is an American adoption of a familiar Russian mode of airing grievances and of protesting against abuses. Professor Hourwich, an able Russian statistician, of the University of Chicago, to whose painstaking researches we are indebted for the most authentic information as to the constitution of the Coxeyite armies, has pointed out that in this respect, as in many others, the Americans are but English-speaking Muscovites. He says :—

"In Russia it frequently happens that the peasants of some remote village or group of villages, finding no relief for their grievances with the home authorities, send their delegates to bring 'petitions in boots' to the seat of the central government. The weary 'walkers,' as they are called in Russia, march thousands of miles, very often begging 'for Christ's sake.' That men should come to the adoption of such methods of petitioning in America is a phenomenon so extraordinary that it deserves study from another than a policeman's standpoint."

The petition in boots has at least succeeded in achieving a phenomenal success. This, no doubt, it owed chiefly to the immense publicity which it secured through the newspapers ; but the art of converting the Press into a sounding-board is one of the

DESIGNS FROM THE "GOOD ROADS"

PETITION TO THE HOUSE OF REPRESENTATIVES.

most indispensable for all those who would air their grievances, and Coxey by instinct seems to have divined how to do it. To the Press the intrinsic importance of subjects is a comparatively trivial detail ; the supreme question is not one of intrinsic importance, but of capacity to yield sensational " copy." The sole test of news value is its selling currency, and any one who wishes to catch the ear of the public must do something, by describing which the keepers of the ears of the said public can make the indispensable red cent. It is as much the business of any one who wishes to secure the attention of the public to devise ways and means of making it profitable to the Press to report him, as it is the business of a candidate to win his election, or of a Minister to secure a majority.

Every one in America knew of the existence of the unemployed. Every newspaper reader was bored to death with discussions as to what should be done with tramps and out-of-works. It seemed almost impossible to contrive any device by which this grim and worn-out topic could be served up in good saleable newspaper articles. But Coxey did the trick. Coxey compelled all the newspapers of the Continent to devote from a column to six columns a day to reporting Coxeyism, that is to say with echoing the inarticulate clamour for work for the workless. That was a great achievement. To have accomplished it shows that Coxey is not without genius. No millionaire in all America could, without ruining himself, have secured as much space for advertising his wares as Coxey commanded without the outlay of a red cent, by the ingenious device of his petition in boots.

A writer in the *Railway Conductor* finds a parallel to the Coxey movement in the march of the Blanketeers, which took place in England in the spring of the year 1817, and thus describes that crusade :—

"The Blanketeers were a body of men who marched to London, much in the manner in which the Commonwealers are now marching to Washington, for the purpose of presenting petitions to Parliament and inducing that body t) accede to their demands for the enactment of certain measures of reform in the government. The movement had its origin among the weavers of Lancashire. Early in March of the year 1817, the 10th of the month, I believe it was, a vast body of working men assembled in St. Peter's Field at Manchester for the purpose of discussing the question of Parliamentary reform which was just then agitating the country, and for the further purpose of organising an army which should march to London and present its petition to Parliament in a body. This meeting was called the 'Blanket Meeting,' because of the fact that those who attended were observed to have a blanket, or large coat, rolled up and strapped, knapsack fashion, to their backs; and, for the same reason, those who participated in the movement were known as 'Blanketeers.' Some carried bundles under their arms; some carried rolls of paper in their hands, supposed to be petitions which had been got ready to present to Parliament upon their arrival in London, and many had stout walking sticks in their hand to assist them on their journey. The magistrates came upon the field where this meeting took place and read the Riot Act. (One week before this, on March 3, the Habeas Corpus Act had been suspended throughout the kingdom, under 'An act to empower his Majesty to secure and detain such persons as his Majesty shall suspect are conspiring against his person and government.')

"The meeting was dispersed by the military and the constables; and no more than three hundred of the Blanketeers, without leaders, and without organisation, began their straggling march toward London. These were followed by a body of constables who apprehended some and induced others to desert, until, when the Blanketeers spread their blankets at Macclesfield, at nine o'clock that night, they numbered less than two hundred. These kept on their march, their numbers meanwhile continually decreasing because of desertions and arrests by the authorities along the line of march, until the 17th of the month, when a mere handful of the original Blanketeer army reached the outskirts of London and concluded to disband without having accomplished their purpose of appealing to Parliament.

"Many of the men went into the Blanketeers movement actuated by the belief that it was the most effective way in which they could exercise their right of petition; but the belief was erroneous; Parliament continued in its vicious course of manufacturing social legislation undisturbed by the Blanketeer movement: and in this respect, also, history will no doubt repeat itself with regard to the Commonwealers and the Congress of the United States."

The origin of Coxeyism, the source and secret spring of all its power, is to be found in the existence of an immense number of unemployed men in the United States. It is indeed startling to learn on the authority of such unimpeachable authorities as *Dunn* and *Bradstreet's,* that last winter there were from three to

four million workless workers in the American Republic. Even if these figures are exaggerated, they
point to the existence of a mass of human misery from
which it had been hoped the New World would be
free. If *Bradstreet's* be right, the Americans had an
army of unemployed last winter as numerous as the
soldiers under the colours in all the standing armies
of Europe. The political economist who waxes
eloquent over the waste of wealth occasioned by the
bloated armaments of the present century, always
reckons the cost of the withdrawal of so many able-
bodied men from productive industry as a heavier tax
than the mere expense of their maintenance. The
United States has no standing army of soldiers to
speak of; but its army of unemployed is indirectly
almost as expensive as our European soldiery. The
workless worker produces as little as the drilled
soldier, and although the manœuvres of the parade
ground are economically valueless, they are superior,
at least in providing occupation, to the condition of
enforced indolence in which the unemployed pass
their time.

Yet America is very wealthy. It is the land of
millionaires. But as in England in 1842, "in the
midst of plethoric plenty the people perish; with
gold walls and full barns no man feels himself safe or
satisfied. Have we actually got enchanted, then—
accursed by some god?" To that question Coxey
and his penniless pilgrims of industry have compelled
all men to make some answer.

Coxey, who has given his name to the movement,
is little more than a figure-head. The real man on
the horse is not Coxey, but Browne; and even Browne
is without influence or authority outside the Ohio contingent of the Coxeyite forces. The movement is not

SOME COMMONWEAL BADGES.

that of any one man. Coxeyism is as little the handiwork of Coxey as the French Revolution was the work of Mirabeau or of Robespierre. Coxeyism is a kind of sporadic growth. The idea of petitions in boots commended itself to widely scattered groups of miserable men, all of whom have but one idea and one prayer. " Work, give us work," is their cry, and as it is to the Government they address their prayer, they set their faces towards Washington.

Every newspaper in the country blames the party to which it does not belong for the bad times. Party politicians in the States habitually speak as if prosperity were in the gift of the Administration. The Federal Government, with its tariffs and its subsidies, is constantly called upon to play the part of an Earthly Providence to the classes. Coxeyism only asks that the same *Deus ex machinâ* which has for a whole generation been invoked to fatten millionaires should exert a little of its omnipotence to secure work for the unemployed. As the Mœnad throng of Parisians led by Demoiselle Theroigne poured tumultuous upon Versailles to demand bread, so Coxeyism, with its multitudinous ragged regiments, bent its steps towards Washington. Versailles is within easy marching distance from the Hôtel de Ville of Paris. In America space is a great obstacle—how great no one adequately realises until he has been there. Hence the great difficulty of Coxey. But from an advertising point of view the parade was all the longer and the more drawn out.

When Coxey started he declared that he would lead 100,000 men to Washington. But it is the custom with agitators everywhere, and especially in the States, where the continental dimensions of the Republic seem to foster a habit of inflated and exaggerated assertion, to adjust their prophecies rather to their hopes than their expectations. In the band which Coxey led in person from Massillon in Ohio to the steps of the Capitol in Washington he never had more than five hundred men, and sometimes he had only one hundred. Of the other armies a similar story might be told. From the obscure and complicated record of the movements of the industrials the only thing that is quite clear is that there were never in the whole Coxeyite demonstration more than ten thousand men on the road at one time.* The various "armies" with their maximum strength may be set down as follows :—

Commander.			Starting Point.				Number of Men.
Coxey ...	...	...	Massillon, Ohio ...	...	...	...	500
Frye ...	...	...	Los Angeles	...	...	...	1000
Kelly ...	...	...	San Francisco	...	...	...	2000
Randall	...	...	Chicago ...	...	...	...	1000
Hogan	...	...	Montana ...	...	...	...	500
—	...	...	Oregon ...	...	...	...	900

Many other "armies" sprang up in May. But the later comers never swelled the total to 10,000 men.

As there were more than five thousand persons receiving relief in Chicago alone last winter, it is evident that the numbers of the petitioners in boots were but an almost infinitesimal proportion to the numbers of the actual unemployed. The army of tramps who are constantly on the road in the States is said to number 60,000.† But the greater number

* The official historian of the Commonweal movement, Mr. Henry Vincent, estimates that twelve of the armies number 7,000, but this is probably an exaggeration.

† The American is slowly beginning to see that the tramp question cannot be solved for ever by the simple process of hustling the tramp on to the next village.

Mr. E. Hofer, in the *Overland Monthly*, proposes a plain but somewhat novel remedy for the solution of the tramp problem. His investigations on the subject lead him to the following conclusion;

"It is the duty of the State, to enact laws that shall regulate the tramp, and protect its citizens against him. Let a stockade of several hundred acres of wild land—timber land

D

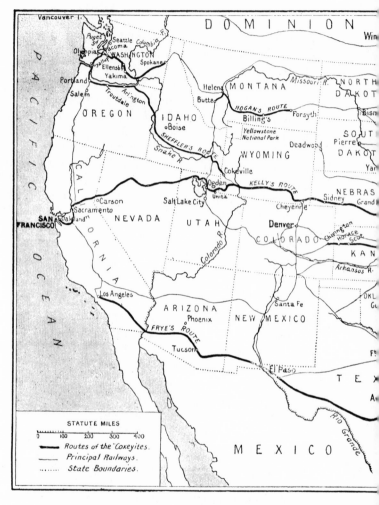

MAP ILLUSTRATING THE ITINERARY C

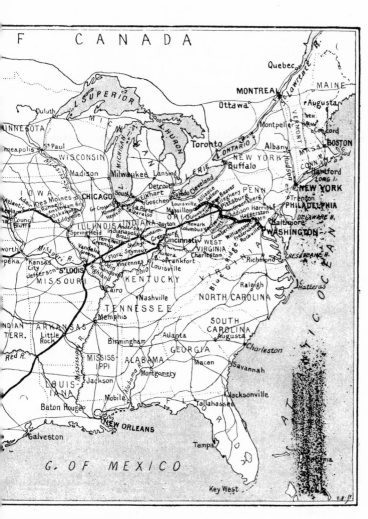

ARMIES OF THE COMMONWEAL,

being diffused in units attracted comparatively little attention compared with the smaller number which was organised and concentrated in half-a-dozen central points.

One very remarkable feature about Coxeyism is the extent to which it is the creature of the Pacific Slope. Browne, Coxey's lieutenant and right hand, brought the idea of a march on Washington from his experiences with Dan Kearney of the Sandlots, San Francisco, with whom he had agitated and petitioned Congress many years ago. The two most formidable armies started from the Pacific Coast—Frye's from Los Angeles, Kelly's from San Francisco. Of the other armies, two took their rise in Oregon and Montana. Coxeyism may indeed be said to be the creation of the Pacific Coast. The only important body of men not directly recruited on the far side of the Rockies, or directly inspired and directed from the Pacific Slope, was Randall's Chicago army. But

---

whenever it can be had—be inclosed and owned by the county in each county in the State. In the other States where this is not practicable, a smaller stockade for other employment must be used. But in the newer States the most profitable employment for compulsory labour must remain the subjugation of wild land. Within this stockade let plain barracks be erected on the cottage plan. By proper direction all this can be done by tramp labour. Let straw and blankets be supplied, and an open fireplace for each cottage. Only the actual necessities of shelter and comfort should be supplied for the novice who is sentenced to the barracks. The plainest and cheapest food should be supplied in abundance, and all tobacco and liquor cut off. A uniform of duck or other material must be supplied, that all may be known by their having the same appearance everywhere, and all other clothing destroyed. A free bath should be supplied, and all required to take it. Their labour should be clearing and tilling the land in this inclosure by hand. There should be no labour-saving machinery employed in a trampery, as this institution might be named. The land shall be cleared with mattock and axe. The soil shall be tilled with spade and hoe, as is done in England and France to this day. This would afford the largest possible amount of labour within one enclosure.

"The sentences to the trampery should come from the county or police courts, and should be indefinite, but never for less time than to make the cure of trampism radical. Whenever the disorganised citizen became organised and capable of self-support and self-direction as a free man, he could be allowed to go on parole. But until then he must lose his identity, his freedom, and his vote, just as completely as the man in the state prison. A system of rewards for meritorious conduct should be invented, to draw out and develop the best services and the best traits of the men. As soon as trusties could be found, they could be let out in bands of ten or twenty to clear lands in the neighbourhood, which work on the Pacific Coast, and on both slopes of the mountains, and in parts of the South, is now done by Chinese labour. Within the stockade his labour could be made remunerative by preparing the wood he cuts for firewood, and the products he grows should be entirely for his own maintenance and support. Then he would simply be not a tax on the rest of the community, as he now is, and that, too, on those least able to bear it. Uniformed, restrained, and employed, he would become self-supporting, —he would cease to be a terror to the community, and would no longer be a burden upon the taxpayer."

even this was brought into being as the direct result
of the presence of Kelly's Californian army in the
neighbourhood. The armies recruited in the Eastern
States were contemptible. There were three score
pilgrims from Boston, and even fewer from Philadelphia. Coxeyism, it cannot be too often repeated,
was local to half-a-dozen states, and these at first
almost without exception the furthest away from
Washington.

Coxey himself, with his Ohio contingent, was
comparatively close to Washington. Comparatively
that is. But when he unfurled the banner of the
Commonweal of Christ at Massillon on Easter Sunday,
Coxey's men had a longer march before them than
that which lay before the Pretender when in 1745 he
came down from the Highlands to march on London.
The roads also were probably as bad between Massillon
and Washington as those which led through Preston-
pans and Derby. But Coxey's base was comparatively
within a stone's throw of his objective. It was far
otherwise with the armies from the Pacific Slope.
When Napoleon left Paris for his fatal march on
Moscow, he had a shorter distance to travel than that
which intervened between the Coxeyites under Frye
and Kelly. The distance between Los Angeles and
Washington, as Frye covered it, was further than
that which stretches between London and Khartoum.
When the Oregon industrials started for the capital,
they had as long a road to travel as an army starting
from Erzeroum on its way to London *viâ* Constanti-
nople. Hence for the armies, with the exception of
Coxey's contingent in Ohio, the possession of railway
transport was indispensable. The petitions in boots
really came to mean petitions on wheels. When the
wheels stopped, the petitions were stuck in the mud.

Petitions in boots are all very well when the distances
are so short that the boots will not wear out. But
when they are longer than the boots will last, why
then a fresh mode of petitioning must be devised;
and it was this necessity which led to the train-
stealing which forms so characteristic a feature of
Coxeyism.

The question as to the constitution of the armies
has been much debated, but one thing stands out
quite clearly. These bands of industrials behaved
themselves with extraordinary moderation. If some
of them occasionally stole a train, they took it as a
necessity of transport. It was borrowing rather than
stealing. They took the loan of the rolling stock for
a time. They stole little else. No bodies of broken,
landless men ever seem to have behaved with a more
scrupulous regard for the rights of property. They
begged—it may be they took collections—but no acts
of robbery are reported by their enemies, nor does
there seem to have been any act of violence perpetrated by the industrials. If they had been lazy
tramps, vicious vagabonds preying upon society, this
extraordinary absence of crime could not have been
recorded. Their behaviour seems to have been
exemplary. "You cannot find so much as a chicken-
feather among my men," Coxey boasted, when he led
his men to Washington past hen-coops innumerable ;
and although in some districts the farmers barricaded
their farms when the army approached, there seems
to have been no acts justifying their misgivings.

From the newspaper reports and from the character
of their leaders, the Coxeyites seem to lie under the
imputation of religious enthusiasm rather than of
irreligious license. Coxey and Browne are both
religious enthusiasts. So is Kelly. One of the chief

pre-occupations of the Coxeyites seems to be preaching and singing hymns. Prayer is not so much practised amongst them. Their camps have been regulated with Spartan rigour. No toleration was shown to drunkenness, and the armies appear to have been singularly free from camp-followers. Poverty does not always bring chastity into its train, but the march of the industrials seems to have been unattended by the contagion of vice which usually marks the trail of armies.

Here are the rules and regulations of the Chicago army, as drawn up by General Randall :—

All members must submit to its discipline, be orderly, peaceful, and law-abiding.

Every member must obey promptly the directions and orders of those who have been elected or appointed to places of authority over them.

A guard will be detailed every day for the succeeding twenty-four hours of a sufficient number of men, to be divided into three reliefs, which shall be under command of the officer of the day.

Every day a sufficient number of men will be detailed to act as police, to see that the camp, barracks, or other place of shelter is kept clean, and to direct men who are thoughtless and careless about their persons to keep as clean as possible.

Every man must keep his person and his immediate portion of the quarters clean, and refrain from boisterous, profane, and obscene talk, and conduct himself in such an orderly, sober, dignified way, whether in or out of quarters, as will inspire the public everywhere that we are American citizens ; that we take pride in our country ; that we have a just sense of our rights under the laws of our land ; and that we are banded together to make the whole people as a jury listen to our grievances.

No person will be allowed in camp except members of the commonweal army and those who have permit or countersign.

No speech-making shall be allowed in camp without consent from the commanding officer.

As all men in the army have joined for " pot-luck," and expect to take it, let there be no grumbling over rations or the quarters furnished to us, no matter what the quality of the one or the inconveniences of the other. We are patriots, and must endure our lot, whatever it may be.

We are, however, fortunately not under any necessity of inferring the nature of the Coxeyites from their general behaviour, or the rules and regulations of their camps. Professor Hourwich, already referred to, subjected 290 members, selected at random from the men under "General" Randall's command, to a close examination, and the results at which he arrived appear to be decisive. The Professor, who was assisted by a sociological statistician, is satisfied that the information which he obtained was thoroughly reliable. The conclusions which he published in Chicago on May 7th are briefly as follows :—

Of the 290 industrials, one-half were American born ; of the other half, the majority were British born. Two-thirds were English-speaking men. They averaged 30 to 32 years of age.

Of 262 industrials, 181 were skilled mechanics, representing 70 trades ; 74 were unskilled, and 7 were tradesmen. The fourth were union men. Of the skilled mechanics, 70 were unionists, and 111 outside unions. Their average wage when at work was—unionists, 10s. per day, non-unionist mechanics, 7s., unskilled labourers, 6s.

Of 115 questions as to education, only two were badly educated. They averaged seven years of school life ; 26 had attended high schools, business and professional colleges, academies and universities.

Of 198 questioned as to politics, 88 were Democrats, 39 Republicans, 10 Populists ; 25 did not vote, while 28 were not naturalised.

One half the non-Chicagoan industrials were married, and had left their families in search of work. One-fourth of 261 had been helped through the winter by charity. The average duration of lack of employment was five months. Two-thirds of them had saved enough to tide them over this period, but their savings were spent. Only five or six appeared to be of questionable character.

It is, therefore, says Professor Hourwich, not the tramp, but the unemployed working man—the unfortunate citizen—who has turned into the ranks of the Commonweal.

The Coxeyites, ridiculed by the classes, have the sympathy of the masses. Organised labour, and labour not organised, has cheered the armies on their way in a fashion that fills Mr. Edward Bellamy, of " Looking Backwards " notoriety, with new hope. Speaking of Coxeyism, Mr. Bellamy says :—

" The most significant feature of this industrial situation lies, not in the numbers of the marching bodies—which, of course, are trifling—but in the fact that it is evident that the labouring masses of people, the working classes, are deeply in sympathy with it. This has been shown, as of course every newspaper reader knows, by a series of demonstrations on the part of the working-men—the poorer classes generally in the great cities, as well as the smaller districts along the line of march. It is also evidenced by the sympathetic attitude of the officials of the Knights of Labour, the Federation of Labour, and the Railway Un'on in the west, and especially in their attempt to assist the armies by the threatening strikes if the latter's demands were refused. I have been much impressed by what the working-men have said to me personally regarding their sympathy with the movement, and while I was prepared for a surprise, it was even greater than I expected. They evidently think it their cause, and believe that these armies are standing for their interests.

"The contemptuous expressions from many sources as to the smallness of these armies seem to be ill-judged. The cost and difficulty of moving even 100 men across the country for 1,000 miles with no organised commissariat, is simply enormous, as any old soldier will testify. That these armies have done what they have done, made the marches they have made, and maintained the good discipline they have, with the resources at their disposition, is an astounding fact, and will be so regarded by future historians. The phenomenon as a whole of the rise and course of these demonstrations is significant not only of a deep discontent on the part of the masses with the way things are going in this country, but also of a loss of faith in the ordinary governmental bodies at Washington. That this loss of faith is well justified no one who has followed the course of our national and State legislatures for a number of years past can question. The government of this country, whatever its nominal form, is in effect the rule of the rich, and not the rule of the people.

So far Mr. Bellamy. Now let us follow in detail the march of the three industrial armies which have attracted most attention—those of Coxey, of Kelly, and of Frye.

When the black - browed Marseillais, who knew how to die, marched across France to Paris to the strains of Rouget de Lille's immortal war-song, they passed almost unchronicled through revolutionary France. That was before the days of modern journalism. When Coxey and Browne on Easter Sunday began their famous march from Massillon to Washington, there were only about a hundred industrial soldiers in line behind the banner of the Army of the Commonweal, but this small force was escorted by no fewer than forty-three special correspondents with four Western Union telegraphic operators and two line men. Never in the annals of insurrection has so small a company of soldiers been accompanied by such a phalanx of recording angels. As a result

every incident in the march to Washington has been
chronicled with a minuteness of detail and, let me
add, with a picturesque exercise of the imagination
which has seldom been surpassed. Before the march
was over twenty-seven of the forty-three specials had
been recalled, but sixteen went over every foot of the
road.

The American reporter will sacrifice everything, even
truth itself, to make his copy readable, and the pictures
which they have given us of Coxey and his strange

GENERAL COXEY OFF TO WASHINGTON.

company are no doubt somewhat highly coloured.
Beneath all their garnishing, however, can be discovered as curious a caravan on a miniature scale as
ever started since the crusade of Walter the Penniless.

The " hundred vagabonds " who started from
Massillon had swollen to six hundred as the army
marched through Homestead—Mr. Carnegie's Homestead—but when the perilous march across the snowy
mountain had to be faced only a hundred and forty
were found in line on the summit. The ranks were

again recruited when the army approached Washington, but they never mustered five hundred after Homestead. What the army lacked in numbers it made up in the originality, not to say eccentricity, of its leaders.

I met Browne at Chicago. He discoursed to me copiously and energetically upon the importance of

CARL BROWNE ADDRESSING COMMONWEALERS.

employing the unemployed in making good roads. I liked the man. He was full of ideas about paper money, on which I could express no opinion—a due regard for my sanity having always restrained me from the discussion of problems of the currency—but I heartily agreed with him as to the desirability of utilising the wasted labour of the community in opening up the country by the construction of passable roads. Browne seemed to me unquestionably sincere, and he was very proud of the extraordinary cartoon which I reproduce here. He was even then in communication with Coxey, and was much elated by his success in inducing the American Federation of Labour to indorse his favourite nostrum of the issue of five hundred million dollar bonds for the construction of roads. Browne was born July 4, 1849, of a fighting stock. His father had served both in the Mexican and in the Union wars. Browne himself had seen life on many sides. By turns printer, painter, cattle rancher, journalist, cartoonist, and politician, he had even more than the ordinary American facility of turning his hand to anything. He had been Kearney's private secretary, and had energetically thrown himself into the agitation against the Chinese. Like many other Americans he was mystical and much disposed to theosophy. He had acquired a strong ascendency over Coxey, so strong indeed that reporters declared Coxey was mesmerised by Browne, and was but the passive instrument of his lieutenant's will.

Coxey was a younger and richer man. Born in Pennsylvania in 1854, he left school when thirteen, and went to work at a rolling mill. He was diligent, and he prospered sufficiently to go into business on his own account in 1879. Two years later he purchased a sand-stone quarry at Massillon, Ohio, and in 1889 added to his other ventures that of owning a stock farm, where he bred horses, in Kentucky. Originally an Episcopalian with musical tastes, he has now become theosophist, and is said to be convinced that he and Browne are between them sharers in the reincarnation of Christ. Coxey wears spectacles, is married, and has six children.

It would need the graphic pen of Carlyle to describe the motley crew which marched out of Massillon on Sunday morning, while the air was full of the chiming Easter bells. First marched a negro carrying the American banner. Then riding on a big grey horse came Browne in his buckskin coat, fringed down the sleeves and plastered with decorations. A broad-brimmed white sombrero covered his head, and round his neck he wore an amber necklace given him by his wife. After him came the trumpeter Windy Oliver, the astrologer "Cyclone" Kirkland, of Pittsburg, and seven musicians of the band. Coxey himself followed the band in a buggy drawn by two bay mares and driven by a negro. In an open carriage behind rode Mrs. Coxey and her sister.

The procession proper was headed by another negro standard-bearer carrying the banner of the Common-weal of Christ with its portrait of the Saviour and the suggestive legend, "Death to interest-bearing bonds!" Then followed the hundred industrials — only one hundred in the whole company. Grimy they were and ragged, but they stepped out bravely behind their banner, caring little for the jeers of the populace, which outnumbered the army by twenty to one. The forty-three newspaper men tramped alongside, while the rear was brought up by a miscellaneous multitude, who tailed off as the snow came down and the mud grew deep in the road.

Honoré Jaxon, the Indian half-breed, Riel's private secretary, was in the army, with his long black hair and striking features. He was in heavy marching order, with blankets strapped round his body, an axe by his side, moccasins on his feet, and a beaded girdle round his waist. Jaxon went more lightly when the

British officers hunted him across the frontier at the time of Riel's rebellion, but notwithstanding his accoutrements he stepped it all the way, and reached Washington before the main column. Another strange figure was the Great Unknown, Louis Smith by name, who subsequently incited to mutiny in the ranks, but who at first was a potent agent in main-

COMMONWEALERS IN CAMP.

taining discipline. He rode backwards and forwards along the column seated in his red saddle, wearing blue overcoat and white riding trousers, distributing badges and exhorting the Commonwealers to stand firm and not to mind the scoffs and the jeers of the world. The impedimenta of the army consisted of a waggon laden with one of Browne's panoramas, with a cover curiously painted in symbolical colours, with a couple of commissariat waggons, on which was inscribed the watchword of the Commonweal.

A circus tent was carried with them, and such rations as they could secure. As a rule the army was supplied with victuals by the people on the way. The reporters complained of having ham and eggs three times a day, but they paid for their fare. The Commonwealers being dependent on charity, often went hungry. They cut their own firewood in the woods, made fires in camp, received their rations in groups of five, took off their shoes, laid down in their blankets, and rested. All along the road the country-folk came to see the show. It was as good as a circus in its way—and, besides, who could say but that it might lead to better times ? So the crowds cheered, and brought crackers and pies and bacon, and the Commonwealers felt encouraged to persevere. Sometimes they enlivened the camp by singing some of the Songs of the Army of the Commonweal. Of these the following sample of Lieutenant Browne's muse will probably suffice :—

AIR—"*Marching through Georgia.*"

Come, rally to our standard every unemployed man to-day,
And show the bloated bondholders we mean just what we say;
One hundred thousand unemployed are marching in array.
We are marching to Washington.

Chorus.

Hurrah, hurrah, our day of jubilee!
Hurrah, hurrah, for the country of the free;
Hurrah for legal tender! No interest bonds for me!
We are marching on to Washington.

Millions of honest citizens can nothing get to do.
Desolation fills our stores, and fields and factories too;
But we are bound to drive it out, old things we'll change to new.
We are marching to Washington.

Corporations fret and fume and prate about their gold,
Many millions now we have that can't be bought or sold;
We'll have no interest-bearing bonds for black sheep in our fold.
We are marching to Washington.

Americans never can be crushed—they know their mighty power;
They've waited long and suffered much ere this triumphant hour,
And from the face of our fair land interest-bearing bonds we'll scour.
    We are marching to Washington.

On the Capitol steps we'll stand, and there our rights demand,
For non-interest bonds let every loyal citizen raise his hand,
For plenty of money and good roads will make a happy land.
    We are marching to Washington.

On Sundays Browne preached. His sermons seem
to be a strange mixture of prophecy and politics, of
theology and finance. Over the head of the preacher
floated a banner bearing the inscription, "The Kingdom of Heaven (on Earth) is at Hand." In one of
the sermons, of which a report has reached us, he
declared the present condition of the country to be the
fulfilment of the revelation to St. John. The horns
of the beast were the seven conspiracies against the
money of the people; the ten horns were the ten
monopolies, foremost among them the sugar trust.
Grover Cleveland had called an extra session of Congress, and by the aid of "that grey-headed rat from
Ohio, John Sherman," had been able to heal the
wounds of the seventh head by repealing the Silver
Purchasing Bill.

Browne is great in Scripture, and his Biblical allu-
sions are quite Puritanic. Here, for instance, is an
extract from one of his general orders :—

We are fast undermining the structure of monopoly in the hearts of the
people. Like Cyrus of old, we are fast tunneling under the boodlers'
Euphrates, and will soon be able to march under the walls of the second
Babylon and its mysteries too. The infernal blood-sucking bank system will
be overthrown, for the handwriting is on the wall.

In his eyes, Coxeyism is the outward and visible
sign of the second coming of Christ. He wrote at
the beginning of the march the following exposition
of his views on this subject :—

The vision of St. John is as clear to me to-day as to him when he saw it
on the Isle of Patmos. All true prophecies must be on the lines of the pro-

jection of human affairs and human nature by one who has a knowledge of both by many reincarnations until reading intuition. Christ taught the "kingdom of heaven is at hand"—meaning undoubtedly, on the lines of reason, that it could come, whenever the people here willed it, through beneficent government—a co-operative system. St. John saw that it was possible for the people, some time by successive reincarnations, to reach a degree of intelligence when they would abolish usury, and the old world (custom) would pass away, and there would be a "new heaven and a new earth." And as that can only be done by legislation, it must come without bloodshed, as prophesied—by peaceable means. So if this really is the second coming of Christ, "coming as a thief in the night" (as prophesied), in the reincarnation of His soul in the whole people, as I feel certain it now is for the first time since His crucifixion, this movement cannot fail. If it is not His second coming, then it will fail. It is plain to me that the fall of the second "Babylon" is to come true, as was the first, as foretold by Isaiah. What is meant by the second Babylon by the author of Revelation is the money power of usury. The very word he uses as a prefix could not apply with such force to anything else—he is speaking of earthly things. We purpose to unite a pure State with a pure religion, both founded on reason—one in all and all in one.

Here we have the familiar tone of the Fifth Monarchy man with a modern accent.

Coxey writes and speaks with less theological fervour. But, like Browne, he is zealous against all interest-bearing bonds. The watchword of the Coxeyite agitation is "Death to the interest-bearing bond!"

Their legislative programme is not limited to the demands of the Good Road Association. They have two Bills before Congress.

The Road Bill provides for the creation of a country road fund of 500,000,000 dols. to be issued in non-interest-bearing bonds at the rate of 20,000,000 dols. a month. The Bill also provides that all work shall be done by the day, which shall consist of eight hours, and that the lowest rate to be paid shall be 1 dol. 50 cents per day.

The other Bill authorises non-interest-bearing loans to states, territories, counties, townships, municipalities, and incorporated towns or villages, for the purpose of making public improvements. Any of these authorities may borrow a sum or sums not

E

exceeding one-half the assessed value of their real estate. The money is to be issued in the form of 1-dol., 2-dol., 5-dol., 10-dol., and 20-dol. Treasury notes, which shall be full legal tender for all debts, public and private. The Government is to retain 1 per cent. for the expense of engraving and printing. The loan is to be repaid in twenty-five annual instalments of 4 per cent. each.

The scheme may or may not be absurd. But something like it would probably be adopted at once if there were to be a rebellion or a foreign invasion; and in the opinion of many the need of finding work for the workless is not less urgent. Europe spends every year in defensive armaments twice as much as the capital sum asked for by the Coxeyites to make roads, which are indispensable for the material development of the country.

The chief incident in the march to Washington was the crossing of the Blue Mountains in a snowstorm. The passage was a good piece of stiff climbing, which was too much for all but 150. Of those who got through Browne said in a general order, "Your names will all be emblazoned on the scroll of fame. As Henry V. said to his men after the battle of Agincourt, your names will be as familiar as household words." A card of merit was issued to all who made the march, in the following terms :—

The Commonweal of Christ : This certifies that John Souther, of group 3, commune 1, Chicago community of the Commonweal of Christ, is entitled to this souvenir for heroic conduct in crossing the Cumberland Mountains in the face of snow and ice, and despite police persecution and dissension breeders.

Their reception varied. Nowhere was it more enthusiastic than at Alleghany City, where the enthusiasm of the populace was in inverse proportion to the hostility of the police. The army was presented

with a new banner, bearing the following inscription
in gilt letters on white silk :—

Pittsburg and Alleghany.   Laws for Americans.   More money, less misery
good roads.   No interest-bearing bonds.

After reaching the Chesapeake and Ohio canal, the
crusaders transferred themselves to two scows, which
conveyed them for ninety miles in two days at so
much freight per ton, each soldier being averaged at
150 lb. net weight.   After they disembarked they
resumed their march to the Capitol.

The purple banner of the Nazarene floated overhead, followed by the white standard of the Pittsburg
and Alleghany men ; but not for all their banners or
for all their eloquence were they allowed to approach
the steps of the Capitol.   The mounted police broke
up the procession and arrested Browne.   Coxey not
being recognised succeeded in reaching the steps,
where however he was seized and removed.   He
handed his written protest to a reporter, and the first
act of the great Coxeyite demonstration was at an end.

Coxey, Browne, and one other of their colleagues
were tried and convicted of trespassing on the grass
in their attempt to make their way to the steps of
the Capitol.   They were fined, and ordered to be
imprisoned for twenty days.   The muse of history
may yet find a theme for bitter irony in the outcome
of this attempt of the Coxeyites to bring before the
Representatives of the Republic the sufferings of the
voiceless thousands of the unemployed.   Imprisoned
for trespass on the grass—upon which they were
driven to tread owing to the action of the police in
blocking the ordinary means of access to the Capitol
—that was the fate of the petitioners in boots !   An
old world despotism could hardly have treated the
Coxeyite petition with more cynical indifference.

The march to Washington from Massillon was child's play compared with the enterprise undertaken by the Commonwealers who started for Washington from the Pacific Slope. The distance—some three

From *Judge*.]   [May 12, 1894.
SQUELCHED.
" We will present a petition with boots on which cannot be pigeonholed."—Coxey.
Uↄ cle Sam.--" I've got some boots on myself ! "

thousand miles—was a longer walk than that undertaken by the Crusaders of the Middle Ages who started for the Holy Land, and the armies no sooner

"GENERAL" LOUIS C. FRYE (CALIFORNIAN DIVISION).

began to march than they discovered it was indispensable they should go by rail. As they had no money to pay for their freight, this necessity led them naturally to seize railway trains. Sometimes they succeeded in inducing the railway companies to carry them. More frequently they seized goods trains and compelled the conductors to bring them along. But for this expedient they never could have crossed the great desert. There were two different bodies: General Frye's, which started from Los Angeles, and General Kelly's, which came from Sacramento.

The following is the text of the Constitution of Frye's army:—

PREAMBLE.

WHEREAS, The evils of murderous competition; the supplanting of manual labour by machinery; the excessive Mongolian and pauper immigration; the curse of alien landlordism; the exploration, by rent, profit and interest, of the products of the toiler, has centralised the wealth of the nation into the hands of the few, and placed the masses in a state of hopeless destitution.

We have only to look upon the history of the past—like causes produce like results. These same causes led to the downfall of Persia, Greece and conquering Rome. The end came when two per cent. of their population owned all the national wealth.

We have reached that point on our own road to ruin where three per cent. of the population own seventy-six per cent. of all the wealth. Witness the abandoning and selling of children by their parents in San Francisco, on the western shore, and the protest against the slave traffic in children from Italy by New York, on the eastern shore of our nation.

This is one of the signs, history tells us, that preceded the downfall of all the past great nations.

The daily grind of pinching poverty, linked with the thought of a hopeless future, kills even the deep maternal instinct. The greatest crime perpetrated by a nation is to allow her people to be idle and sink into debauched servitude. The strange tragical questions confront us on every hand—

Why is it that those who produce food are hungry?

Why is it that those who make clothes are ragged?

Why is it that those build palaces are houseless?

Why is it that those who do the nation's work are forced to choose between beggary, crime or suicide, in a nation that has fertile soil enough to produce plenty to feed and clothe the world; material enough to build palaces to house them all, and productive capacity, through labour-saving machinery, of forty thousand million man-power, and only sixty-five million souls to feed, clothe and shelter? Recognising the fact that if we wish to escape the doom of the past civilisation something must be done, and done quickly.

Therefore we, as patriotic American citizens, have organised ourselves into an Industrial Army, for the purpose of centralising all the unemployed American citizens at the seat of government (Washington, D.C.) and tender our services to feed, clothe, and shelter the nation's needy, and to accomplish this end we make the following demands on the Government :—

1st. Government employment for all her unemployed citizens.

2nd. The prohibition of foreign immigration for ten years.

3rd. That no alien be allowed to own real estate in the United States.

CONSTITUTION.

ARTICLE I.—NAME.

SECTION 1.—This organisation shall be known as the United States Industrial Army.

SECTION 2.—It shall have the power to make its own Constitution and Bye-Laws and elect its own officers.

ARTICLE II.—HOW COMPOSED.

SECTION 1.—This army shall be composed of American citizens over sixteen years of age, or those who have declared their intentions to become such.

ARTICLE III.—OFFICERS.

SECTION 1.—The officers of the army shall be a general, five aids, a quartermaster general, brigadiers, colonels, captains and sergeants.

SECTION 2.—The general, quartermaster-general and five aids shall be elected by the army; brigadier by his brigade; colonel by his regiment; captain and sergeant by their company.

ARTICLE IV.—THE GENERAL AND STAFF.

SECTION 1.—The general and staff shall have the supervision over the army, and see that the constitution is carried out; grant commissions to recruiting sergeants, and have power to revoke the same.

SECTION 2.—The general and staff shall constitute a court-martial. The accused to have a right of an appeal to a vote of the army against their decision.

SECTION 3.—Officers to hold office during good behaviour.

ARTICLE V.

SECTION 1.—Fifty men shall constitute a company; ten companies a regiment; five regiments a brigade.

ORDER OF DISCIPLINE.

Roll call twice a day, when practicable. Drill once a day, when practicable. Any disobedience of orders shall be sufficient grounds for expulsion from the army. Each regiment to have its own rules of order in conflict with the order of the army.

Adopted at Los Angeles, Cal., March 5, 1894.

Kelly's was larger and more formidable than Frye's. It was twice threatened with Gatling guns—at Sacramento and at Utah. It travelled alternately on foot, by rail, and in flat-bottomed boats, which it built on the Des Moines River. It was sometimes menaced by the authorities, and then fêted by the people. The Pacific armies said little about good roads. Their cry was State aid for the irrigation of the desert. They do not seem to have been acting in concert with Coxey, and General Kelly expressed himself freely in criticism of Coxey's tactics. The most notable feature about their movements was the sympathy which they commanded along the line of their march.

Not even the seizing of trains and the general dislocation of railway transit could alienate the support of the masses. Mr. Sovereign, General Master Workman of the Knights of Labour, with the support of Mr. Debs, of the Railway Labour Union, threatened to tie up all the roads of Iowa if the armies were not allowed facilities across the State. The Knights of Labour and the populace generally stole a train at Council Bluffs, which they generously presented to General Kelly, who, however, refused to accept the gift. In securing that train, a son knocked his father off the engine, of which he was conductor, and helped to take the engine to the camp. Professor Bemis, of the University of Chicago, told the ministers of religion in that city that if the Coxeyites were locked up, "it would be like firing a volcano." "Recent extensive tours," said Mr. Sovereign, of the Knights of Labour, "convince me that the temper of the unemployed is not to be trifled with and goaded by the civil authorities." The American Federation of Labour, a body corresponding to our Trades Union Congress, endorsed the demand for good roads.

In regard to the attitude of labour toward the movement, Samuel Gompers, president of the American Federation of Labour, said :—

"The working people are becoming convinced that it is the duty of a democratic government to see to it that every one of its citizens is given an opportunity to work. Coxeyism is becoming a great eye-opener to organised labour. The rich are becoming too overbearing, and with their trusts and syndicates they are squeezing the labouring classes a little too tight. It is no more than right that they should lend a little of their surplus wealth to the government, without interest, as a buffer to the startling condition of affairs brought about by the hard times. However, what I am angered most

"GENERAL" CHARLES T. KELLY.

about is the position some of the authorities have taken in attempting to intimidate the Coxeyites and induce them to return home. This is altogether too un-American to be thought of or tolerated for a moment. The Coxeyites have just as much right to petition Congress in a way that suits them as have any other honest and peaceable American citizens."

Still more significant was the open encouragement which they received from the governors of certain Western States. Governor Waite, of Colorado, publicly declared that if he were called upon to order out the militia against them, he would only order out the commissariat department. Governor Hogg, of Texas, roundly sided with the army against the railway companies. The railway which brought them to Texas ought, he said, to carry them out of it, unless they wished to remain in the State. He accused the railway authorities of endeavouring to force the men to commit a crime by switching them off in the desert, where they could get neither food nor drink. If they were starved into capturing a passenger train and obstructing the United States Mail, the Federal soldiers would then be called upon to furnish troops to keep the mails moving. Governor Hogg continued :—

No armed force while I am governor will be permitted to shoot down men who commit no greater offence than tramp and beg to keep from starving. If these men were violating any criminal law of our state, I should unhesitatingly have them arrested and punished; but they are not. There is no criminal law in Texas nor in any other state, so far as I am advised, that punishes a man or any set of men for taking free rides in people's carriages or railroad cars.

That was tolerably strong. But the public official declaration of Governor Lewelling, of Kansas, is even more significant :—

The Coxey movement is a spontaneous uprising of the people. It is more than a petition; it is an earnest and vigorous protest against the injustice and tyranny of the age. The demonetisation of silver has been the last straw upon the backs of an overburdened and long-suffering people, and they have taken this method to protest and to assert their manhood and independence. The depth of this movement is not comprehended by the politicians of the old dispensations. It is awe-inspiring, and, believing as I do in divine interposition in the affairs of men, I cannot fail to see an inspiration beyond mere enthusiasm,

This body of men is not a mere aggregation of tramps. Some of the best blood and bone is enlisted, and the wonderful discipline, the patient suffering, the steadfastness of purpose all go to show that this ghost of the "Hunger Demon" will not down at the bidding of plutocracy. The followers of Peter the Hermit were a rabble of men, women, and children. Here we see a vast army of untrained men, all under conscious and willing discipline. It is the marvel of the times, and foreshadows a change in the politics of the government of this nation.

And what is more significant, the spirit of the times will demand fair play and just treatment of these men. The person or party that does them violence in this, their right of petition, will go down before a wave of public indignation which has never been paralleled. Here in Kansas the people should hold public meetings and petition Congress to afford the industrials food and shelter, and give a patient ear to their demands. If this is really a government of the people, shall Congress not at least give ear to such a mighty voice?

If these men are an army of tramps and vagabonds, they are none the less representative in character; and if the government crucible has forced the people into pauperism and vagabondage, still the people shall rule, and thus the voice of vagabondage representing the majority must and shall be heard.

Here indeed is "the marvel of the times foreshadowing a change in the politics of the government of this nation." These Governors of Colorado, of Texas, and of Kansas represent territory covering 440,000 square miles, double the area of the whole German Empire. They were elected by the free vote of three millions of citizens. They represent the law, they answer for order. They are the executive that must answer for order. Confronted by the advancing armies of Coxeyism, that is what they say.

Nor is it only Governors of Western States who sympathise with the Coxeyites. In Chicago an army of a thousand men was recruited to welcome General Kelly, an unfortunate army which set out gallantly to walk to Washington and went to pieces by the way, torn by internal dissensions and maltreated by the Indiana police, who were furnished with raw hide whips for the service. In Oregon a Commonweal band seized a train, was captured, and went incontinently to gaol. A division of Frye's army under one Galvin seized a train in Ohio, and only surrendered under threat of a loaded Gatling.

The dread lest Kelly's men would seize a train paralysed the train service on the Rock Island Railway, and yet when Judge Hubbard called out the National Guard to protect the railroad, the citizens of Council Bluffs hanged him in effigy, and passed a resolution intimating their desire that he should leave the city at once. A newspaper reporter at Council Bluffs, describing the state of public feeling, says :—

Should there be a move to force the order for the army to move on or should it disband there will be trouble. The people of this city and Omaha are in sympathy with the Commonwealers, as was evinced yesterday when they marched through the streets. Men cheered them on their way, and women were crying over the sad sight of such a crowd of able-bodied men, many with families, out of employment and homeless. If they are fired on by the militia, the sentiment is at such a pitch that Kelly and his army could be reinforced with ten thousand people in two hours.

The discipline and enthusiasm of Kelly's brigade is notable. The men have slept night after night on the bare earth without blankets. " Visitors to the camp," says a reporter, " have noticed the constant and severe coughing that is going on there. Last night General Kelly gave to a sick comrade the last blanket he had, and passed the night on the ground. Eight men were removed from their beds on the earth this morning by the local hospital corps." Notwithstanding this the army pressed steadily on. Kelly sometimes made them tramp twenty miles a day across American roads in spring time, and once made a forced march of forty miles.

The stories with which the American papers have been filled for the last month of the seizure and recapture of railway trains form a very remarkable chapter in the annals of modern romance.* It is

* The most picturesque and romantic incident in the train stealing was the forced loan of a train that was taken by two young ladies out of sheer sympathy with Kelly's sick soldiers. The story as it is told by the official historian Vincent is as follows :—

An incident connected with the capture of the engine and train in the Union Pacific transfer yards at Council Bluffs, April 20, was generally overlooked at the time by the newspaper

MISS HOOTEN AND MISS HARPER.

amazing that so much train-seizing, train-chasing, and
train-capture could have gone on for a whole month
with so little loss of life. A band of one hundred or
two hundred men seizes a train, and, in reckless
defiance of time-tables and traffic managers, steams
out eastward, pursued after a time by another train
laden with armed men ; while in front the railway
company exhaust the ingenuity of their engineers in
throwing obstructions across the line. Sometimes
they tear up fifty yards of the permanent way, at
other times they screw a rail across the track, but
their favourite device was to create an improvised
barricade by derailing a locomotive and planting it
across the line. The Commonwealers never seem
to run into these obstructions. They discover them
in time, tear up the rails over which they have passed,
improvise a short semi-circle of railway round the
obstacle, and steam gaily on, leaving the obstructions
behind them to impede their pursuers. After a time
the forces of law and order overtake them ; they
surrender ; they are sealed up without food or water
in goods waggons, and carried off to gaol. But that

correspondents. Kelly and his men were encamped at Weston, fourteen miles east of the city.
The railroad managers and state officials had turned a deaf ear to their entreaties for transportation, and the indignant citizens had risen *en masse*, as it were, to demand that a train be
provided for the army. The demand was in vain, and when the crowd took the matter in its
own hands and went to the railroad yards to steal a train, it was headed by two young women
of Council Bluffs—Annie Hooten and Edna Harper. They led the attack, which resulted in
the capture of the engine, and went with the train to Weston, where they offered it to General
Kelly. Kelly refused the offer. Warrants were obtained for the arrest of the girls, but they
escaped, and afterwards joined the army on its trip across the state of Iowa. They declared
their intention of accompanying the army to Washington, and a suitable conveyance was
obtained for them. They were present at the big public gathering held in the opera house at
Atlantic, Iowa, on the evening of April 25, and were induced by the citizens to get upon the
stage and tell the story of how they captured the engine. They pushed their way to the stage,
where their courage seemed to forsake them, but finally Annie Hooten, with the other standing
beside her, said, in an abashed way: "You want to know how we stole the engine. Well, I
will tell you how we stole the engine, though I never stood up before an audience before. We
heard that there were sick men at the camp at Chautauqua, and we wanted to help them.
We were excited and did not know what to do, and then we stole the engine and ran it down to
the camp, and had the sick men put aboard and hauled them back to the city. That is the
way we stole the engine. We did not know it was wrong then, but somebody afterward told
us it was wrong, so we are sorry we did anything wrong. That's how it was. We wish to
thank the citizens of Atlantic for receiving the army so kindly, for you must know we consider
ourselves part of the army, as we are going through to Washington with it." This was
received with rapturous applause, and the meeting ended.

in no way deters other bands from repeating the same manœuvre the very next day. It is simply marvellous that with such a campaign going on day after day, in a dozen different states, so few men have been killed. The authorities arm their men with repeating Winchester revolvers ; many of the Commonwealers have six-shooters. Yet no one gets killed ; and all this fooling with rolling-stock so far does not seem to have produced a single serious accident. The powerlessness of the railways to prevent this lawless appropriation of their property by bands of Commonwealers so numerically insignificant is one of the most serious and significant features of the agitation.

After the arrival of the Coxeyites at Washington, there was a good deal of discussion in the press and elsewhere as to the significance of the movement.

The *North American Review* for June published three articles upon Coxeyism by three representative Americans, all of whom take a very serious view of the movement.

Major-General Howard, writing on the significance and the aims of the movement, says :—

The Coxey movement is unique in its inception, different from any other in the history of our country, and, indeed, quite unlike ordinary revolutionary experiments. The attempt to affect United States legislation by organising the unemployed into peaceful hosts and marching them, without previous furnishing of supplies, by the precarious means of begging their way for hundreds of miles, to the Capital, appears to ordinary minds the height of absurdity. Yet notwithstanding an almost unanimous press against their contemplated expedition, notwithstanding the discouragement by members of Congress with hardly a dissenting voice, and all legal checks upon them by State and United States executive power, Coxey's first contingent is already in Washington, Kelly's from San Francisco at Des Moines, Ia.; Frye's, organised in Los Angeles, Cal., is in Pennsylvania ; the Rhode Island body, calling itself a delegation of unemployed workmen, has passed New York; and many other companies under different designations are organising, or have already accomplished miles *en route.*

General Howard endeavours to comfort himself by reflecting that Coxeyism is not so serious as the revolutionary movement in Europe, but he thinks that something should be done. He says :—

> It seems an absolute necessity that the holders of capital and labour should come to a cordial, mutual understanding; and certainly the day is not far distant when there will be a competent tribunal established by our Congress to adjust questions of difference and secure co-operation without resorting to the dangerous and costly methods of strikes and peremptory discharges.

Mr. Byrnes, Superintendent of the New York police, takes an even more serious view of the situation. He says that the movement is the most dangerous that the country has ever seen since the Civil War. If there is no law to check it, he thinks that one ought promptly to be passed, for the movement is illegal, un-American, and odious, and should have been put a stop to long ago. Coxeyism is spreading the socialistic doctrine that the majority may be ruled by the minority ; and if it is carried out much further, the United States will fall into a chaos in which mobs will be fighting mobs everywhere. He points out that the Coxeyites in Montana mobbed a United States marshal and his deputies, captured a train on the Northern Pacific and started east, compelling the railway company to clear the track in order to avoid a frightful collision. A United States regiment had to be called out to seize them.

Mr. Doty, Chief of the Bureau of Contagious Diseases, calls attention to the danger to public health that is involved in Coxeyism :—

> It is easy to understand that as a means of increasing contagious diseases throughout the country, Coxeyism is an agent of the most vicious type.

With the following practical suggestion Dr. Doty concludes his paper :—

> It seems strange that, while religious and other societies, philanthropists and rich men, are cudgelling their brains to find the best method of improving the lowest class, the important necessity of public baths should not occur to

them. These should be built on a large scale, with every possible convenience, even to a barber's shop, where a tramp could occasionally have his hair cut and face shaved, which luxury he is at present deprived of. The baths should always be opened and made attractive. When this is done, there will be fewer Anarchists found, and fewer hospitals needed.

Senator W. V. Allen, the Populist leader, thus expressed himself to the American editor of the *Review of Reviews,* who asked him if he were sponsor for Coxey. The Senator replied :—

" Not in the least. I disapprove utterly of the marching of these industrial armies toward Washington, and see nothing to commend in Mr. Coxey's financial proposals. This movement is in no way connected with Populism, and the Populist party is not responsible for it. It might naturally be true that these men should look to the Populist party as the advocate of remedies for the conditions out of which their grievances arise, but that is all. I look upon Coxeyism as I do upon the foam that accumulates upon waters that are lashed by storm. It is simply the lighter part—the floating evidence that there is commotion in the water beneath, and that something under the surface, rocks perhaps, disturbs the calm. It has no other significance to me It is like an unsightly eruption on the body politic, that is symptomatic of something wrong in the system. The boil on my hand is not the evil, but merely the evidence that there is impurity in the blood that flows hidden in the veins. So it is with the Coxey movement. Here are a lot of fellows that are out of employment. They know that they want work. They talk more than they reason. One fellow says it is this that will give relief, and another says it is that. There is no particular significance in their demands. Their idea in marching on to Washington is to demand that the Government should do something to afford relief. But all this is only the logical consequence of those conditions of which I have been speaking. I have never been out to see the Coxey army, and have no sympathy with the movement or with its specific purposes. I had never heard of it until I read the newspaper accounts. I think it wholly visionary ; but whether visionary or not, I would make the same arguments for the right of Mr. Vanderbilt in a peaceable manner to present his grievances, if he had any, that I would make, and have already made on the floor of the Senate, for Coxey. In this country m n are upon an equality of rights, and they must be treated alike. This is a far as I have ever gone in behalf of the Coxey people."

Dr. Shaw, my American Editor, who visited the camp at Washington in June, says :—

I was reminded by the Coxey camp of certain romantic characteristics that pertained to some of the attempts many years ago in the West to establish phalansteries on the Fourier plan, and that have marked other detached projects in the line of communism. The Coxeyites had pitched their tents around three-and-a-half sides of a nearly square field, the middle of which had been converted into an excellent baseball ground. Good ball players were numerous among them, and spirited match games seemed to be a part of each afternoon's diversion. In the stream hard by were plenty of fish ; and Chief-Marshal Carl Browne had procured seines with which it was

F

proposed to obtain an abundant supply of that kind of food. The various squads of Commonwealers were vieing with each other in the decoration of their tents and booths. They were laying out ornamental flower beds, and making much ingenious preparation of a festive nature in view of the approach of the 4th of July. They were all comfortable, and, so far as one could learn, were nearly all of them members of skilled trades. Most of them appeared to be from twenty to twenty-five years old. Inasmuch as the times were dull at home and they were out of work when they started for Washington, and inasmuch, furthermore, as they were not obliged to give support to dependent women or children, they felt at liberty to prolong somewhat indefinitely their quixotic sojourn at Washington. They were intelligent enough to enjoy the great notoriety they had attained. There was not a sick man in the entire camp, and not a particle of evidence of grief or distress or crushed spirits. The leaders were probably perplexed; but as for the men in the ranks, they were well aware that when the times improved, or the Coxey business was played out, they could find work at their trades. A good many of these men were from the industrial towns of Rhode Island and Connecticut, while Philadelphia was also well represented. It was evident enough that so far as anything serious was concerned, the movement had fallen completely flat.

Nevertheless we have no desire to belittle that movement unduly or to refuse recognition of the fact that there are deeply serious conditions out of which it has in part come. The return of a brief season of prosperity may obscure those conditions somewhat, but may not remove them. It is the business of the statesman, the journalist, and the intelligent citizen to face these conditions frankly and earnestly in order that Coxeyism may not return to plague us in some more dangerous form. It is gratifying to believe that there is not so much distress throughout the country as there was three months ago. But we ought not lightly to forget how widespread and how painful that distress was through a period of about half a year. We cannot count forever upon the buoyancy of American conditions.

The historian of the Commonweal movement, in closing his narrative in June, says :—

Probably not less than twenty-five expeditions are now on foot in as many parts of the country, while others, as at Chicago, are rapidly organising with a view to the strengthening of the present forces. The magnitude the movement has already assumed is a matter of surprise to all, especially to those who are not in sympathy with it. That which was regarded at first as an amusing joke has become a most grave matter to the people of the entire country.

The latest reports from Washington indicate that the administrative authorities are beginning to make ready for meeting the responsibilities which may grow out of the gathering of the Commonweal. It is advised by the officers of the War Department that Coxey's men be treated as free citizens, who have a right to enter the city and remain in it as long as they are obedient to the laws of the country. General Schofield has been directed to remain in Washington, in anticipation of any emergency. The result of interviews with nearly fifty of the Senators, is that the Commonwealers are clearly within the law in their movement upon Washington. The health commissioner has announced that he will meet the various arrivals on the district line with a corps of assistants and examine every person, to see that he is free from disease, and upon the discovery of any contagious disorder will quarantine the entire body until all danger shall have passed.

As the result of the approach of the forces, the Capitol officials have begun to be more stringent as to admissions to the Senate gallery, permitting only such to enter as have cards of admission, and fresh ones must be had upon each separate visit. It is stated that a similar order will prevail in the House at an early date. Woodley Park, which immediately adjoins the summer residence of President Cleveland, has been tendered to General Coxey for occupancy by his army, and he has accepted the same; the owner having offered it free of charge for an indefinite period.

Reports received at police headquarters, at Washington, show that the growth of the several armies is more rapid as they converge nearer to the National Capitol, the aggregate number of Commonwealers being nearly seven thousand; this embraces but twelve of the moving bodies. The authorities quoted express the opinion that the number of the Commonwealers will swell to exceedingly large proportions, if there are no difficulties in the way of securing sufficient food at Washington. There is no likelihood of Federal troops being brought before the scene at Washington, so it is semi-officially stated, unless the local police are unable to properly handle the matter. There is undeniable evidence that the concern already expressed at Washington is growing in intensity as time passes, and that the success which has followed the movements of the Commonweal up to the present has afforded great encouragement to the discontented in the various towns and cities of the Union who are likely to follow in the footsteps of those who have gone before.

Journalists laugh at Coxeyism. The labouring people sympathise, and in the end it is the latter who will prevail. We are not unfamiliar with similar petitions in boots in London. Lazarus showed his sores in Trafalgar Square, and the unemployed tramped their shoes off their feet in 1886–7, demonstrating their desire for work. London newspapers, with one or two exceptions, scoffed and flouted the agitators. The metropolitan police broke up the processions and cleared the Square amid the cheers of Dives and his myrmidons. John Burns and Cuninghame Graham were flung into prison, and for a time there was peace, the peace and the silence of the grave. But in two short years London elected its first County Council, and John Burns fresh from prison became the most influential member of the new governing body. The men of Trafalgar Square became the rulers of Spring Gardens, and the greatest movement of our time in the direction of municipal socialism is being conducted at this moment in the name of the London Council

COXEY'S CRAZY CHASE.—THIS IS WHAT COMES OF PREACHING "PATERNALISM."

by the representatives of the army of discontent which bivouacked at the base of Nelson's Column only seven years ago.

There is something so abhorrent to human reason in the waste of the labour of a million willing workers in a continent which has not yet decent roads through its most populous districts, that everyone must sympathise with the attempt by pacific, although irregular, methods to force the subject upon the attention of the Government. Coxey may be mad, and Kelly may be visionary, but America needs good roads and the arid lands of the West await irrigation. General Frye's demands are more extensive. He wants Government employment, the prohibition of all immigration for ten years, and the prevention of all aliens holding land in the United States. If a hostile power were to invade the United States, the necessity of repelling the enemy would compel the Government to find means wherewith to utilise this waste mass of human force in making fortifications, roads, and other indispensable necessaries of successful war. But as there is no enemy in the field save Hunger and Cold, the Government is paralysed. It has neither funds nor initiative now.

So it has come to pass that these workless workers are endeavouring, more or less aimlessly, to force on a crisis that may be as effective although not so bloody a stimulant to action as actual war. They realise, do these unemployed industrials, that governments when threatened with destruction by war can find at least rations for all the troops they can raise. What then if they are equally threatened by armies of industrials marching resolutely onwards to the capital? Of the capacity of these industrial armies to place whole districts in a state of siege, there is already evidence enough and to spare. The seizure of railway trains, the suspension of traffic along whole lines of rail, the calling out of the militia, the parading of Gatling guns, the pursuit and capture of trains by United States cavalry, all this may be regarded as but playful, somewhat tragically playful reminders that even in a free Republic the condition of the government going on is that men must somehow or other be fed. What will be the end of it all who can say? No prophecy can be made with any degree of certainty, excepting this, that the end is not yet. A revival of trade may postpone further developments at present, but if all the lessons drawn from past history are not mistaken, Coxeyism will in future assume much more menacing dimensions, unless, forestalling the evil betimes, the Americans decide upon adopting a policy which will give the workless something better to do than the organising of petitions in boots.

CHAPTER III.—THE HIGGLING OF THE MARKET—
AMERICAN FASHION.

THE ruins of Finchale Abbey, on the river Wear, still
remain to attest the sanctity of the north-country
ascetic whose shrine it was in days of old. In his
hot youth the saint, before he became a saint, was
permitted by the grace of God (so runs the ancient
legend) to see a vision of Hell. The sight trans-
formed his life. From that moment he abandoned
his sins and endeavoured by the cruellest mortifica-
tion of his body to testify to the sincerity of his
repentance. When he had looked into Hell he saw
that it was the Hell of Extremes. Side by side with
the conventional blazing fiery furnace there was a
place of intense cold, full of thick-ribbed ice, and
driving hail, and biting winds, so bitter that he could
not say which was worse to bear, the Hell of Heat or
the Hell of Cold. But ever afterwards he sought to
inflict upon himself at Finchale some foretaste of the
doom of the damned. In high noon in hottest
summer he would lie blistering and scorched on the
heated rocks. In midwinter he would sit up to the
neck in a hole broken in the ice of the frozen Wear.
And when the country folk would expostulate with
him as he lay baking in the sun, he answered nothing
but " I have seen greater heat." In like wise when
in winter they adjured the saint to come out of his
bath-hole in the icy river, as the cold was too great
for mortal man to bear, he would murmur, " I have
seen greater cold."

This north-country tale comes back to me when I hear Englishmen groaning about our labour troubles. For I have been in the United States, and when I hear our labour men declaiming against the tyranny of capital, the despotism of employers, and the grievances inflicted upon workmen, I reply, with the saint of Finchale, "I have seen greater tyranny." So, in like manner, when employers denounce the violence of high-handed unionists and the unreasonableness of strikers, I shrug my shoulders and reply, " I have seen worse violence." For, as I have said, I have been in the United States, and in industrial matters our American kinsfolk are where we were forty or fifty years ago when rattening was the first word of an outlawed unionism and murder the ultimate argument against the blackleg. What Sheffield was in the palmy days of Broadhead and Crookes, before the Royal Commission was appointed which revealed the secrets of a unionism resting upon the foundation of assassination—preached as a virtue and practised as a necessity—so Pittsburg is to-day, and when we say Pittsburg we say Chicago, Denver, or any other great industrial centre. Hence, when an Englishman returns from the United States to the worst strike region in the United Kingdom he is conscious of an immediate and unmistakable change for the better. Our difficulties are bad enough, but they are as moonlight is to sunlight, as water is to wine, compared with the industrial feuds which rage on the other side of the Atlantic.

I can best illustrate this by briefly stringing together a few of the incidents of the labour war which has been raging for the last month or two in the coke and mining industries of America. As my object is to describe the temper of the disputants rather than to discuss the merits of the dispute, I will not confuse the issue by details as to the points of difference between the parties. Nothing is more misleading than the dissertations upon rates of wages in one country addressed to readers in another land, where no one knows anything about the purchasing value of the money discussed. It may be taken for granted in every case that the workers and their employers are at variance because they differ as to their respective shares of the profits of their industry. Times are bad in the United States ; the unemployed are numerous, and the employers, confronted by cut-throat competition between themselves, seek to cut prices by cutting wages. Against this the workmen rebel, and an industrial war ensues, which is called a strike or a lock-out, according to the sympathies of the speaker. This may be taken for granted as the ordinary groundwork of all the disputes to which I am about to refer. A very interesting article might be written describing the points in dispute and the final settlement of the great strike in the bituminous coal trade, which began in April, paralysing the industry of nearly 200,000 miners, and a far greater number of others whose work depends upon coal, but for that I have no space, nor would it be so useful, on the whole, as the illustrations which I proceed to give of the mode in which industrial warfare is carried on in the land of " Triumphant Democracy."

Here, for instance, is an episode culled from the newspapers, describing the strike in Mr. Carnegie's country—the State founded by William Penn on principles of peace, brotherhood, and good-will. It is interesting in many ways. It shows the ordinary methods of compulsion employed by strikers, the means of resistance resorted to, and the results which follow. When the strike was declared, the men in several mines refused to join in the movement. They preferred to continue at work ; they had no quarrel with their employers, and they went down the mines as usual. The strikers decided that they must be brought into line. This was effected by methods hardly distinguishable from those of civil war.

The strikers organised a small Army of Intimidation, about 500 strong, at Uniontown, Pennsylvania. This army was as destitute of uniform and of discipline as the first tumultuary levies of the French Revolution, but, like the *sans-culottes*, it had grim resolve in its heart to use the weapons which it held in its hand. The Army of Intimidation, operating from its base at Uniontown, had its plan of campaign, its leaders, and its arsenal. Its soldiers were armed not merely with clubs, according to the ancient tradition of all such irregular levies, but also with revolvers. With these they marched from mine to mine to "persuade" the men at work to join the strike. Arguments as to the holy cause of the brotherhood of labour, which might otherwise have fallen upon deaf ears, became singularly persuasive when accompanied by the click of the revolver. The mere sound of their approach sufficed in some cases to close the mines, the miners flying to the open country to escape with their lives. In other places, where they did not rightly appreciate the moral earnestness of the strikers, conviction was borne in upon them by clubbing. The Army had closed several mines in this way when the mine-owners thought it necessary to act on the defensive. As there are no police to speak of and no soldiers, the sheriff, to whom they appealed for protection, enrolled deputy sheriffs or, as we should say, special constables, and despatched them to protect life and property at the threatened mines. These deputies, armed with Winchester repeating rifles, garrisoned the mines. What followed bears a curious resemblance to the skirmishes that marked the beginning of our civil war in the seventeenth century, when Roundhead and Cavalier in turn made sallies upon each other's strongholds, and either carried the place by a sudden rush or were beaten off after an exchange of shots with a man or two killed or wounded. The Army of Intimidation on April 4 marched from Uniontown to Fairchance, closing with violence all mines that lay on the line of march. Rainey's mines, however, they were compelled to leave working, as they were guarded by a strong detachment of deputies armed with Winchesters. At McClure's works shots were exchanged, some of which slew a Hungarian in the intimidating army. Another intimidator was shot at the Donelly and Mayfield mines which were garrisoned by Englishmen. At the Davidson Mine, a little further on, the army was more successful. They looted the works, drove the miners out, destroyed the engines and buildings. A shot was fired which enraged the conquerors. Bent on vengeance, they dashed up the tip, where the chief-engineer Paddock was standing. Paddock tried to escape amid a fusillade of stones and bullets. He fell shot in the back of the head. His pursuers pounded him with stones and clubs, and then to "mak' siccar," three of them carried the bleeding body to a window, and flung it out on to the ovens, forty feet below. The army then, glutted with vengeance and flushed with victory, evacuated the wrecked mine, and marched on. But the sensational incident of the murder of chief-engineer Paddock succeeded in doing that most difficult of all things, it roused phlegmatic and apathetic American sentiment. Telegrams announcing his death were despatched all over the district, and at Connellsville, where they possess a lock-up, "conservative citizens began to talk lynch law." They did more than talk. A body of citizens, armed with guns and revolvers, started in pursuit under the county detective, to avenge the death of Paddock. After a hot chase, they came up with the rear guard. A skirmish ensued, in which the Avengers shot two of the Intimidators dead, and took eleven of them prisoners, whom they brought back in triumph to the lock-up. Another batch of fifty-three were brought in later. "A large crowd gathered and loud cries went up for the blood of the captives." But they were safely housed in the lock-up. Thirty more were captured, and then the president of the Miners' Association was arrested at Uniontown. Altogether 150 men were placed under arrest.

The Army of Intimidation was by no means intimidated. The same telegram that reported the arrest of the miners' president added that 3,000 strikers were on the march to the Moyer works. At Broadford, two strikers were killed and one fatally wounded, "bringing the total to six men killed by bullets in one day." At night the scene in the mining region resembled a seat of war. 1500 strikers, mostly Hungarians and Poles, encamped near Scottsdale, and through the night the blaze of a hundred camp fires marked the bivouac of the intimidating force. Rainey's works, bristling with the Winchesters of determined deputies, were menaced by 1200 men; but ultimately it was decided to place them under guard. At this time it was computed 10,000 men strikers were encamped for purposes of intimidation around the Rainey Mines. All this occurred in the early days of April, before the great coal strike had begun. A month later, on May 4, another ugly outbreak occurred. At the Painter Coke Works in Fayette Co., the strikers stormed the place, knocked down the engineer, beat him into insensibility with heavy clubs, and were on the point of cutting off his head with an axe when they were driven back by officials armed with Winchesters. A dozen men and women were wounded before the works were cleared. Connellsville, the scene of the rally of conservative citizens a month before, was still in a disturbed state. The prompt action of the Coal Company in arming a large force with Winchesters somewhat discouraged the strikers, who, instead of attacking the works, contented themselves with marching backwards and forwards before the works displaying red flags. But although discouraged, the strikers were not cowed. On May 23, the Army of Intimidation was got together again in Uniontown, as may be seen from the following entry :—

"Nine hundred miners started at midnight of the 23rd for Stickle Hollow to attack the Washington Coal and Coke Company's works. Several contingents joined them, making altogether 2000 men with bands, guns and clubs. Waited for the men to come up from the mines, and as they appeared, they summoned them to quit work. As they were doing this, the deputies appeared from ambush behind a car, and poured a volley into the midst of the strikers. They fled, but were pursued by continuous volleys from the deputies, who numbered seventy-five. Five strikers were shot dead, and several wounded. Deputies say the strikers also fired.

"At Fairchance the Frick Company have manned their pit with armed deputies."

In such fashion, in the Pennsylvanian coke region in the year of grace 1894, do employers and employed seek to adjust their differences.

It will be said, and with justice, that the Pennsylvania coke district has been stuffed with foreign immigrants, and that it is unfair to refer to this strike as a typical American labour dispute. It is no doubt true that the most of the intimidatory armies of Pennsylvania were Hungarians or Huns, as the Americans style them, and Poles. The American Protectionist of those parts, having secured a heavy duty on all imported goods by pretending that a high tariff was necessary to enable him to pay high wages to American labour, no sooner secured his tariff than he imported thousands of Huns and Poles, on whom there was no import duty, in order to undersell the American workman. Hence the presence of these foreign elements which undoubtedly contribute considerably to the bitterness of the industrial war. An ugly illustration of this occurred at Detroit in April. A wages dispute between the Detroit municipality and their workmen led to an attack by 700 Poles upon the sheriff and his deputies, which resulted in the killing of two men and the wounding of fifteen others. The sheriff himself was almost killed. He was knocked down and hewed at with pick and shovel on his head and body. An artery in the leg was severed, and he was not expected to live. But although it would be a mistake to debit all the outrages to the foreigner's account, there is no doubt that he is always an element of danger. This comes out very clearly in the history of the great coal strike, which was declared on April 11.

The struggle in the bituminous coal trade attained the dimensions of a national dispute. The States involved were sixteen in number, but the chief seats of the strike were in Illinois, Ohio, Indiana, Pennsylvania, and West Virginia. Of 189,000 miners, 178,000 came out on strike, voluntarily or otherwise. The Union ordered a universal strike. Mines that were working at Union rates were laid idle equally with those where reductions had been made. "The fight for living ·wages is a general fight, and no local settlements will be authorised or recognised," was the dictum of President McBride. Until a general settlement has been declared, " coal must not be loaded at any price, or for any purpose." Naturally many miners who were working at Union rates did not see the sense of coming out. Hence the necessity for the tactics which were employed, and very generally employed, to enforce obedience to the orders of the Union. The following are a few of the incidents in the course of this strike extracted from a diary compiled from the *Chicago Herald :*

" April 23.—Mob of 1500 miners marched to La Salle, Ill., to prevent tl e miners working. A riot ensued. Most of the men carried revolvers stilettoes, and daggers.

" 200 miners crossed over into Western Virginia from Ohio, and forcibly took the men from the pits.

"April 26.—Acting-Governor Gill ordered out five companies of the Chicago Militia to be in readiness to protect the mines. The miners march-ing on La Salle had seven brass bands, a drum and five corps, and seven commissary waggons. 100 teams of people followed them, making a pro-cession three miles long.

"April 27.—3000 miners, chiefly foreigners, marched into Teluka, I l., carrying pistols and clubs, and armed with dynamite bombs. They came in six divisions of 500 men each. The coloured miners work; the Unions do not protect the blacks, who are denied admission to the Unions. The miners were persuaded away from Teluka.

" May 3.—Mesaba Iron Company, fifty-eight, mostly Finns, secured ex-plosives, with the avowed purpose of blowing up people in Virginia, Minn., and the neighbourhood.

"At Peoria, Ill., 600 miners, armed with clubs, and followed by twenty-five carriages, compelled several mines to close.

" Finns ugly at Virginia, Minn. 1000 strikers met the regular troops, who had been called out, at the depôt.

" May 5.—Strikers shot by Marshal Free at Mountain Iron, Minn. Twenty minutes after the Marshal left the town a mob of 500 strong, armed with crowbars, axes, Winchesters, and ropes, took possession of the place.

" May 6.—The Coal Company at Stanton, Ill., received a consignment of arms. A fence built round the collieries, and other fortifications made in anticipation of trouble.

" May 7.—At Birmingham, Alabama, 200 strikers went to Price's mine.

Put dynamite under the boiler and engines, and blew them up, then destroyed the property of the mining company. They then marched on, blowing up a car loaded with timber on their way. They let the other cars down a hill, and wrecked them.

"May 11.—The strikers at Pana, Ill., broke into the powder house, filled sections of the gas-pipe with powder, and then exploded it under the windows of the working miners. Notices, 'If you don't quit work it will be murder,' posted over the town.

"May 12.—At Oskaloosa, Iowa, 500 strikers, with brass band and leaders on horseback, marched in double file, ordered the American Coal Company's men out.

"May 20.—At Birmingham, Alabama, a mob of strikers went to a miner who refused to come out. As he unfastened the door they fired a volley, riddling him with bullets. He died instantly. The mob then entered the house, firing right and left.

"May 21.—Strikers. 200 strong, each carrying a heavy club, called at all the smaller mines at Danville, Ill. They said, 'Now, you fellows, look out! After this no more talk goes. We will fix you if you take another pound of coal out.' All the tools in Beard's mine were stolen, and thrown into the Vermilion River. The tools and cars at another mine were destroyed, and the track torn up.

"At Breeze 250 miners arrived, with two waggons and provisions and tents, and camped near the West Mine, to see that no one went to work.

"At Stanton, the Consolidated Coal Company ordered a shipment of Winchesters, 100 shells containing 5 drachms of powder and several ounces of shot, all that could be had at St. Louis. A like shipment ordered from Chicago. The Citizens' Defence Organisation is organised in squads, each under its leader. Drilled daily.

"May 23.—600 strikers on their way by train from Missouri to Leavenworth, Kan., to induce 800 miners, whose wages were increased, to join the strike. Alarm bells will be sounded; 500 citizens with arms will meet the sheriff at the Court House, and receive strikers.

"At Pana, Ill., 800 men are at work in the mines : 1000 strikers massing in the district to turn them out. The Coal Companies received shipments of revolvers, Winchesters, and ammunition. Guns kept in the mine. Miners all armed and prepared. Citizens organise to defend the miners.

"At Danville, Ill., 1000 strikers compelled 200 men to leave work and join the strike. The 1000 miners were armed with knives, pistols, and clubs. They also had a covered waggon filled with rifles. Principally Hungarians, with bottles of whiskey in their pockets or in their hands. The sheriff had only 35 deputies. The deputies collapsed.

"At Evansville, Ind., 200 strikers attacked 30 workers, severely beating and bruising the non-Unionists. The strikers came with waggons laden with provisions and Winchester rifles. After a fight, in which two men were killed and five wounded, the mine was shut down. The strikers camped at its mouth, supplied with six weeks' provisions and firearms.

"At Pana, Ill., 500 strikers threatened to kill the men engaged in putting out the fires in the mines. Striker arrested and liberated from prison by the mob.

"At Kangli, near Streator, Ill., 30 strikers attacked six workers. The manager fired on them, whereupon the strikers hunted them into the woods, threw the boiler and engine down the pit, and smashed everything they could.

"May 24.—At La Salle, Ill., Sheriff Taylor, while protecting the County

Cabon Coal Company, was attacked by several hundred strikers with revolvers, stones, &c. The sheriff, two deputies, and five miners were wounded. Many arrests made. Telegraphed for militia. 500 miners, armed and organised in Spring Valley, marched to release prisoners. Sheriff removed in closed carriage to escape murder.

"At Pana the Citizens' Protective League of 600 members organised. 2000 strikers threaten to attack. Injured the electric light plant. Town in darkness. Preparations made to receive them with three volleys from a thousand Winchesters.

"250 strikers, with pistols, knives, and clubs, marched from the neighbouring mines to Carterville. Superintendent of police, supported by a crowd armed with Winchesters, rifles, muskets, and pistols, leave Carbonville for the scene of action.

"May 25.—At La Salle six companies of the National Guard encamped on the hills. 600 strikers attack, but are driven back with fixed bayonets. Militia occupy a position of great strategic strength.

"At Stanton, Ill., the last of the forty-eight mines of the Consolidated Coal Company closed as the forces at the disposal of the Company inadequate to protect mine. Train derailed by strikers near Mount Olive.

"200 strikers on their way to Ottawa, Ill., hunt miners from Gorfat mine, burn waggons, tools and clothes, knock in props at the main entrance, pits cave in. Every road leading into Ottawa is now picketed with heavily armed men. If the strikers approach, fire bells will be rung and hundreds of citizens will rally with rifles and shot guns.

"Miners congregate at Pana, Ind., from all sides. 2000 from the South, 1000 North. 300 deputies, composed of the best citizens, bankers, merchants, journalists, &c., prepare to receive them. 700 men still at work.

"At Birmingham, Ala., 700 State troops ordered out.

"At Brookside strikers try to blow up a water main, were fired upon, six wounded.

"May 26.—At La Salle at ten o'clock at night five explosions heard. An attack expected, but nothing occurred.

"At Lad, Ill., 400 drunken armed strikers seized Burlington freight train and came on to Spring Valley towards La Salle. Six companies of troops marched out to capture train. They had their sides 'bulging' with ball-cartridge. Dispersed the strikers, capturing three prisoners. Police report that the strikers have thousands of pounds of dynamite. Mine owners unable to account for fully ten tons. None of the local papers publish the news, the *La Salle Tribune* saying that if anything appeared reflecting upon the foreign element they would be blown up with dynamite. Governor Altgelt all day receiving telegrams for troops, arms, and ammunition."

Until the middle of May the tactics of the strikers had been chiefly confined to intimidating non-Unionists and closing mines by force. The last weeks of May saw a new and very serious development in the shape of a blockade of the railways. No one who has not been in America can adequately realise the extent to which civilisation is an affair of railroads. Railways in England were conveniences of communication. In the United States, especially in the Western States, they were necessaries of existence. The miners' strike, by creating a coal famine, threatened society with a danger which was enormously intensified by the action of the miners. Finding that, notwithstanding all their efforts, some mines continued in operation, they decided to institute a coal blockade of the railways. Their leaders repudiated the policy, but it was none the less carried out.

Gangs of miners encamped upon the main lines of railway in Indiana and Illinois, piled railway tires across the track, and compelled every train to pull up for examination. If there was no coal on board, it was allowed to proceed. If there were any coal cars, they were side-tracked or ditched before the rest of the train was permitted to pass the obstruction. Here are a few entries relating to this portentous development of industrial war :—

"May 25.—At Evansville, Ind., the strikers stopped coal trains.

"At Shelburne, the strikers will allow no more coal to pass.

"At La Salle an Illinois Central freight train was wrecked by strikers piling railway tires on the rails. It was intended to wreck the express train, because the Illinois Central was using coal from the La Salle shaft. English-speaking strikers unable to control the Russians, Poles, and Belgians.

"Thirty car loads of coal side-tracked, on the East Illinois Railway at Lifford, Ind., by the strikers.

"At Minonk, Ill., the strikers decide to stop coal on the Illinois Central.

"May 26.—At Brazil, Ind., strikers capture a car of coal, side-track it, and leave it in charge of fifty women.

"May 27.—At Minonk, Ill., 200 miners, Poles, Belgians, and Hungarians, encamp at junction of Sante Fe and Illinois Central. Only trains without coal allowed to pass. Bonfires are blazing at the crossings within a block of the sheriff's headquarters.

"May 28.—Two hundred militiamen arrive and go into camp. They form up on either side of the junction at Minonk, so as to allow a coal train heavily guarded with deputies to pass. A man attempted to alter the switch, and was fired on by the deputies.

"Miners at Wenona, Ill., chiefly Poles, placed rails on the track, and prevent the passage of any coal train. The sheriff at first powerless to prevent them. But at night he fired on the strikers, and dispersed them. The miners pulled out the pins from the couplings.

"At Mount Olive, Ill., the strikers tore up the Maddison Coal Company's track, and destroyed the line.

"May 29.—At Mount Olive, Ill., the Chicago express was almost wrecked by obstructions placed on the line by strikers.

"At Yellow Creek, O., miners attempted to board the night express. The sheriff, however, with over fifty deputies, guarded the train, and beat them back seven times before the train could start again."

So ruthless were the miners that it was with the utmost difficulty permission was secured for the miners to extinguish a fire which broke out in Spring Valley mines. The English-speaking miners rushed to put the fire out ; the foreign element resolved upon letting them burn. Permission was refused to the town of Des Moines to obtain the coal necessary to keep the city waterworks going. The Illinois Lunatic Asylum at Kaukakee, in which were 1100 inmates, ran short of coal. To save the miserable lunatics from perishing of cold, the strikers at first permitted them to have some coal ; but, on second thoughts, strike policy triumphed over humaner considerations, and the permission given on the 21st was rescinded on the 29th. *Per contra*, permission was given to McBride, the president of the strikers, and also a brewer, to obtain coal for his breweries, where he had 15,000 dollars' worth of beer which would have spoiled if no coal could have been procured.*

The state of latent civil war which these industrial disputes bring to the surface was most vividly illustrated in the strike among the gold and silver miners

* The *Chicago Herald*, dated June 7, has the following headings : "Two miners shot. Deputies guarding the Ohio River Bridge fire into an approaching party. Besides those killed, four of the strikers are wounded in the fusillade. Twelve hundred State militiamen ordered out by Governor McKinley to quell the riotous workmen. Lawless bands are stopping trains, and defying officers. Other conflicts expected." That relates to Ohio. The news from Indiana is as follows : "Fighting in Indiana. Fusillade near Farmersburg. Engineer stoned to death by miners. Martial Law proposed." Illinois is no better : "Killed in a riot. One man slain and three fatally wounded in a fight with strikers near Peoria. Desperate gang charges a barricaded mine. The invading army applies the torch, and destroys property worth 30,000 dollars."

of Colorado. The dispute began about the eight-hours day. The miners were working nine hours. They demanded an eight-hours day, with three dollars wage. The owners offered them a day of eight-hours and twenty minutes. This the men rejected, and then added to their original demand a claim to be allowed to elect their own superintendent, or, as we should say, manager. This being clearly inadmissible, the strike was declared.

In recounting the incidents of this local struggle, it is difficult to believe that we are writing of an industrial dispute. The whole story is one of war and of the incidents of war. We read of forts and cannon, of Gatlings and of Winchesters, of revolvers and of dynamite, of cavalry and militia, and even of the formal exchange of prisoners of war.

When the strike was declared 1200 miners in the neighbourhood of Denver, Colorado, withdrew to the level summit of two hills named respectively Bull Hill and Battle Hill, and there they threw up two regular forts, which they armed and provisioned for a siege. Bull Hill is described as a lofty peak commanding the whole country. The top is quite level, and several mining towns are within artillery range of the fort. It is well supplied with food, giant powder, dynamite and ammunition, but report was doubtful as to water.

From this position of vantage the miners made war upon the mines in their vicinity which continued at work. The manner of their warfare may be gleaned from the following extracts from the diary of the campaign :

"May 24.—At Cripple Creek, Col., seventy deputies left to guard the mines at Victor, four miles distant. Twenty were surrounded and disarmed by the strikers. Twenty-three reached the Independence mines, where they were surrounded next day by 300 strikers. The alternative was offered them of surrendering, or to be blown up with giant powder which was enclosed in beer casks with fuses attached. They surrendered.

"May 25.—One hundred and twenty-five deputies came from Denver to Cripple Creek. They found the shaft-house blown up with giant powder, machinery ruined and shaft-house burned. The deputies fortified themselves with timber near the railway track awaiting attack. Strikers have 400 Winchesters and 800 revolvers of an improved pattern, with abundant ammunition.

"May 26.—At Denver, Col., seventy-five strikers at early dawn stole a construction train, and coming upon a bridge guarded by seven deputies, a fight began in which two men were killed and several injured. Governor Waite ordered out the entire militia of the State, including the light artillery, with Gatling guns and smooth bores. The deputies, 350 in number, have a cannon. Miners threaten to hurl dynamite down upon the deputies.

"May 27.—President Calderwood of the miners proposes an exchange of prisoners. Miners had captured the superintendent of the Spring mines and two men, holding them as hostages. Six hundred armed deputies with two Gatlings have arrived.

"May 28.—The miners at Cripple Creek descended from their fortress and raided two towns for firearms and hostages. They have placed pickets round their camps and refused to allow strangers to pass the lines. A miner had his horse shot under him for not halting when summoned."

Heavy firing occasionally was exchanged between the miners and the deputies, but to little purpose. At last, on June 4, the deputies, with a Parrott and a Gatling gun, decided to storm the strikers' camp. But what would almost certainly have been a bloody and desperate battle was averted by the Governor of the State. He undertook to mediate between the miners and the deputies, and the quarrel was ultimately arranged, the miners undertaking to give eight hours' full work, exclusive of twenty minutes for lunch.

It is a melancholy and an alarming record. The mere brute violence which is everywhere rampant is bad enough, but that is, by no means, the worst feature of the story. What is far more appalling is the utter paralysis of public and moral authority. Arbitration neither side appears to have thought of. The public contented itself with keeping a ring, watching with pitiless curiosity the combatants worrying themselves to pieces like wild beasts in the arena of the Colosseum. So far as can be seen from the American papers, the Christian Church made no effort to compose this fatal strife.

Where moral authority is not, resort to Gatlings and dynamite seems to many the only alternative. The great mischief in America is the absence of trust, the rooted disbelief in the honesty and good faith of anybody. Rightly or wrongly, American workmen seem to be convinced—I have heard picked leaders of American labour assert it again and again—that no award, no agreement is ever respected by their employers a day longer that it suits their interest to keep it. Bad faith on the part of the employers is balanced by murder and outrage on the part of the employed, while the Church, which should be the conscience of the community, is seared as with a hot iron by a conventional indifferentism to the affairs of this world.

The Pope, in his famous Encyclical on Labour, laid down doctrines which all Christian Churches every-where would do well to lay to heart. But nowhere is there greater need of the preaching and the teaching of that sound doctrine than in the United States to-day. " Blessed are the peacemakers, for theirs is the kingdom of Heaven," does not seem to offer sufficient inducement to Christian men to compose these industrial feuds. Perhaps they will wake up to a sense of their duty and their responsibility, when they discover that the failure to make peace not merely forfeits the kingdom of Heaven, but inevitably turns the kingdom of this world into a kingdom of Hell.

PART II.

JUST BEFORE THE BATTLE.

CHAPTER I.—THE SEAT OF WAR.

CHICAGO is the only American city which has had anything romantic about its recent history. The building of the city, and still more its rebuilding, are one of the romances which light up the somewhat monotonous materialism of Modern America. Its surprising growth is one of the wonders of the nineteenth century, although it is not so great as the growth of London. More than thirty years ago a young Kaffir who had visited London described, on his return to South Africa, his impressions of the city. He said that London, the great place of the English, was greater than all the great places of other countries. " Their cities," he said, " are like children to London. Paris is large and so is Berlin, but London is the mother and could hold one in each arm." As the Kaffir said of Berlin and of Paris, so I may say to-day of New York and of Chicago. They are great places, but they are as children compared with London ; London is the mother, and she could hold one of them in each of her arms. The population of Chicago is 1,400,000, and the population of New York 1,800,000, while that of London, at the census of 1891, was 4,200,000. The two great cities of America rolled into one are not equal to the great Babylon on the Thames. London, the Americans will be prompt to reply, has had a thousand years in which to grow, whereas Chicago is but the seedling of yesterday. That is no doubt true. In the year 1812, when the Pottawatomie Indians massacred the white inhabitants of fort Dearborn, three years before the battle of Waterloo, the population of London was about a million. Eighty years ago, Chicago started with nothing, whereas London had a million of inhabitants. In the eighty years which have passed since then, London has added to her population three millions, whereas the total population of Chicago to-day is barely half that number. So far as the building of a new city is concerned, London has beaten Chicago twice over. The only difference is that, whereas Chicago started with nothing, London had a huge nucleus of a million inhabitants. Still the fact remains, that in the 688 miles composed in the metropolitan police district, three millions of people have come to live in 1894, which is as much a new population as that which is to be found in the city on the shores of Lake Michigan. This is a very remarkable fact, look at it how we please. There is nothing which the visitor hears more constantly in Chicago than the assertion that great allowances must be made because of the newness of the city. Seventy years ago, you are told, there were only a few log huts upon the site of the present city, where you, to-day, have a population rapidly mounting up towards two millions, for whom it was necessary to create houses, streets, railways, and all the necessities of civilised existence. That is, no doubt, true ; but it is equally true that London has had to create in the same period houses, streets, railroads, and all the appliances of civilisation for twice as many people as those which inhabit Chicago. New London—that is

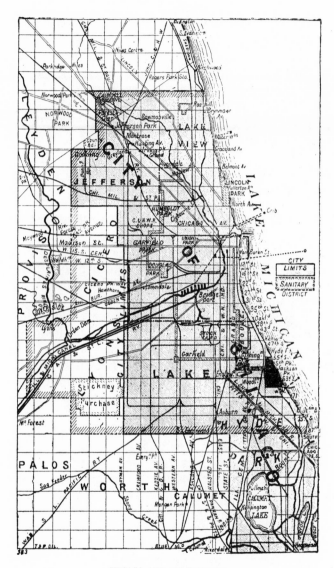

CHICAGO AND ITS VICINITY.

to say, the city which has come into existence outside the old London of 1812—is twice as great in mere numbers and many times greater in other things than the city of Chicago. Therefore, even in the phenomenal aggregation of population within the lifetime of a single individual, London has no reason to fear comparison with Chicago.

The growth of London is even more remarkable than that of Chicago, because Chicago started with no dead weight in the shape of a debased, pauperised, and degraded class such as has swarmed from times immemorial in the slums of London. The builders of the new Babylon on the Thames which has sprung up around our capital had not the immense advantage of virgin soil and a territory upon which the city builder could lay out his plans as he pleased, without fear of vested interests other than those of the prairie wolf and the wandering Indian. The result has been that our English Babylon is not so much a building as a growth. Chicago is laid out in regular parallelograms, a city made by the surveyor and the architect, who, with practically unlimited space in which to build, have mapped out the city with a carpenter's rule, with straight avenues running north and south, intersected at right angles by equally straight streets running east and west. In the blocks made by the intersection of these thoroughfares, the citizens reside in dwellings planned out with something approaching to the geometrical monotony of a honeycomb. In London there is nothing of this. From the parent stock branches have been thrown out in all directions, and it would be as idle to attempt to reduce greater London to mathematical exactitude as it would be to rule straight the branches of an oak-tree. North and south, east and west, the great umbrageous growth of the city has spread, covering whole counties with its shadow, and lacking, until quite recently, any common centre, or any consciousness of civic existence. In this, Chicago had advantage of London. Far more than any city, excepting Paris, Chicago has a civic consciousness. Londoners live in London, but Chicagoans both live and believe in Chicago. The city has become to be, in a kind of a way, a substitute for a deity. In this the Chicagoans resemble the ancient Romans, whose devotion to their seven-hilled city was even greater than that which the Chicagoans pay to the city which they have reared on the level marsh on the edge of Lake Michigan. There is some hope that the London County Council may succeed in creating a more vivid sense of civic consciousness in the heterogeneous conglomeration of humanity which looks up to the civic Parliament at Spring Gardens. But that is still to come.

Chicago spreads over nearly 200 miles of territory. The area patrolled by the Metropolitan Police is 688 square miles. But, whereas the builders of the new London have paved their city and made it habitable, the greater part of Chicago is still half-baked. One of the most interesting pictures of Chicago of to-day is contained in the report of the postmaster of the city. He contrasts the difficulties of postal service in Chicago with those which exist in the eastern cities, and points out that of the 2400 miles over which his carriers have to deliver letters, 800 are unpaved. An unpaved street means that in winter the houses stand on the edge of strips of morass, while in summer they are swept with dust storms which would facilitate the acclimatisation of the citizens in the desert of Sahara. So at least they say, for as I was not in Chicago during the summer,

I can only speak of the dust at second hand. The Windy City, however, has an unenviable pre-eminence in this respect. As it is with paving, so it is with sewage. The mayor mentioned to me casually that there was an area within the city limits of ten square miles in which a hundred thousand people were living, and which had no main drain. It will probably remain without one until an epidemic of cholera or of typhoid forces the necessity of sanitation upon the inhabitants. The side walks in Chicago are for the most part made of wood. There are 3000 odd miles of side-walk constructed of wood, 241 of stone, and 333 of concrete. Almost the only natural obstacle in the city which interferes with the regularity of the streets is the Chicago River, a narrow but extremely useful inlet of the lake, which winds its way through the heart of the business portions of the city, and necessitates the construction of no fewer than 54 bridges and three tunnels. This river Chicago has succeeded in polluting as foully as London polluted the Thames. Lake Michigan, into which the sewage of the city flows, is also the source of the water supply, the water being pumped from intakes situated four miles from the shore. This arrangement, however convenient, is only temporary. A great canal is now in process of construction, which will conduct the sewage of the city overland until it reaches the Mississippi River, when it will be finally deposited in the Gulf of Mexico. Notwithstanding these drawbacks, the health of Chicago is exceptionally good. The death-rate is one of the lowest of any of the great cities on the American continent, and is frequently as low as, or even lower, than that of London. The numerous open spaces and the wide streets make it impossible to keep out the fresh air from the prairies on one side and the lake on the other, and the fact that the city has been peopled by the healthiest and most adventurous members of every race, tends to give it an enviable pre-eminence among American cities, and counterbalance its natural disadvantage of being situated on a marsh.

The last day I was in Chicago, I ascended the Auditorium Tower, which may be regarded as the Chicago substitute for the dome of St. Paul's Cathedral. The Auditorium building, with its observatory

THE AUDITORIUM HOTEL.

tower, is about one of the ugliest pieces of architecture which was ever reared, either in the Old World or the New. There is a tendency on the part of architects in the New World to imitate the Aztecs in the huge savage clumsiness of their edifices. It would, however, be cruel to hold the Aztecs responsible for the monstrous hulk of hewn stone from which the weather man keeps watch and ward over the Lake Shore City. It was a dull day, although the air was bright and keen. There was sunshine on the lake, which brought into all the more vivid contrast the

murky, wreathing pall of smoke which covered the
city. Chicago, unlike its eastern rivals, burns a soft
coal which produces even more smoke than that which
is vomited forth from the innumerable chimneys of
London. On one side there stretched, as far as the
eye could see, a vast expanse of bright blue water,
unflecked even by a single wreath of smoke, while on
the shore stretched inward, as far as the eye could
reach, there was nothing but a confused chaos of
chimneys of factories and dwelling-houses belching
forth smoke which the wind seemed unwilling to carry
away, but which coiled among the roofs of the houses,
and concealed from view all but those immediately
below. It seemed as if all the Kingdom of Heaven lay
stretched out on one side, while on the other was the
smoke of Tophet. London has no such dark canopy
of smoke as that which broods over Chicago. London,
of course, has its fogs. Therein we enjoy a pre-
eminence in discomfort and gloom in which we have
no rivals. A light grey fog settled down on Chicago
shortly after I came to the city, and the papers were
good enough to say that a London fog had been laid
on for my special benefit in order to make me feel at
home. It seemed to make them uncomfortable, but
it was no more a London fog than a London office
building is a Chicago sky-scraper. It was a tolerably
thick, grey, misty fog, in which it was somewhat
difficult to find one's way, but it did not bear even the
remotest resemblance to the Egyptian darkness which
often shrouds London streets in sulphurous gloom.

Two-thirds of Chicago is built of wood. That, in
itself, is sufficient to make a great difference between
it and any English city. There are spacious boulevards of villa residences built of solid stone, but even
in the heart of the city, side by side with eighteen

and twenty-storied buildings, are to be found wooden
shanties, as if to emphasise, by way of contrast, the
difference between the old city and the new.

From the point of view of the city builder, Chicago
holds a unique place. Long ago she found it necessary to raise the level of her streets, and then compelled the houses to follow suit. Chicago not merely
hoisted huge edifices into mid-air in order to build in
one or two stories, but she put her houses upon wheels
and trundled them along her streets, and this she did
not merely with wooden shanties, but with houses of
brick and stone. Her latest triumph has been the
adaptation of iron to the work of building and the
universal use of the elevator, which enables people to
live nearer the stars than mortals have ever done
before with ease and comfort. These immense sky-
scrapers of twenty and twenty-two stories are singularly lightly built. They are indeed little more than
so many Eiffel Towers, enclosed in veneering of stone
or terra-cotta, but standing four-square to all the
winds that blow, and yielding less to the violence of
the blizzard than the ordinary three and four-storied
houses. As Chicago is built on a marsh, there is no
natural foundation on which to rest these huge edifices,
and therefore it is necessary to build them on artificial
foundations of railway iron and cement, spread on
the ground some forty or sixty feet below the surface
of the soil. From this iron and cement foundation a
framework of steel is built as high as the building
regulations of the City Council will permit. When
the slender masts of steel are run up to the requisite
height, they are fastened together by girders, and
then the ingenious builder begins putting on his
veneer of marble, brick, or stone. As each story is
finished the outside casing rests upon the flange of

the girder, so that there is nothing to hinder the work going on at each story at the same time. One of the first sights I saw in Chicago was the building of one of these sky-scrapers from the top downwards. The buildings when completed are sometimes as ugly as sin, and resemble nothing more than huge packing cases pierced with windows. In other cases, however —notably in the Woman's Temple and the Columbus Memorial Building—they have rather an attractive appearance. Under the roof of a single building are domiciled whole colonies of industrious human ants : lawyers, doctors, dentists, business men of every description, are all to be found next door to each other, and the elevators are continually flitting from the roof to the basement. The Masonic Temple, the tallest of the tall buildings of Chicago, requires the service of fifteen elevators, and even if the city regulations did not forbid the carrying of the buildings much higher, they would be limited by the fact that as they require two elevators for every three stories, if you were to carry the buildings much higher, the whole of the space would be taken up with elevators, and none would be left for use as offices. The larger buildings are all heated throughout by radiators, which are regulated by electricity. Thermometers are fixed in every room, and the moment the temperature falls below a certain number of degrees the heat is turned on at the radiator, and continues until the temperature is raised and the thermometer detaches the electrical arrangement and the heat is shut off. These radiators are in use night and day.

The system of telephone service, expensive but indispensable, enables the citizens to overcome the obstacles of distance which intervene between their residences. All the business of the town is crowded together in the centre of the city, where this gigantic ant-heap of humanity transact the business of half the continent. This congestion of population in the business quarter, and its wide diffusion over nearly two hundred square miles on property which lies within the city limits, brings to the front the problem of rapid transit, of street railways and elevated roads. All American cities are more or less confronted with the same problem as Chicago. In New York, which has both cable cars and elevated roads running the whole length of the Island, to say nothing of the limitless water transit on either side, they are proposing to construct a new elevated railroad which will whirl the citizens at express rate through mid-air, and at the same time they are proposing to dig and hew an underground railway through the heart of the rock on which the city stands. Chicago has no water transit worth speaking of, for they have not yet utilised the lake as a means of communication between north and south. The immense width of its streets, which in some places are almost a Sabbath day's journey across, naturally suggests street railways, and so far as the outlying districts are concerned the street-cars and the elevated railways which are constructed, or in process of construction, solve the problem. The chief difficulty, however, is in the heart of the city, where the traffic is congested, and where all the lines north and south and west meet and centre. Many ingenious methods have been suggested—underground electric railways, although they would have to be borne through bog, and would have to avoid the foundations of the sky-scrapers which reach some forty or sixty feet below the surface of the ground ; and another proposal which is peculiar to Chicago, in the shape of circulating sidewalks. It

H

is an adaptation of the idea of the elevated railways, the only difference being that the whole roadway circulates at varying rates of speed. The platform, of course, is stationary ; then you step on a second roadway which progresses at the rate of three· miles an hour, from this you step upon another roadway which is going at the rate of from five to six miles an hour, and you then take your seat on yet another, which is circulating at the speed of eight miles an hour. You go through the same gradations in reaching the stationary sidewalk from which you descend to the level of the street. The scheme at present is only on paper. It is doubtful whether its promoters will be able to overcome the opposition of the property holders and residents on either side of the streets, who have no desire to see this circulating platform running over the level of the street on a line with their first-floor windows. At any rate, its construction would probably be postponed until some arrangement has been come to by the railroads, and the street railroads combine so as to provide a common centre and interchange of fares between all sections of the town. At present the rule in America seems to be almost universal of having only a single fare for any distance. This single fare is five cents, the universal nickel which corresponds to the English penny, although it is nominally worth two-and-a-half times as much. You can travel from the centre of any city to its circumference without having to pay more than five cents, and you pay the same amount if you go a single block. The people who go a block pay for those who go to the outskirts of the town.

The necessity of street-car locomotion caused by the concentration of population in the business districts, and its scattering over wide areas outside that district,

makes a railway franchise as valuable as a gold mine.
Chicago is served by three street railways, which last
year paid respectively nine, eleven, and twenty-four
per cent. on stock which is said to have been largely
watered. The revenue of the street railways was
larger than the total amount which the City of
Chicago is allowed to levy by its charter in taxation
upon the real and personal property of the citizens.
The cars are worked by cable and by horse, but there
is a great prejudice against the introduction of the
electric trolley into the heart of the city. The cable
is a great improvement upon the horse-car, but none
of the cars are constructed like our omnibuses—why,
it is difficult to say. On the west and north the
double-decked system would be impossible owing to
the fact that the cars have to pass the river in tunnels,
and these do not leave room enough for the double-
decked arrangements. But on the south side, which
is the most profitable of the roads, the cable could
take a double load just as easily as a single. The
overcrowding of the cars, as it is, is simply frightful.
At the rush hours, as they are called, in the morning,
middle day, and evening, the cars are packed about as
full of people as the beehive in swarming time. The
seats are all occupied, the platforms at either end are
crowded, and the gangways down the centre of the
cars are packed as full as it is possible to pack them
by persons holding on by straps. Overcrowding there
would be in any case, but the extent to which overcrowding is carried on in Chicago is due to the rapacity
of the street railway companies, who cynically reply
to all complaints that it is the people who hang on by
the straps who make their swollen dividends. No
one is more ruthless than a railway corporation which
has bought the right to ill-use and oppress the public

by the simple process of corrupting the elected representatives of the people in the City Council assembled.

In an American city a street railway is worth more than a gold mine, and the way in which this valuable municipal asset is flung away by the trustees of the people is one of the grossest scandals of American life. The track is vilely laid, and one of the commonest sights in Chicago is a loaded cart upset in the street, one or both of the wheels having been wrenched off by the attempt to get off the track on to the roadway. The cars are often abominably overcrowded. In the main streets the endless cable supplies motive power; the cross streets are served by horse-cars, while in the outskirts the admirable electric trolley ministers to the convenience of the citizens. The fare is uniform, $2\frac{1}{2}d.$ any distance, long or short.

Many of the private palaces in Chicago are marvels of luxury. Mr. Potter Palmer's residence on Lake Shore Drive is a magnificent reproduction in the New World of the best that the Old World can offer in architecture and in art. It is a palace worthy to be the seat of the uncrowned queen of the American Republic. Of the newspaper offices, the *Herald* is the newest, the most magnificent, and the best equipped. The hotels are brilliantly illuminated with the electric light, but I was only four months in America, and it takes longer than four months for an Englishman to become acclimatised so far as to feel at home under the autocratic despotism of the American hotel clerk.

Chicago supplies its own water from the lake into which, at present, it empties its sewage, diminishing the evil consequences of this by drawing its water from an intake four miles distant from the shore. It is endeavouring to deal with the street sewage

question by diverting the course of the Chicago River
so as to pour all its sewage into the Mississippi
valley, and ultimately into the Gulf of Mexico. This
gigantic piece of engineering is in full progress, and
will take several years before it is completed. In the
matter of electric lighting, Chicago takes the lead of
all the places I have ever visited. They are more
lavish in their use of electricity as an illuminant than
either New York, Paris, or London. The main streets
are also lighted by electricity controlled by the municipality, which has obtained from the legislature the
right to manufacture electricity for its own use ; but
so jealous are the joint stock companies, or corporations as they are called in America, of the municipality, that the City Council, although it has plant
large enough to supply private consumers, is forbidden to do so. That is to say, it may light the
streets and it may also illuminate buildings belonging
to the city, but although the plant is standing idle
half the time, and it could immediately cut the price
of electricity, it is forbidden to do so, not merely out
of regard for the vested interests of the existing corporations, but in order to safeguard the speculators
who have hitherto been able to exploit the community by supplying the community with electricity.
In England we spare the vested interests, but with us
the vested interests must be in existence. It is only
in America where a municipality is crippled by a
regard for vested interests which have not yet come
into being.

Chicago does not yet own its own gas, and is
plundered accordingly by the Gas Trust, which deals
with its customers in a high-handed fashion, which,
if human curses could be as effective as witches' male-
dictions, would have sent the directors of the gas

companies into irremediable perdition. The other
corporations from which Chicago suffers most are
the steam railways, whose iron tracks cross the city
in every direction at level grade. There are three
thousand miles of steam railroads within the city
limits, and there are not three thousand miles of
streets. These railroads have bought their way into
the city by bribing the aldermen, and are still engaged in the work of obtaining the city territory for
their own purposes.

Chicago is horribly paved. Most of the side walks
are constructed of wood, and the majority of the
streets are not paved at all. The arrangements for
cleaning the streets which are paved is primitive in
the extreme. The idea of sweeping the streets from
end to end every day has not yet dawned upon the
imagination of the wildest municipal reformer in
Chicago. Even last winter, when an army of three
thousand unemployed were set to work on cleaning
the streets, and some streets were cleaned which had
never been before since Chicago came into existence,
there were whole stretches of streets where the snow
and mud lay for weeks and weeks untouched. The
street railways, of course, had to clear their tracks,
which they did by the simple process of hitching a
snow plough and a brushing machine upon the cable
and transferring the snow from the centre of the
streets to the side of the tracks, where it remained
piled up in small mountains, to the infinite disgust
of the inhabitants on either side. According to the
city ordinances the street railways are required to
remove the snow from the streets, but as they calculated that it would cost about a hundred thousand
dollars to do the work, they came to the conclusion
that it was better to leave it undone, with the result

that the long-suffering people rose in revolt in several streets and piled the snow across the tracks, effectually blocking the traffic. This led sometimes almost to riots, which required the intervention of the police to put a stop to.

The boulevards and avenues were an exception to the rest of the streets ; they are asphalted, and form an admirable causeway for cyclists and for driving. They are planted with trees, and constitute a most attractive feature of the city. The universal use of soft coal blackened the buildings almost as much as in London. The difference between Chicago and some of the eastern cities which burn nothing but anthracite is very marked.

The fire department of Chicago is probably the best in the world. The lesson of the great fire taught the citizens that they must at any rate rescue that branch of the city service from the devastating blight of the spoils system. The organisation of the department is almost perfect. The discipline and *esprit de corps* of the firemen are beyond praise, and the annals of human heroism contain few finer or more terrible stories than those in which the fire-kings of Chicago sacrificed their lives. They have four firemen per 10,000 inhabitants, more than double the London proportion. Each citizen in London pays 6*d.* per head to the Fire Brigade, and his share of the annual loss by fire is 5*s.* ; but the Chicago poll-tax is no less than 4*s.*, and the annual loss per head by fire is over 14*s.* Such, at least, are the figures given by Mr. Pickard, of Chicago, in a recent number of the *American Journal of Politics.*

Another admirable institution of the City of Chicago which might be adopted with advantage in our English Babylon is that of the police patrol waggon.

At almost every block, certainly on every beat, the constable on patrol has a call-box by which he can telephone to the nearest police-station for assistance. Whether it is an incipient riot that is to be quelled, a drunken man to be conveyed to the station, or the victims of some accident to be carried to the hospital, there is no need for him to leave his beat. A single word through the telephone, and in a minute or two the clanging bell of the waggon is heard as it dashes down the streets as hard as two galloping horses can take it. Three or four policemen are in the waggon, a small mobile force constantly held in readiness to be hurled at the gallop in any direction at a moment's notice. Before the crowd has had time to realise what is the matter, the patrol waggon is on the spot, the ringleaders are under arrest, and the waggon—with the captives—is rattling back to the police-station, leaving the patrol man free to resume his usual round.

The police force of Chicago consists of 2,726 men to 1,600,000 ; that of London, of 13,314 men to five millions population. All the policemen in Chicago carry stout clubs and loaded revolvers, with which, on occasion, they do not hesitate to shoot. The policemen are, on the whole, a fine body of men— Irishmen, for the most part ; they have heavy work to do, and they do it very well under difficulties almost inconceivable by the London constable. They have immense power, and they use it after the usual fashion of policemen, to levy blackmail. The whole force is poisoned by politics, and its *morale* is greatly injured by the impossibility of obtaining justice against anyone who has a political pull. Justice, in the English acceptation of the word, is simply unrealised even in dreams in Chicago police courts, which, however, are no worse, if, indeed, they are not better, than the Justice Shops which correspond to our County Courts.

The municipal ordinances of the City of Chicago are excellent. The only trouble is that they are not enforced. The law is explicit in forbidding saloons to keep open after midnight. But any saloon-keeper who stands in with the police never shuts his doors all night long. The law is severe against opium joints. But the pig-tailed heathen plies his trade under cover of police protection, for which, of course, due blackmail must be paid. But the most flagrant scandal of all is the case of the gambling hells. Gaming houses run wide open night and day in Chicago, although the law of the State of Illinois and the municipal ordinances of the City of Chicago expressly forbid gambling. There are said to be from 1,500 to 2,000 gamblers, regular professionals, who live and thrive in Chicago upon the profits of the gaming hells. One of these establishments which I visited had four faro, four roulette, five poker, and two hazard games running. Its wage bill is said to amount to £36,000 per annum.*

* As this is a kind of curiosity in its way, I extract the figures as given in the *Interocean.*

THE WEEKLY PAY ROLL OF VARNELL'S GAMING HOUSE AT 119, CLARK STREET

Twenty-four faro dealers	...	... at	$40	$960
Twelve roulette croupiers	...	... „	35	420
Six hazard men ...	...	... „	35	210
Nine card dealers	...	... „	35	315
Three floor walkers	...	... „	50	150
Three managers...	...	... „	75	225
Three doorkeepers	...	... „	30	90
Two barkeepers ...	...	... „	20	40
Six porters ...	...	... „	8	48
Eight outside men	...	... „	30	240
Forty cappers, bottlers, and bouncers ...		... „	15	600

$3,298 per week, or
$171,496 per annum

This is only one of scores of establishments running wide open in Chicago, under the eyes of the police, every man of whom is sworn to enforce the law by seizing all the instruments of gaming, and arrest gamblers wherever he can find them.

Nothing can be greater than the contrast between the awe in which the politician in London regards the Nonconformist conscience and the absolute indifference with which the Chicago politician regards the Christian sentiment of the community. So far as politics—city politics—go, you might imagine that there were no churches in Chicago, and that Mr. Moody had no existence. The churches and Mr. Moody may have saved the souls of many excellent citizens, but they have most egregiously failed in saving the city administration from going headlong to the devil. The saloon keepers and the gamblers run the city. Of the sixty-eight aldermen who occupy seats in the City Hall, not more than eighteen can, by any stretch of charity, be described as honest men. Several of them are saloon keepers; some are either gaming-house keepers, or are hand in glove with gaming-house keepers. Fifty of them are admittedly in the market ready to sell their votes and trade away the property of the city to the highest bidder. All this is notorious and undisputed. Yet the Boss of the Boodlers, the head of the ring of corrupt aldermen, was elected by a majority of two to one in his ward last month, although twelve brother boodlers disappeared from the council at the same time. All the arguments of all the reformers do not weigh a cent against the alderman's distribution of Christmas turkeys, and the persuasive arguments of hard cash. Bribery at elections is general, treating universal. The whole municipal administration is run on the

spoils system, and when I was in Chicago every nurse
in the lunatic asylum was sent packing in order to
make room for the nominees of the new Republican
Commissioners who had succeeded in the Democratic
majority.

It is this which is the pestilent, poisonous gan-
grene of Chicago. Compared with that festering
corruption which eats into the whole of the city
administration, the houses of ill-fame are comparatively respectable institutions. Yet, although there
are a few efforts made to reclaim the poor Magdalens
of the Levee, not a single missionary effort has been
put forth to rescue the boodlers of the City Hall.
What is still more strange, as yet not even the most
languid attempt has been made to turn the rascals
out. " What is the use ? " says cynical Chicago.
" If we get rid of this crowd, we should get a worse
crew in their place."

Chicago has at present the good fortune to have a
capable, resolute, honest, young Mayor, who is heroic-
ally fighting against immense odds the battle of
municipal honesty and, of course, reform. But as he
is a Democrat the Republicans stand aloof, and as he
is a Catholic the Protestants of the A.P.A. persuasion
hold him in holy horror. For both religious bigotry
and partisan rancour are far more rampant in Chicago
than in London. There is a curious renaissance of
Titus Oates and of Lord George Gordon visible all
over the North-West. Chicago is not a religious city
as a whole, and what religion there is seems to be
largely Catholic. There are double as many attend-
ants at Catholic churches as there are in the
Protestant places of worship. Almost all the offices
are held by Catholics. This is, for the most part,
not because they are Catholics so much as because

they are Irish. The Irish, being forbidden to rule their own country, have recouped themselves by ruling the great American cities. Mr. Pocock, writing in last month's *Forum*, points out that the Irish, although in a minority everywhere, have for years past held almost a monopoly of municipal offices in the following cities :—

New York	Boston	Troy	Kansas City
Brooklyn	Chicago	Pittsburg	Omaha
Jersey City	Buffalo	St. Paul	New Orleans
Hoboken	Albany	St. Louis	San Francisco

In Chicago, the Irishman is everywhere to the front, and the Catholic Archbishop Feehan does not stretch out a finger to keep him in the straight path. The Mayor, although born in Buffalo, is a John Patrick Hopkins. The Chief of Police, Mr. Brennan, is a member of the Clan-na-Gael, who was born in Ireland. The City Treasurer was born in Ireland. The Chief of Detectives is Jno. D. Shea, an Irish-American, and so forth, and so forth. One-half of the aldermen and two-thirds of the policemen are Irish. They run the city, and are far more important in their own eyes and other people's than they are anywhere else in the world. So convinced are some of them as to the supreme position of their race, that I had some difficulty in persuading an Irish housemaid that the Pope was not an Irishman. Her disgust at learning that he was only a Dago — Chicagoan for Italian—was as suggestive as it was amusing.

Chicago is interesting to Englishmen because it is the only city which has taken a part both directly and indirectly in English affairs. It was in Chicago that the Clan-na-Gael organised the dynamite campaign, and it was from Chicago that they despatched some twenty emissaries charged with instructions to destroy the public buildings and the public men of England in the cause of Irish nationality. The Clan-na-Gael is still a power in Chicago. The mayor is reputed to be a member of its organisation, and the chief of police undoubtedly is one of the clan; but the feuds which divide the Irish in Chicago, and which came to a head in the murder of Mr. Cronin, still exist. Mr. Gladstone's name is one to conjure with among the Irish of Chicago, and the more reasonable were disposed to accept the Home Rule Bill as à pledge of the reunion between the nations. But the indirect influence of Chicago upon us is even greater. Chicago, as the head and centre of the great central states, has done more to force the Irish question to the front by its cheap beef than by all its dynamite. It was the slaughter-houses of the stock-yards which cut to the root of Irish landlordism, and for the matter of that of English landlordism also. Not until the next century has dawned shall we be able to realise adequately the extent to which Chicago and the Chicago exporters of beef, pork, and wheat have undermined the ancient social organism of the United Kingdom.

When I was a boy New England was the centre of interest to Old England. The group of poets, essayists, and philosophers which lived at Boston were the best known of all Americans. One by one these great ones have died, and now Oliver Wendell Holmes almost alone remains. Later Henry Ward Beecher and Goff represented another section of American life which influenced directly and indirectly the social, religious, and intellectual life of the Old World. But they have gone, and now there are only two Americans who are sufficiently well known by the masses of the English people to be able to fill the largest hall in any city in which they choose to speak. Both of these are from Chicago. One is Mr. Moody, and the other is Miss Willard.

The future of Chicago is an additional reason for regarding with intense interest the course of affairs on the shore of Lake Michigan. Professor Badcock, a scholar and an historian, who has devoted many years to the problem of the probable centre of the American continent, has written a treatise in which he claims to demonstrate that, from every consideration—historical, ethnographical, ethnological, and political—the future centre of the American Republic must in time come to be found near the southern end of Lake Michigan. Without following the Professor through his elaborate calculations, it is obvious that a city which stands mid-way between the great lakes system of the north and the immense waterway of the Mississippi and Missouri, which, despite all the disasters which have befallen it, and the jealousy and opposition of rivals, has forced its way to the first place but one in the American continent, and which has as its only rival a city situated on the rim of the continent, is not likely to fall behind in the race for the possession of the capital of the New World. Unlike New York, which has only an island to live upon, and which cannot spread beyond a certain circumscribed area, Chicago threatens in time to cover the whole of the state of Illinois. It has space enough on the shores of Lake Michigan for the population of ten millions which is predicted for it in the course of the next fifty years, when the transoceanic canal is constructed, which will enable the steamers of all countries to discharge their cargoes at the wharves of Chicago. Even now, if New York is the mistress of the Eastern States, Chicago is not less easily queen of the Central and Western States. From Chicago emanate influences which are felt in every farmstead from the lakes to the Gulf.

Chicago is singularly deficient from the English standpoint in many necessary institutions. It is almost incredible that such a city, so great and prosperous, should be so miserably devoid of the appliances of civilisation as we understand them in the older world. In the whole city there is scarcely a place where you can wash your face excepting in a public-house. The first public bath was opened shortly before Christmas. No one is permitted to bathe in the lake, there are no coffee palaces, teetotums, or anything of that kind in the whole of the city. There is a public library with four branch reading-rooms and many places of call throughout the city, but of institutions such as the People's Palace and the Polytechnic and the old Mechanics' Institutes, there are practically none.

For the common man in Chicago, either in recreation or refreshment, or almost anything, the saloon is almost the only institution which cares for his material wants. The churches may save his soul, but they take very little account of his body ; while they damn the saloon keeper vigorously enough in theory, they allow the saloon keeper to run the machine pretty much as he pleases, nor do they demean themselves so far as to enter into competition with him on his own ground. The necessity of fighting the saloon by putting something better in its place is beginning to be recognised, however, and one of the most gratifying signs of the times was the launching of the scheme of the People's Institute in connection with the popular but temporary institute which is carried on on the West Side by Bishop Fallows and the Rev. Dr. Clark.

If such an institute were established in every one of
the thirty-four wards of the city, Chicago would have
done something practical towards meeting the great
social needs of the labouring population upon whose
industry depends so much of her greatness. Hull
House, which may be regarded as a superior and more
social Toynbee Hall, has been and is one of the chief
hopes of the future of Chicago. The best hope for
Chicago is in the multiplication of Hull Houses or
branch establishments affiliated with the central institution in all the slum districts of the city. It would
be difficult to imagine a greater contrast between the
worthless society woman who devotes her days to
pleasure and her nights to more or less pleasurable
dissipation, and the patient laborious Christlike work
of Miss Addams and her coadjutors in Hull House.
Beginning with small things, they have gradually ex-
panded and developed their beneficent activities until
they have made Hull House the social centre of the
whole district. Whether they be Bohemians, or
Poles, or Jews, or Italians, the friendless populations
in the vicinity find a ready welcome and a sympathising hearing from the inmates of Hull House.
The place simply swarms with clubs of all kinds.
The gymnasium is an admirable institution for the
training of both sexes. A New England Kitchen
teaches by example the value of scientific cooking,
and there is a well furnished library and artistic
picture gallery, and a charming *crêche* ministers to the
needs of the people in every direction, while dispen-
saries, savings banks, and co-operative institutions
flourish amain. The place is a stronghold of women,
especially among women, and there is no place in
Chicago where all that makes for progress has such
ready and energetic help as from Hull House.

Chapter II.—The Millionaire and His Model Town.

Mr. George M. Pullman, whose refusal to consent to arbitration was the cause of the recent industrial war, is the man who has made the Pullman car a household word in every land for its convenience, its comfort, and its luxury. Unlike Mr. Field, who is said to be a leap-year politician, voting only once in four years when a President is to be elected, Mr. George M. Pullman is an active Republican, well known in Washington, and much esteemed by party treasurers, to whose campaign funds he has been a liberal contributor. Mr. George M. Pullman, in addition to many acts of private charity, is notable among the millionaires of Chicago as the man who, taking a hint from Krupp, endeavoured to found a town in his own image. The town of Pullman, which was named after the author of its being, is a remarkable experiment, which has achieved a very great success.

Unlike Mr. Field or Mr. Armour, Mr. Pullman has built up his fortune without resorting to the more ruthless methods of modern competition. Indeed, his career is notable as an instance of competition by high prices rather than by low. Mr. Field wiped out the retail storemen, and Mr. Armour the small butchers, by underselling them. Mr. Pullman has undersold no one. He has always succeeded, not by producing a cheaper article, but by producing a dearer ; but the higher-priced article was so much better that Mr. Pullman succeeded in establishing a virtual

monopoly of one of the most highly-specialised busi-
nesses in the world. This is the more remarkable
because Mr. Pullman was not originally a mechanic.
He was merely a man of reflective mind, of native
ingenuity, and of great persistence. The inconvenience
of a journey on the cars before the Pullmans were
invented turned his attention to the possibility of
making the sleeper as comfortable in the cars as in a
hotel. The moment he set to work to realise his idea
he was confronted with the fact that it could not be
done " on the cheap." Nothing daunted, he decided
it should be done at a high price if it could not be
done at low. The first Pullman car which he constructed and put on the rails cost 18,000 dollars to
build, as against 4,000 dollars, which was the price
of the ordinary sleeper. Railway men shrugged
their shoulders. It was magnificent, they said,
but it was not business. A palace sleeping car,
at 18,000 dollars could not possibly pay. Mr.
Pullman refused to be discouraged. " Let the
travelling public decide," was all he asked; " run
your old sleepers and the new one together; I will
charge half a dollar more for a berth in the Pullman
and see which holds the field." The verdict of the
public was instant and decisive; every one preferred
the Pullman at the extra price, and the success of the
inventive car-builder was assured. He has gone on
step by step, from car to car, until at the present
moment he is said to have a fleet, as he calls it, of
nearly 2,000 sleepers, which are operated by the
Pullman Company. They have besides 58 dining
cars and 650 buffet cars. Altogether the cars which
the company operates number 2,573.

Other competitors have come into the field, but
Mr. Pullman deserves the distinction|of having placed

GEORGE M. PULLMAN.

every railway traveller under an obligation by acting as pioneer of commodious, luxurious, and safe railway travelling. After building his cars in various parts, Mr. Pullman decided finally to centralise in the centre of the American continent. Carrying out his decision, he naturally fixed upon Chicago as the site for his works. The Pullman Company was incorporated with a capital of 30,000,000 dollars, the quotation for which in the market to-day is twice that amount. From the first year of its existence, says the writer of "The Story of Pullman," proudly, it has paid its quarterly dividends with the regularity of a government loan, and its $30,000,000 of capital has a market value of $60,000,000, while its stock is so largely sought as a rock-ribbed security for the investment of the funds of educational and charitable institutions, of women and of trust estates, that out of its 3,246 stockholders, 1,800 are of this class, and 1,494 of these 1,800 are women. He took up an estate of over three thousand acres round Lake Calumet, which is fourteen miles from the centre of Chicago, and which was at that time far outside the city limits. There, following the example of Messrs. Krupp at Essen, he set to work to construct a model city in his own image. The car-works were, of course, the centre and nucleus of all. In these gigantic factories, where 14,000 employees work up 50,000,000 feet of lumber every year, and 85,000 tons of iron, they have a productive capacity of 100 miles of cars per annum. Their annual output, when they are working at full stretch, is 12,500 freight cars, 313 sleeping cars, 626 passenger cars, and 939 street cars.*

* The statistical data were given by the Pullman Company in " The Story of Pullman."
   Total amount of lumber used annually by the Pullman Company, about 51,000,000 feet.

MAIN ADMINISTRATION BUILDING, PULLMAN.

Mr. Pullman's ambition was to make the city which he had built an ideal community. In order to do so he proceeded in entire accordance with the dominant feeling of most wealthy Americans by ignoring absolutely the fundamental principle of American institutions. The Autocrat of all the Russias could not more absolutely disbelieve in government by the people, for the people, through the people, than George Pullman. The whole city belongs to him in fee simple ; its very streets were the property of the Pullman Company. Like Tammany Hall and various other effective institutions in America, not from the broad basis of the popular will, but from the apex of the presiding boss. Mr. Pullman was his own boss. He laid out the city, and made the Pullman Company the terrestrial

Total quantity of iron used annually, about 85,000 tons.

Total number of employees (July 31st, 1893), 14,635.

Total amount of wages earned daily by Pullman employees, $24,965.63.

There are operated by the Pullman Company 2,573 sleeping, parlour, and dining cars. Of these 650 are buffet cars and 58 are dining cars.

During the year ending July 31st, 1893, the number of miles run by Pullman cars was 206,453,796, and there were carried 5,673,129 passengers.

About 9,000 meals are served daily in Pullman dining and buffet cars.

There are about 33,000,000 pieces of Pullman car linen laundried annually.

Mileage of railroads under contract, 126,975.

The longest regular, unbroken run of any cars in the Pullman service is from Boston to Los Angeles, 4,322 miles.

The total producing capacity of construction shops per annum is 12,520 freight cars, 313 sleeping cars, 626 passenger cars and 939 street cars. Coupled together these cars would make a train over 100 miles in length.

If all the lumber used annually in Pullman shops alone were delivered on one train, the train would consist of 5,000 cars and would be thirty-five miles long.

The Pullman savings bank has 2,000 depositors, and their deposits amount to $632,000, an average per person of $316.

The average wages per day for workmen of all classes in Pullman shops, including boys and women, is $2.26.

The Town of Pullman has eight miles of paved streets, and 12,000 inhabitants, of whom 6,324 are operatives.

Of the 2,246 Pullman employees who live on the borders of the town, about 1,000 own their own homes.

All the sewage of the Town of Pullman is collected in a 300,000 gallon reservoir under the water tower, and pumped to the Pullman produce farm three miles away.

providence of all its inhabitants. Out of a dreary, water-soaked prairie, Mr. Pullman reared high and dry foundations, upon which, with the aid of his architect and landscape engineer, he planned one of the model towns of the American continent. Here was a captain of industry acting as the city builder.

Here is the Pullman Company's own account of the Town of Pullman :—

Mr. Pullman fixed upon the vicinity of Lake Calumet, fourteen miles away, in the heart of the city, as the site for his works. Here he purchased 3,500 acres, which has since increased in value proportionately with Chicago's remarkable development. The entire tract is now embraced within the boundary limits of the great city. Even now, the Pullman district is a centre, around which there is a connected girdle of thickly populated communities. At a very early date the beautiful town of Pullman, with its shaded avenues, its glimpses of bright water, its harmonious groupings of tasteful homes and churches and public buildings, the whole coloured here and there with the green of lawns and the bloom of clustered banks of flowers—at a very early date all this will be as a bright and radiant little island in the midst of the great tumultuous sea of Chicago's population; a restful oasis in the wearying brick-and-mortar waste of an enormous city.

And then, too, at its very door will come, not long hence, the bulk of Chicago's manufacturing commerce. It is only a matter of a short time when Lake Calumet, along which the Pullman land stretches for miles, will become an inside harbour. The thirty million bricks per year which the Pullman Company is now manufacturing are made of clay taken from the bottom of the lake, and in the meantime the Government is dredging out the river which connects Calumet with the thousands of miles of waterway of the great chain of lakes which lead to the ocean and to the world beyond seas.

What this land, which a dozen years ago was bleak, sodden prairie, will represent when this comes to pass, and great ships are moored to its miles of water front, is an interesting item in speculations upon the marvellous probabilities of Chicago's future growth. The day is not only coming, but is near at hand, when the $30,000,000 present capital stock of the Pullman Company will be covered, and more than covered, by the value of the 3,500 acres of land on which is built the town of Pullman.

Of the details of how Pullman was constructed; of how the dreary, water-soaked prairie was raised to high and dry land; of how the entire town was planned and blocked out in all its symmetrical unity of purpose by Mr. Pullman himself; of how the architect and landscape engineer, working together, carried out the details of the plan to their harmonious and beautiful conclusion—all this has been told and retold in the scores of studies of Pullman which have appeared in print on both sides of the Atlantic.

In the same publications there have appeared minute descriptions of the system by which the sewage of the town is collected and pumped far away to the Pullman produce farm; of how every house and flat, even to the cheapest in rent, is equipped with the modern appliances of water, gas, and internal sanitation; of how grounds for athletic sports were made; all the merchandising of the town concentrated under the glass roof of a beautiful

arcade building; a market house erected that is the ornament of one of the
handsomest squares in the town; churches built; a beautiful school-house
put up, in which there attend nearly a thousand scholars; a library founded
of over 8,000 volumes; a savings bank established, paying a liberal rate of
interest and conforming in its regulations to the greatest convenience of the
wage-earners; a theatre provided that is an artistic gem.

All this has been detailed so much at length that there need be to it only a
passing reference. With these details in mind, imagine a perfectly equipped
town of 12,000 inhabitants, built out from one central thought to a beautiful
and harmonious whole. A town that is bordered with bright beds of flowers
and green velvety stretches of lawn; that is shaded with trees and dotted with
parks and pretty water vistas, and glimpses here and there of artistic sweeps
of landscape gardening; a town where the homes, even to the most modest,
are bright and wholesome and filled with pure air and light; a town, in a
word, where all that is ugly, and discordant, and demoralising is eliminated,
and all that inspires to self-respect, to thrift, and to cleanliness of person and
of thought is generously provided. Imagine all this, and try to picture the
empty, sodden morass out of which this beautiful vision was reared, and you
will then have some idea of the splendid work, in its physical aspects at least,
which the far-reaching plan of Mr. Pullman has wrought.

It was not a philanthropic, but a business experiment, and none the worse on that account. The
great principle of *quid pro quo* was carried out with
undeviating regularity. If every resident of Pullman had gas laid to his house, he was compelled to
pay for it at the rate of 2 dollars 25 cents a thousand
feet, although the cost of its manufacture to the
Pullman Company was only 33 cents a thousand
feet. Ample water supply was given, with good
pressure, but of this necessary of life the Pullman
Company was able to extract a handsome profit.
The city of Chicago supplied the corporation with
water at 4 cents a thousand gallons, which was re-
tailed to the Pullmanites at 10 cents per thousand,
making a profit large enough to enable the corporation to have all the water it wanted for its works for
nothing. Thus did the business instinct of Mr.
Pullman enable his right hand to wash his left, and
thereby created at the very threshold of Chicago are
object lessons as to the commercial profits of municipal socialism. But between municipal socialism,
representing the co-operative effort of a whole com-

ARCADE THEATRE, PULLMAN

munity voluntarily combining for the purpose of making the most of all monopolies of service, and the autocratic exploiting of a whole population of a. city, such as is to be found in Pullman, there is a wide gulf fixed.

As a resident in the model town wrote me, Pullman was all very well as an employer, but to live and breathe and have one's being in Pullman was a little bit too much. The residents in the city, he continued, "paid rent to the Pullman Company, they bought gas of the Pullman Company, they walked on streets owned in fee simple by the Pullman Company, they paid water-tax to the Pullman Company. Indeed, even when they bought gingham for their wives or sugar for their tables at the arcade or the market-house, it seemed dealing with the Pullman Company. They sent their children to Pullman's school, attended Pullman's church, looked at but dared not enter Pullman's hotel with its private bar, for that was the limit. Pullman did not sell them their grog. They had to go to the settlement at the railroad crossing south of them, to Kensington, called, because of its long row of saloons, ' bumtown,' and given over to disorder. There the moral and spiritual disorder of Pullman was emptied, even as the physical sewage flowed out on the Pullman farm a few miles further south, for the Pullman Company also owned the sewerage system, and turned the waste into a fluid, forced through pipes and conducted underground to enrich the soil of a large farm. The lives of the working men were bounded on all sides by the Pullman Company; Pullman was the horizon in every direction."

All this provoked reaction, and a feeling of resentment sprang up in the model city against the too

ARCADE PARK, PULLMAN.

paternal despotism of the city builder, and so it came to pass that the citizens by a vote annexed themselves to Chicago, of which it is now part and parcel. This was a sore blow and a great discouragement to Mr. Pullman. But no annexation can destroy his control over the town. It is still the property of the corporation of which he is the controlling mind.

How little he foresaw the dispute which has convulsed the industry of the United States may be gathered from the following complacent reflections with which the Pullman Company conclude their " Story of Pullman " :—

On the business theory that the better the man, the more valuable he is to himself, just in that proportion is he better and more valuable to his employer; on this simple business theory an attempt has been made to surround the working men in Pullman with such influences as would most tend to bring out the highest and best there was in them. So far from starting with the theory that these working men are weaklings to whom things are to be given, and who must be held up and supported lest they fall, the starting point is in exactly the opposite direction. The assumption is that the Pullman men are the best type of American workmen, who stand solidly and firmly on their own feet, and will work out valuable and well-rounded lives just in proportion to their opportunities. By the investment of a large capital, it is found possible not only to give them better conditions than they could get elsewhere, but to give those conditions at prices wholly within their power to pay ; and yet sufficient to return a moderate interest on the investment, and so sustain it and make it enduring. That is the whole Pullman proposition in a nutshell. With philanthropy of the abstract sentimental sort it has nothing to do. With the philanthropy which helps men to help themselves, without either undermining their self-respect, or in the remotest degree touching their independence or absolute personal liberty — with philanthropy of this type it has everything to do.

To measure the actual effect of the conditions which exist at Pullman, it is only necessary to look at any representative assemblage of the Pullman workmen. During the eleven years that the town has been in existence, the Pullman working man has developed into a distinct type—distinct in appearance, in tidiness of dress, in fact in all the external indications of self-respect. Not only as compared with the majority of men in similar walks of life do they show in their clearer complexions and brighter eyes the sanitary effects of the cleanliness and the abundance of pure air and sunlight in which they live, but there is in their bearing and personal demeanour what seems to be a distinct reflection of the general atmosphere of order and artistic taste which permeates the entire town. It is within the mark to say that a representative gathering of Pullman workmen would be quite forty per cent. better in evidences of thrift and refinement, and in all the outward indications of a wholesome habit of life, than would a representative gathering of any corresponding group of working men which could be assembled elsewhere in the country. Nor do the benefits that have been brought about stop at mere external indications. The Pullman workman has a distinct rank of his own, which is recognised by employers everywhere in the United States, and which makes him universally in demand and sought after. There is, as a matter of fact, hardly a great producing centre in the country, in the fields reached by the great Pullman industries, to which Pullman men have not been brought by special inducements of promotion or wages.

The story of the town of Pullman is but a repetition on a large scale of the story of the building of the first Pullman car. The same organic solidity of structure, the same faith in the intrinsic commercial value of the beautiful, which entered into the one entered into the other. The Pullman car solved the problem of long continuous railway journeys, and the town of Pullman along new lines, gives a hope of bettering the relations of capital and labour. The issue of this last is a question of the future, but it is at least a legitimate subject of speculation, whether what the car wrought in one direction, with all its attendant and lasting benefits to humanity, may not in some sort, on a broader scale, and with benefits to humanity even more far-reaching-and enduring, be repeated in the great field where the town of Pullman now stands as the advance guard of a new departure and a new idea.

In brief, the Pullman enterprise is a vast object-lesson. It has demonstrated man's capacity to improve and to appreciate improvements. It has shown that success may result from corporate action which is alike free from default, foreclosure or wreckage of any sort. It has illustrated the helpful combination of capital and labour, without strife or stultification, upon lines of mutual recognition.

I have quoted what Mr. Pullman thinks of himself and the town which he has built. It may not be without interest to see what is thought of Mr. Pullman, not by trades union agitators, but by a Methodist minister who, on May 21, deemed it his duty to preach in the Methodist Church of Pullman on the text " The labourer is worthy of his hire."

I cannot keep still and smother my convictions You need not fear that the company will retaliate upon us as a church for anything I may say. It dare not in the face of public opinion. And, let me add, if the fears of some of you should ever be realised, better a thousand times that our church be disorganised by the company than that we truckle to them, forego the God-given and American right to free speech, smother our convictions, muzzle our mouths, fawn beneath the smiles of any rich man or corporation. Better to die for the truth than be surfeited by a lie.

Suffer a word regarding Mr. Pullman himself. I have nothing to say of him that savours of fulsome eulogy or nauseating praise. I will not speak of him as a philanthropist, for I have never seen nor heard of any evidence of this. I will not speak of his services to his age, because I know of none I will not refer to his services to his country, as history is silent thereon.

After referring to Mr. Pullman's admitted ability as a business man, raising himself from a poor boy in a country town to his present position as head of a great manufacturing industry, Mr. Cawardine said :—

In this age of rapidly increasing fortunes, when men become rich in a day by speculation, rearing a fabric of success upon the ruin of others, I am willing to accord him all honour; but when Mr. Pullman as a public man stands before the world and demands of us that we regard him as a benefactor to his race, as a true philanthropist, as one who respects his fellow men, who regards his employees with the love of a father for his children, and would have us classify him with such men as George Peabody, Peter Cooper, and George W. Childs, I confess, as a minister of the gospel, delivering my message in the shadow of these deserted shops, I fail utterly to see the point. The facts are not in accordance with the assertions made. If he is all this, then let me ask him a question or two :—Why does Mr. Pullman, in the midst of a hard and rigorous winter, when the hours of work were few and the wages at their lowest ebb ; when whole families were in want; when the churches burdened with their heavy rents were seeking to relieve the poor, and that noble organisation, the Woman's Union—which we were not allowed to call the "Relief" Union for fear of hurting Mr. Pullman's pride—was doing all it could to help the destitute ; why was it that our cry for help was unheeded and no large amount was given by Mr. Pullman or by the company ? Why did he permit one of his officials to publish a statement that there was no destitution in Pullman, and that there could not be as long as $720,000 was deposited in the bank to the credit of the labouring men, a statement which I have reason to believe was, in effect, false and misleading?

Why does not Mr. Pullman do something for the moral and educational development of this place ? Why does he extort such exorbitant rents from the churches of this community ? Why does he not assist the Young Men's Christian Association just a little? Why does he not give us an emergency hospital, of which we stand so much in need ? And, last not least, why, let me ask, does he not as a man of flesh and blood like ourselves, bring himself into a little closer contact with the public life of our town, cheer his employees with his fatherly presence, and allow the calloused hand of labour occasionally to grasp the gentle hand of the man who professes to be so intensely interested in our welfare ?

Never until George M. Pullman can give a satisfactory answer to these questions will I account him a benefactor to his race, a lover of his kind, a philanthropist, or one who has done anything for posterity which will cause mankind, when his dust slumbers beneath the sod, to rise up and call him blessed.

The great trouble with this whole Pullman system is that it is not what it pretends to be. To a casual visitor it is a veritable paradise ; but it is a hollow mockery, a sham, an institution girdled with red tape, and as a solution of the labour problem most unsatisfactory.

The great trouble with the town of Pullman, viewed from the standpoint of an industrial experiment, is that its deficiencies overbalance all its beauties. It is the most un-American town in all America. It belongs to the map of Europe. It is a civilised relic of old world serfdom. To-day we behold the lamentable and logical outcome of the whole system.

So far Mr. Cawardine, who besides uttering these remarks, entered upon an exhaustive disquisition on the causes of the strike.

Chapter III.—Labour and its Leaders.

In no country is the lot of a labour leader a happy one. It is peculiarly unenviable in the United States. The universal suspicion is especially rife among the Labour Unions. As an eminent labour leader said to me, the moment a man by industry, character, or genius raises his head one inch above the dead level of mediocrity he is at once marked down, his every action is misinterpreted and every evil motive is imputed to him by those who imagine that his rise implies their fall. Nevertheless the position of leader never seems to go a-begging. The Labour Party in America at the present moment has no fewer than four distinct chiefs.

To begin with Chicago, which has its Trade and Labour Assembly, its Parliament of Labour, representing or attempting to represent all the unions in the city. The leading spirit in this assembly is Mr. William C. Pomeroy, who is also general organiser for the Federation of Labour.

Mr. Pomeroy is a Kentuckian, of some education and wide reading, with a natural genius and magnetic power which stood in small need of book training. He is in many respects the most remarkable personality in the camp of labour in Chicago. His address of welcome to the Federation of Labour was unique. His position—idolised by some, detested by others, and distrusted by most—is exceptional. It might be made commanding. All that he needs to attain to any position for good to which he might care to

WILLIAM C. POMEROY

(General Organiser of the American Federation of Labour).

aspire is the command of the confidence of his fellows. On the day when Mr. Pomeroy is trusted in America as John Burns, for example, is trusted in England, the labour men will not need to look further for their leader.

Mr. Pomeroy is much the most eloquent of the representatives of labour to whom I had the pleasure of listening during my stay in America. His oratory is, perhaps, too rhetorical for English ideas; but he is a son of the South, and he has all the exuberance of rhetoric which seems to belong to the southern races. He has some taste in letters, and he was passing through the press when I left Chicago a somewhat notable novel entitled "The Lords of Misrule," which is not merely a scathing indictment of the capitalist system, but a prophecy of the evolution of the social and political forces in the United States. Mr. Pomeroy is a man who has thought much, his reflections are original, and his conclusions such as naturally attract attention. He is no Socialist, but a strong trades-unionist of the old school. In his novel he sketches the evolution of a socialist state of society which has as its natural and inevitable result the paralysis of all human exertion, the mainspring of improvement being cut by the dead level enforced by the socialist state. He does not regard socialism as the ultimate outcome and solution of the problems of society. His views are somewhat pessimist. He thinks that the socialist state would gravitate into militarism, and out of militarism would come the division of the American continent into two or three rival states. Whatever we may think of Mr. Pomeroy as a seer of events still in the womb of the future, there is no doubt but that he has reasoned out his conclusions with a great deal of

K

thought, and he has presented them in a form which can hardly fail to command considerable attention, not merely among the readers of " Looking Backwards," but also among the more select circle of political students and sociologists.

Mr. Pomeroy openly declares that he is a disciple of Tom Paine, and in the last speech which I heard him deliver he roundly declared that the gospel according to Tom Paine was the only gospel which was believed in by the American working men. Notwithstanding this, he introduced into his speech a very fervent declaration of his devotion to Christ, " whose church was the world, whose pulpit was the breasts of men, and whose religion was humanity." " No wonder," he declared, " that the sons and daughters of toil cheer His name. Nor can you," said he, " separate Christ from His Church ; " but his conception of the church differs widely from that of orthodox Christendom. Christ's church, according to Mr. Pomeroy, is " within the inner temple of the pulsating hearts of the peoples of the world, and in listening to His sermons they forget those of the salaried soothsayer." Notwithstanding this denunciation of the " salaried soothsayer," Mr. Pomeroy concluded his speech by an impassioned appeal to the churches to produce a new Peter the Hermit who would preach a new crusade for the redemption not of the Holy Sepulchre but of the desecrated temple of humanity. " Peter," said Mr. Pomeroy, "must come from the churches. We want their help, and they will not follow Peter of our raising." A notable declaration, and true withal.

Mr. Pomeroy was one of the chief founders of the Modern Church, a curious institution which is not unlike our Labour Church, but which only meets every other Sunday. Its gatherings alternate with the

fortnightly meetings of the Trade and Labour
Assembly in the Bricklayers' Hall. This church has
no creed, no parson, and no collection. Notwithstanding this, Mr. Pomeroy, like many other working
men, is still in the stage in which the infliction of
summary punishment upon the scab and the blackleg
is not merely regarded as a venial offence, but as a
positive duty. Their argument is on this wise. The
employers in defence of their interests and property
employ hired ruffians such as the Pinkertons and the
Coal and Iron Police to coerce and if needs be to kill
unionists, therefore the unionists are justified in self-
defence in treating those workmen who accept the
protection of the Pinkertons as traitors to their order.
As I said in writing on the Brotherhood of Labour in
my book, " If Christ came to Chicago " :—

There is ample need for the advent of a Peter the Hermit if the social crisis
in America is not to culminate in bloodshed. The working people without
allies have given no hostages to fortune, and have no visible reason for
refraining from violence. It is true that violence will injure them in the
long-run far more than it can help them; but like all men who suffer and
who are weak, they think more of the immediate winning of a strike by knocking a few " scabs " on the head than of the permanent loss which such violence
inflicts upon their cause. The fact that large numbers of labour men are at
this moment in what in England we call the Broadhead stage of development
—Broadhead being the secretary of the Sheffield Cutlers' Union, who used
to hire men to kill and maim scabs or blacklegs—simply proves that they are
more or less outlawed.

If they were within the pale, if they had churches to back them, and newspapers to plead for them, and courts to do them justice, and their own trusted
representatives on the bench and in Congress to see fair play, they would have
long ere this emerged from the stage of incipient Thuggee in which many of
them dwell. As they have no church to help them, they clutch the revolver;
and in default of an impartial judge to appeal to on the bench, they fetch the
" scab " a clout over the head with a sandbag or a club. Every time they do
this they supply Mr. Carnegie and others with plausible justification for the
use of Pinkertons and of Gatling guns, and public opinion even among those
who are most sympathetic is driven over to reinforce the enemies of labour.

At the same time it is obvious enough that violence,
although mistaken in the long run, may, and often
does, win temporary victories. A case in point
occurred during a strike while I was in Chicago.

Some builders who were engaged in finishing one of the lofty buildings, the peculiar characteristic of Chicago, had a quarrel with their workmen. There is no necessity here to go into the merits of the dispute. The workmen asserted very loudly that the employers in question were violating a distinct understanding by virtue of which wages had been settled for a period within which the dispute as to wages arose. Workmen in Chicago always assure you that no employer dreams of keeping an agreement, no matter how solemnly it may have been arrived at or how carefully it may have been defined, any longer than he sees it to his interest to do so. This strike was mentioned as a case in point. There were any number of unemployed men in town who would gladly have taken the work in hand at any wages that might have been offered them. The moment these scabs or blacklegs were introduced the building was invested by unionist pickets, and if any stray blackleg could be caught alone on leaving his work he was pretty roughly handled. The beating and rough handling of blacklegs was defended as a necessary act of war. It is curious as indicating the state of things in this great American city that the police, for reasons of their own, were undisguisedly in favour of the strikers. The city treasury at that time was very short of money, and it had been proposed that the police should share in the general cut in wages, to which all the officials from the mayor downwards submitted. The police objected, and the force was full of incipient revolt when this strike occurred. A fellow-feeling makes one wondrous kind, and the police, over whose head was hanging the Damocles sword of a ten per cent. reduction in wages, fraternised with the strikers, whose assaults on the blacklegs they were officially instructed to repel. There is reason to believe that both the mayor and the chief of the police had reasons of their own for not wishing to quarrel with organised labour, and as a result, and after a few days' resistance, the builders gave up the fight avowedly because they were unable to obtain police protection. A friend of mine who called at the headquarters of the unionists on the day of their victory, found them naturally very exultant. He asked them how it was that they were able to make such short work of the blacklegs. One of the pickets explained ingenuously that the police were of course compelled to intervene whenever there was a conflict in the streets, but that as the assault almost always took place in a more or less tumultuous crowd, in the midst of which the policeman was compelled to use his club, and, said the picket naively, " they usually contrived that the club fell upon the heads of the blacklegs and not on ours." It was only a comparatively trivial strike, but it illustrates one of the reasons why violence in trade disputes is not regarded as being such bad policy as it is in England.

I first saw Mr. Pomeroy when he was presiding over the Trades and Labour Assembly on a Sunday afternoon. The Labour Parliament of Chicago is not the most orderly of deliberative assemblies, and I could not help admiring the skill and energy with which Mr. Pomeroy handled the gavel. " I wish you were Speaker of the House of Commons," said I to him. " Faith," said he with a smile, " and so do I." He is a man of ready wit and has supreme confidence in the magnetic and intellectual ascendency which he exercises over his fellows. He has a great eye for effect and an innate power of command. For years he has taken a leading part in good and ill repute in the labour unions, and is in thorough accord with the general feeling of his class, that Capital is the enemy. In the minds of the labour leaders the struggle for improved economic conditions is the present-day version of the War of Independence. To such men Carnegie is much more detestable than George the Third, and the Battle of Homestead is in the direct line of succession of the more famous battle of Bunker's Hill. Of this a curious illustration occurred at the eleventh annual meeting of the Illinois State Federation of Labour, which was held last year at Galesburgh. At that meeting Mr. Pomeroy was deputed to present a gavel to the chairman, Mr. Madden, of the Typographical Union, then acting as President of the Federation. He said :—

I am delegated by Mr. John W. Connorton, of Chicago, to present a gavel to the President of this body. It is a gavel of historic interest. Various parts of it were made from a rifle captured from a Pinkerton detective during the battle at Homestead at the time of the great strike. The barrels, the stock, the screws were all put to service in the gavel. A brass button with the letter "P" on it is sunk into the mallet. The handle was made from the wood of the tree under which Major Andre was captured and where the three revolutionary heroes refused to accept his bribe. On the gavel is engraved this inscription : "Captured Homestead, 1892. Presented to M. H. Madden, President Illinois State Federation of Labour, by John W. Connorton."

Mr. Pomeroy's conception of the position of affairs is best stated in his own words. He was a member of a special committee appointed last July to draw up an expression of the opinion of the Trades and Labour Assembly on the pardoning of the anarchists by Governor Altgeld. This statement, although couched in the somewhat hyperbolical style of the American orator, is well worthy the attention of those who wish to understand the real sentiments of the American working-man. Omitting the first page or two, in which Mr. Pomeroy traced the struggle of man for freedom from the days of the Thirty Tyrants to the French Revolution, he says :—

The Greek thought himself free until his bonds were dangled before his eyes. The Roman felicitated himself on his citizenship and limited franchise, and the Frenchman grew intoxicated in the frenzied belief that he had given liberty to France. But the scales fell from their eyes, and they knew that they had been following phantoms, and they saw that they were still slaves.

In our own Republic, wrested from the mother country by the valour of patriots, the star of liberty arose above a sunset of blood and carnage. The world has gazed on in wonderment at the giant strides of the young nation toward the goal of success. But we have achieved commercial greatness at the expense of true liberty. Our grand ship of state, with sails full set, approaches the breakers. Ahead are hidden reefs and mighty whirlpools. Already she begins to swerve from her channel, and sails must be furled or she goes aground. Those in command have thrown aside the compass and are guiding by the dangerous magic of the mighty dollar. And we on board gaze aloft at her spreading sails, and seeing not the approaching storm, hearing but the sighing of the winds, with cheeks ruddy from the kisses of the lulling zephyrs, dream on and on the sweet dream of peace, while conditions shape themselves for strife. We see the grand structure which bears us on, and grow proud, and mayhap arrogant. We see not the barnacles which eat their way through her staunch-looking hull. We salute the flag at the masthead, and with tears of joy and swelling heart boast of our beautiful ship, of her mighty power, of her splendid crew.

We exult too much of a condition which no longer exists, and declaring ourselves a liberty-loving people, imagine that we are a liberty-enjoying people. We embrace the shadow of a fast vanishing substance and smile in our felicity while we delude ourselves with adoration for flags and fireworks. We fondly imagine that each fold of our banner contains a mystic potency, guaranteeing something or other for our welfare, and at each report of the Chinese cannon our spirits rise to a point of almost fanatical exhilaration, and our hypnotism is complete. We point with scorn at the shortcomings of other lands, and compare our "glorious achievements" and "heretofore never enjoyed citizenship" with what we term the age of tyrants and oppressors. Yet from the thirty tyrants of Greece, Caligula, and Nero, with their Prætorian guard, to Bonfield, Schaack and Grinnell, though a wide step in the cycles of time, shows no improvements for the better in methods of persecution and tyranny, the perceptible difference being the additional refinement displayed by the moderns in vouchsafing a trial to their foredoomed victims, before a prejudiced judge and a packed jury.

From the Brazen Lion of Venice, with its depository for anonymous denunciators dooming to death by the stealthy stiletto-wielder, to Pinkerton, with his hireling spies, fomentors of trouble and bearers of false-witness, is but a change from one system of strangling liberty to another, equally as abhorrent, equally as vile ; the difference being that the assassination was accomplished in the name of an absolute monarch of a subdued people, while the Pinkerton works solely at the dictates of the man of money, and under the flag of freedom.

From Boadicea, weeping for her daughters outraged before her face by the Roman camp followers, to the American mother of toil, who sees the conditions so swiftly changing that her offspring must shortly sell honour to maintain body and life together, may appear a far-fetched comparison, yet the close observer of the trend of affairs can, without being too imaginative, see himself at this day confronted with this very sad condition; the perceptible difference being that the daughters of Britain's Queen were made the victims of a savage warfare waged by a relentless enemy in an age of barbarism, while the daughters of the American poor are becoming the forced victims of necessity in an age of civilisation and in a land of plenty.

From the blood-sweating slaves in the mines of Siberia to the blood-sweating slaves in the mines of Pennsylvania and Spring Valley is no wide sweep of thought, and both exist painfully apparent, the one vieing with the other in the horrors of human servitude. True the flag of the Czar of Russia guards one, while the flag of the Czar Necessity upholds the other. One exists under an absolute monarchy, the other an absolute despotism, the only observable distinction being that Siberia furnishes food and shelter for its bond slaves, while this can hardly be claimed for the bond slaves of America.

From the bastille of France, now vanished, to the bastilles of America, plainly apparent in the Pinkerton sweat-boxes, is but a transference of despotism from the soil of France to the soil of the United States. From the militarism of Germany to the militarism of Cœur de Alenes is but a single step, and that step planted on the necks of American freemen. From the Mameluke guards, stabbing and slaying at the dictates of a tyrant, strangling freedom of speech at the nod of a dictator, to the money-purchased thuggism of this modern and enlightened Republic is many strides in advance, both in time and in atrocity. And nowhere in history can we find examples of wanton bloodshed and murder so vividly depicted as meet our horrified gaze right here in our own land, in our own time, in this age of commercial ascendancy and Christianity. For example, we mention East St. Louis, the Union Stock Yards, the Black Road, and the more recent butcheries at Homestead and Lemont. The ancient Mamelukes were given immunity by an absolute despot. The modern Mamelukes are put aboard train and deported to another State, and, unwhipped of justice, grow in power. True, the ancient Mamelukes seized as their own the land which had fostered and maintained them, and the growing strength of their modern compeers points the possibility of some such enterprise on their part.

And summing up the evidences of the damning decay of the fabric of our inherited liberties, retrospecting on things that were, and analysing things that are, we must truthfully admit that we have been derelict in protecting and fostering our sacred heritage torn from the womb of a thousand battles. Condemning anarchy, we must necessarily condemn the conditions whence it springs, and condemn the absolutism which is its other extreme. One must perish with the other, but neither by the other. Palaces must not be erected for the one and prisons for the other. The perpetuation of one means the perpetuation of the other. Both must be eliminated along constitutional grounds, and the cause of their existence accompany them.

Before the tribunals of justice all men must be on an equality. The blind goddess must indeed be blind. Public clamour, so dangerous to the preservation of the rights of man, must have no voice within the hearing of the judgment seat. No classes must be known, no beliefs aired as criminating or exculpatory evidence. Acts must be proved, not inferred. The ermine must remain as unspotted as the summer snows on the mountain peak; as fixed as the polar star, as unchanging as the decrees of fate, as unswerving as time itself must Justice tempered with mercy be decreed.

Therefore we deem this epoch propitious for a note of warning sounded in the ears of our fellow-workers. We believe the time is at hand when organised labour, loyal to the principles of freedom as enunciated by Patrick

Henry and Thomas Jefferson, should give the alarm which we hope may result in a restoration of our common country to the paths of true liberty, wherein, as Jackson declared, "Every man and each man in this country by the eternal must and shall be free."

Working to the accomplishment of this end, thoroughly aroused to the necessity for immediate action, fully aware of the danger of procrastination, and determined to recognise and utilise all honourable expedients toward attaining our object, and cheerfully hailing those signs of the changing times which tend to a recovery by the people of their just rights, and ever ready to lend honour to whom honour is due, ever ready to award approval for all actions in accord with justice and humanity. . . .

The remainder of the message, which is written by Mr. Madden, eulogises Governor Altgeld as the embodiment of all that has descended from the fathers of the revolution.

I may add in concluding this very brief sketch of Mr. Pomeroy and the Trade and Labour Assembly, that quite recently Mr. Pomeroy, Mr. Madden, and some other members of the Illinois Federation of Labour and the Chicago Trades and Labour Assembly struck out on a new line in attempting to provide for planting out of the unemployed on the land. Such at least was the original idea, but the scheme as at present formulated is more interesting as an attempt to establish an ideal community than as a practical proposal to plant the surplus population of the cities upon the land. The following account of their scheme is taken from the *Chicago Herald* of June 10 :—

The members of the Chicago Labour Organisations have organised an association for the purpose of acquiring possession of four square miles of land in the territory owned by the Land of Sunshine Company in Southern California, this to be subdivided into tracts of twenty acres each with the exception of a square in the middle, which will be held in common and adapted to the general use of the land owners.

In the centre of the smaller square will be a circular park, bordered by the main street, facing which will be the residences. It is the plan to build in this park the village building and school, the stores occupying one block and the shops another. These will be under the immediate control of the land owners organised into a democratic form of government and controlled as are public buildings in the city. Behind the circle of dwellings will be a comparatively small strip of land devoted to kitchen gardening and pasturage. From this circular drive-way, which is the border of the village park, it is planned to build eight roads that will reach to the sides of the tract. Four of these will stretch diagonally from the drive-way to the corners of the tract. The other four will connect the drive-way with the points marking the middle of each side. Another road will divide the sides into quarters and join the main diagonal roads in the middle. Between these roads 112 plots of twenty acres each will be laid out, each one facing on a roadway, and the farthest side of the one on the remote edge of the tract will be but 280 rods from the dwelling.

"It has been our experience," said M. H. Madden, president of the association, "that the principal reason labouring men who have lived for years in the city object to becoming farmers is the fact that were they to make such a change it would necessitate their living on a farm remote from neighbours. This is the one great objection brought by the men and the members of their families. In this plan the objection is obviated. The men can not only live together, but they will not be compelled to be too close together. They will live facing beautiful grounds, which is much better than the way most of them now live in congested districts and poorly-constructed houses. By the plan we present the people will be given plenty of breathing room, and at the same time will be afforded the pleasure of one another's society. It is the plan to construct in the centre of the ground a school building and build up an excellent educational institution, and have as well a theatre and halls for public meetings. The government of the village will be the same as the government of any village. Every resident will have a voice and vote in its affairs. There is every promise that we will have excellent success with the plan. We not only hope by this that we may establish this little village, where the poor man can be contented, but that we will demonstrate the feasibility of the plan, and that others like it will become established, to the end that the population that is now drifting to the cities may be turned back and the country districts have at least their share of the population.

"The lands we visited in California pleased us very much. The soil is very productive and systems of irrigation have been made very complete. The twenty-acre tracts raising fruit will support a family well and yield a profit."

Under the plan as formulated ninety acres will be devoted to the dwelling circle and parks, 170 acres to the pasturage and gardening grounds. The individual holdings will amount to 2,200 acres. Not more than one tract will be sold to any one person, so that the village will contain no aristocrats.

Mr. Pomeroy is the General Organiser of the American Federation of Labour, a body which corresponds to our Trades Union Congress. It met last year in Chicago. The president of this federation is Mr. Samuel Gompers, the following account of whom recently appeared in the American *Review of Reviews*, from the pen of Dr. Albert Shaw :—

In Clinton Place, New York, a few doors west of Broadway, and a few minutes' walk from the offices of the *Review of Reviews*, one finds on the lintel of an old house, once a residence but now an office

building, a modest sign that reads : " The American
Federation of Labour, Samuel Gompers, President."
The halls are rather dark and dingy, and one climbs
two flights to find the rooms of the Federation.   But
the journey will be worth while if the caller is fortunate enough to find Mr. Gompers at his desk.   He is
not prone to careless absence from his place of work,
but the manifold duties of his position frequently
take him to distant parts of the country.   The
quarters of the American Federation are unadorned
enough to allay any suspicion that the chief officers
of this great combination of the trades unions of the
country are disposed to revel in luxurious appoint-
ments.   Everything is as severely plain as it can
be ; and the stiff common chairs invite no loiterers.
Order and system are evident at a glance, and the
experienced observer is quickly satisfied that the
affairs of the Federation are in methodical and competent hands.

Mr. Samuel Gompers has been heard by many
audiences besides those composed of working men
and members of the constituent orders of the Federation.   He is a short but massively framed man of
perhaps forty-five years, with a strong and handsome
face and suave manner, a business-like yet not too
abrupt deportment, and a diction as discriminating
and clear as one is taught to expect from a college
professor.   Mr. Gompers certainly exhibits great gifts
of lucid expression, whether on the platform or in
private conversation.   He possesses a singularly well-
balanced temperament, the key to which seems to be
a cheerful optimism tempered by natural caution and
held in bounds, though not repressed, by experience
and responsibility.

Mr. Gompers represents trades unionism upon its

best established lines. He was born in London forty-four years ago, and at ten years of age was put at work in a factory, continuing his elementary studies at a night school. He left the shoemaker's trade,

SAMUEL GOMPERS.

which he did not like, and was apprenticed to learn the trade of a cigar maker. At thirteen he was brought to the United States, and became a member of the International Cigar Makers' Union. He assumed activity in that body, and as a delegate to

the early conventions of the American Federation
of Labour was recognised as a natural leader and
intrusted with various offices, and soon with the
presidency. As an editor of labour papers, he has
earned the right to rank with the successful journal
ists of the country. At present Mr. Gompers' journalistic labours are confined to the editing of the
American Federationist, a monthly magazine that is
the official organ of the Federation of Labour. Its
first number appeared in March, 1894. It is intelli-
gently and broadly edited. Its articles are short, but
pithy, and from good sources. For example, the
opening contribution in the June number is from
Tom Mann, the English labour leader; Grace H.
Dodge writes of working girls' clubs; Alice L. Wood-
bridge of women's labour; Edward Thimme of child
labour; and there are many other admirable bits of
contribution, correspondence and editorial comment.
Miss Frances Willard sends the *Federationist* a hearty
greeting, and every page of this June number indi-
cates breadth of view on the part of the editor, and a
desire to bring the labour movement into the intelligent sympathy of right-minded men and women
everywhere.

It is for the peaceful and lawful evolution of industrial conditions that Mr. Gompers has always
stood. He has never for a moment swerved from the
doctrine that the policy of the labour movement, as
represented by trades unionism, should aim always to
secure high wages and a reduction in the hours of
labour, these two things meaning improved conditions
and surroundings that must have far-reaching and
beneficent results. The competitive industrial system
seeks to conquer the markets of the world by selling
cheap, Mr. Gompers would declare ; and hitherto the

burden of this competition has been placed chiefly upon the shoulders of labour. The combination of workmen in trades unions is for the purpose of throwing back part of this burden upon the shoulders of the capitalist class, who in order to still compete must be content with smaller profits. He has been described in a labour paper as "an eminently practical man, belonging to that school of unionists who believe in high dues, thorough organisation, perfect discipline, sick benefits, death benefits, out-of-work benefits, travelling benefits, and maintaining an aggressive position at all times for higher wages and shorter hours of labour."

The American editor of the *Review of Reviews* made Mr. Gompers a neighbourly call the other day to exchange views with him upon the coal strike, and upon various questions of the day that have to do with the prevailing social unrest.

"I see no immediate or early possibility," said Mr. Gompers, "of a complete agreement, in settlement of the coal dispute, that shall include all the States and mining districts that are involved. The effect of the uncontrolled competition of the Southern Illinois district with those that lie beyond it, north, south, west and east, is such that for the present a settlement all along the line seems to be out of the question. There is nothing to do but to close the strike by separate agreements in the different coal-mining territories involved, and then proceed to bring the Southern Illinois miners into a state of more perfect organisation so that in future their district may not be a source of disturbance to the coal-mining interests of the entire country.

"But," Mr. Gompers continued, "although this year's coal strike is not to be terminated upon principles as sweeping in their application as one could desire, I wish to say emphatically that I regard this great strike, in spite of its numerous unfortunate incidents, as an essentially fortunate thing, not only for the cause of organised labour but also for the general economic and industrial interests of the United States. The financial panic of last year, with its attendant industrial depression, led a general attempt on the part of capital engaged in the employment of labour to sharply curtail the consuming power of the masses of the people by diminishing their ability to purchase—that is, by a general reduction of wages. This movement against labour made its way through various great fields of employment. In the railroad world it was resisted by the strikers on the Great Northern system, whose final success in arbitration has helped to check the downward tendency. But the most typical instance of the aggressive movement among the employing class against the workers was in the mining field and especially in that of bituminous coal mining. The great strike was a notice served upon capital that the whole world of organised labour had determined to take a stand, to face about, and not only to resist further aggression but to endeavour to gain back some of the ground that had been lost. With the success of this stand, —for the miners have in most of the districts concerned gained all or a considerable part of their demands,—it is evident that there is a turn in the tide. Wages in general are not to decline any further, but on the contrary are to tend upwards. And with better pay the people will require larger supplies of standard commodities and the wheels of industry will be quickened in many directions. It is not true," Mr. Gompers further continued, "that the miners have really suffered anything in the loss of wages during the weeks of enforced closing down of the mines. They will gain back all the time apparently lost by more steady employment hereafter. It is only approximately a certain volume of output that the country can consume in any case, and if through a strike the miners can secure a higher wage per ton it is clear that their total wages upon a year's output will be increased by so much."

Mr. Gompers was asked to express himself as to arbitration in industrial disputes, and especially as to the possibility of some form of compulsory arbitration. He replied that he was most assuredly in favour of arbitration :—

"As for 'compulsory arbitration,' however," he continued, "the two words seem to me antithetical. Arbitration always involves a compromise. The conditions under which it usually comes about are those which have led each of the parties in dispute somewhat to fear and somewhat to respect the other. The employing interest is usually the stronger. But when, through careful organisation, the employees attain a position which commands the respectful attention of the representatives of capital, it becomes possible to confer together successfully and to secure a reference of disputes for the desired settlement by arbitration. I see no means by which legal compulsion to arbitrate could be made really beneficial to the party that is usually the weaker. It would be an instrumentality that might react dangerously against the progress of organised labour. The labour movement has too much at stake and has too slender means at its command to indulge in dubious experiments. The weapons that it now uses have been tested by long experience, and their use is understood and also their limitations."

Against the idea that an occasional outbreak or scene of disorder in connection with a strike was the essence of the labour movement, Mr. Gompers protested earnestly :—

"The real labour movement," said he, "goes on unnoticed by the newspapers and unwitnessed by the public. At this moment, while we discuss the question, there are probably thousands of committees of trades unions and labour organisations in conference with employers in the shops and counting rooms of the country. For every strike that occurs, scores of questions are settled by quiet conference between groups of organised working-men and their employers. The strikes are unfortunate and to be regretted, but they are a part of the existing industrial order and serve their purpose. They should not be indulged in without great caution, but sometimes they are necessary, and their general result is beneficial upon the whole. It is always to be noticed that employers fight most stubbornly and ruthlessly in their first experience of a strike. They are much more disposed to negotiate and compromise when subsequent disputes arise."

With regard to the attitude of the American Federation of Labour upon public questions, Mr. Gompers stated that the order is committed to the doctrine of the free coinage of silver at the ratio of one to sixteen, regardless of the success of attempts to secure international agreement. He regarded Coxeyism and the industrial army movements rather as evidences of social unrest and incidental phenomena than as occurrences having any primary or vital significance in themselves. With Mr. Coxey's doctrine of non-interest-bearing bonds Mr. Gompers could find no theoretical fault. In fact, his words were friendly rather than otherwise for the financial propositions that Mr. Coxey has advocated. As a practical matter, however, he did not consider that proposals to deal radically with the currency and the national debt are timely or advisable. In a general way, the American Federation has for some years been committed to the doctrine of an income tax. Mr. Gompers expressed himself as personally adverse to the exemption line in the pending bill, and as in favour of a tax that should reach all incomes of self-supporting men, no matter how small. He would, however, employ the principle of a graduated tax, increasing the rate as incomes increased which were therefore better able to contribute to the public treasury.

The interview was ended by the following statement regarding the aims of the Federation :—

The American Federation of Labour actively participates in every effort made by thinking men to secure amelioration in their condition, economically, socially, and politically, and often initiates movements tending towards those purposes. But the organisation, as such, is particularly committed to the shorter hours movement, or what is more popularly known as the Eight-Hour movement, the leaders all agreeing that the movement which gives the workers more leisure brings more intelligence and consequently more independence, more sterling qualities of character and truer progress. The Federation has accomplished wonders in this movement for a shorter workday, and millions of workers now enjoy countless golden hours of rest, leisure, and opportunity as the result of the concentrated efforts of 1886 and 1890.

The American Federation of Labour dates from about 1880, and is therefore some fourteen years old. It includes about seventy-five distinct trades unions, with an aggregate membership of from six hundred thousand to seven hundred thousand individuals. Some of these unions, like those of the carpenters, bricklayers, cigar makers, coal miners, iron moulders, steel workers, and printers, are very large and strong ; while others, owing to the nature of the craft which they represent, are small in membership, though often very complete and effective in organisation.

The only other labour organisation in America which can compare with the Federation of Labour is the Knights of Labour. This organisation, in 1886 had not fewer than 700,000 members, 600,000 of whom had joined in the course of that year. But American labour unions fluctuate very greatly, and the Knights of Labour are a very signal illustration of this fact. In 1880 they numbered 300 in Chicago, in 1886 they rose to 22,000, in 1893 they had fallen again to 300. When I left Chicago they were prospering, and their numbers were estimated at 40,000. Mr. Powderly, who until quite recently was the Grand Master Workman, has been expelled the order. The rock upon which the Knights split was their antagonism to trades unions, a rock which they have assiduously endeavoured to avoid under the guidance of the present Grand Master Workman, Mr. Sovereign. Mr. Detweiler, a well-known Chicago unionist,

L

writing on the work of the Knights in the past, says :—

Since the first general assembly of the Knights of Labour, many reforms that are of direct value to the labouring classes have been accomplished. Labour bureaus have been established in nearly all the Northern States. Laws for the sanitation, safety and comfort in workshops, factories and stores have been adopted. Trades unions have become recognised social factors ; weekly pay-days have been largely adopted. Child labour has been regulated to some extent, and good men and women are still doing earnest and excellent work in that direction. The inhuman method of working convicts by contractors is being rapidly abolished. Laws to prohibit the bringing of foreign labour under contract to the United States have been passed. A fair effort has been made to enforce these laws. The hours of labour have been shortened to a greater extent than casual observers would imagine. There are probably 500,000 workmen in the United States who labour only eight hours a day, and as many more whose hours of toil have been reduced from twelve, fourteen, and sixteen hours to ten. All this may be said to be a direct result of the agitation inaugurated and largely directed by the Knights of Labour.

The printed cards of the organisers of the Knights, some of whom I had the advantage of meeting when in Chicago, set forth that they secure their members $4, or 16s. a week, sick benefit, and $50, or £10, for funeral expenses.

THE KNIGHTS OF LABOUR

Is the greatest labour organisation the world has ever seen.

It is the only organisation which, while striving to secure for wage-workers the best possible terms as to wages, hours and conditions, aims at reforming the causes of industrial injustice.

It secures to each trade and locality absolute control over his own trade or local affairs, yet its perfect organisation enables its members to act unitedly and promptly, therefore effectively, when concentrated action becomes necessary to remedy injustice or to resist oppression.

It is pledged to work for the overthrow of the capitalistic system of production and exchange, yet realising that reforms can only be beneficial and permanent when they rest upon the convictions of a wisely educated people, it seeks to accomplish its objects only by appeals to reason and conscience—never by force.

It is a secret organisation only as far as secrecy is necessary to protect its members from wrong and persecution, and can never be used to shield wrong-doing.

Its doors are open to all who labour honestly and usefully, either by hand or brain, without question or discrimination on account of creed, race, or nationality.

The present strength of the Knights of Labour is estimated at 325,000. One great difference between the Knights of Labour and the Federation of Labour is that the Federation objects to uniting men in any other than strictly class organisations, whereas the principle of the organisation of the Knights is that their component minor bodies should include labouring men of all conditions. In this they resemble the American Railway Union, with which, in June last, they formed a hearty alliance, being affiliated and conjoined for the purpose of uniting the members of both organisations in a close bond of harmony for the better advancement of the world of labour. The Knights in one respect are better than any of the other labour organisations, inasmuch as they resolutely refuse to make any distinction as to the sex, race or colour of their members. In politics the programme of all these associations is practically the same, although it must be admitted that for the most part it is in the air, and cannot be regarded as counting for very much with the caucuses which draw up platforms for the two parties which divide American politics between them. The last approved programme is as follows :—

We re-affirm our allegiance to the principles set forth in the Omaha platform, and recommend to the favourable consideration of the People's Party State Convention the following platform of the Federation of Labour, adopted at Chicago December, 1893, and thus secure the union of all labour and farmer organisations for the purpose of consolidating and uniting the active industrialists and agriculturists in one harmonious political party :—

1. Compulsory education.
2. Direct legislation.
3. A legal eight-hour work day.
4. Sanitary inspection of workshop, mine, and home.
5. Liability of employers for injury to health, body, or life.
6. The abolition of the contract system in all public work.
7. The abolition of the sweating system.
8. The municipal ownership of street cars and gas and electric plants for public distribution of light, heat, and power.
9. The nationalisation of telegraphs, telephones, railroads, and mines.
10. The collective ownership by the people of all means of production and distribution.
11. The principle of referendum in all legislation.

L 2

I now come to the American Railway Union, which is playing the most conspicuous part in the present strike. I had not the good fortune of meeting Mr. Debs, whose name has become so familiar to newspaper readers ; but I had a long and interesting conversation with his right-hand man, who shares with him the notoriety and the peril of arrest for the part which he has taken in the present strike. Mr.

EUGENE DEBS.

Rogers, the editor of the *Railway Times*, is a very sensible, straightforward man, whose ambition it is to convert the *Railway Times*, which is at present a fortnightly paper, into the daily organ of the railway employees.

Eugene Debs, of Terre Haute, Indiana, like Mr. Gompers, was born in England, and has brought his English common-sense to bear upon the organisation of railway employees. He has long been recognised as one of the ablest men engaged in the labour movement. He was Secretary of the Brotherhood of Locomotive Firemen and editor of the *Locomotive Firemen's Magazine*. For years he has recognised the fact that the railway employees were powerless until they were combined. Before the formation of the American Railway Union each class of railway employees had its own union, and they very frequently refused to act together, with the result that they were defeated in detail. There was no need for the railway magnates to resort to the usual expedient of dividing in order to conquer, for the unions were so bitterly divided among themselves that the companies had it all their own way. In the old days the locomotive engineers would have nothing to do with the locomotive firemen, and the switchmen consorted with none but switchmen, the railway telegraphists were equally exclusive, while the railway trainmen and the railway conductors practised the exclusive policy as far as they could. Frequent attempts were made to federate these bodies so as to have a supreme council, but the federated unions were so jealous of their council that the efforts came to nothing. Mr. Debs, after much studying of the causes of this failure, came to the conclusion that a closer union of the rank and file was necessary and that the power of the officers must be curtailed. He wanted an organisation which would reconcile the two apparently contradictory principles of strict trades-unionism and general organisation of all the men. He conceived the plan of organisation to consist of lodges, which were composed exclusively of the several branches of the railroad service, but were united as lodges of one general body, the idea being that to each branch of the service should be left the adjustment of such matters as affected that branch peculiarly and exclusively and could be handled by it without outside assistance, the general body being called upon to take charge of all matters of common interst to all railroad men, and to back up any individual branch if it proved to be too weak by itself to enforce such demands as the organisation at large might consider proper and just. In a general way the idea is similar to that which underlies the American Federation of Labour. It combines the trades union principle with that of the Knights of

Labour, which is expressed in the words "an injury to one is the concern of all."

Having conceived this idea, Mr. Debs set to work to realise it. He is an eloquent man and an energetic organiser, and he had his paper, the *Locomotive Firemen's Magazine,* with which to enforce his views. After pointing out to the railway employees that the result of his scheme would increase their strength, and at the same time reduce their contributions to the central fund, he succeeded in securing recruits by the thousand, and at the beginning of this year the American Railway Union, one of the largest labour unions in the country, of which he is president and founder, was accomplished. The following is his declaration of principles, which is not only interesting in itself, but sets forth on the best authority the views of some of the ablest labour men in America on the present position of labour on the railways.

In the creation of a new organisation of railway employees, certain reasons prompting the movement are demanded and should be set forth with becoming candour.

The number of employees now in the service of the railroads in America has been variously estimated from 800,000 to 1,000,000. It is safe to assume that this vast army of employees is, at the present time, not less than 1,000,000.

Accepting the highest claims of the various railway organisations as a basis of calculation, less than 150,000 of these employees are members of such organisations, leaving more than 850,000 who are not enrolled in the ranks of organised labour.

To state the proposition concisely, organisation is union. It is a self-evident truth that "in union there is strength," and conversely, without union weakness prevails; therefore, the central benefit to be derived from organisation is strength,—power to accomplish that which defies individual effort.

Experience, the great teacher, whose lessons, sooner or later, must be heeded, points out with unerring certainty the defects, and demonstrates the inefficiency of the organisations as they now exist:

First.—They do not provide for all classes of employees, it being shown that 850,000 of them, or eighty-five per cent. of the whole number, remain unorganised. These may be divided into three general classes: (1) those who are eligible but decline to join; (2) those who have been expelled because of their inability or refusal to bear the financial burdens which membership imposes, and (3) the multiplied thousands in various departments of the service who are totally ineligible, there being no provision for their admission.

These facts, in the light of thirty years of organisation, establish, beyond all controversy, the truth of the declarations herein set forth, and emphasise the demand for an order in which there shall be room and protection for all whose hearts throb responsive to union sentiments, and whose desire it is to march under union banners in the great struggle for the triumph of union principles.

Second.—The existing organisations, designed to promote and preserve harmonious relations between employer and employee, have met with only limited success, if, indeed, it can be shown that any progress in that direction has been made. Never has there existed that mutual confidence without which it were misleading to assume that peace, amity and good-will prevail. At best, therefore, this relation, between employer and employee has been little better than an enforced compliance with conditions rarely satisfactory to either party.

Third.—What must be said of organisations which have failed to establish friendship and good-will even among themselves? From the first there have existed antagonisms and jealousies, culminating in warring factions instead of a harmonious whole. Organisation has been pitted against organisation, bringing upon themselves not only disaster but lasting reproach.

Fourth.—Protection is the cardinal principle of the present organisations ; but they do not protect. Since " an injury to one is the concern of all," a failure to protect all is an exhibition of a purpose without the power to enforce it, and this fact emphasises the necessity of the federation of organisations, but which under existing conditions is impracticable, if not impossible.

Fifth.—It is universally conceded that one of the most serious objections to the existing organisations is their excessive cost to the membership, the sum totals of which, were the facts known, would amaze the labour world. So enormous have they become, that tens of thousands, unable to bear the burden, have been forced back into the ranks of the unorganised.

Sixth.—Another defect in existing organisations is their secrecy, as for instance, the secret ballot, by virtue of which thousands of worthy applicants have been excluded. The air of mystery surrounding their proceedings is not calculated to inspire confidence. On the contrary, in the relations between employer and employee, in carrying forward great enterprises in which the people at large are profoundly interested, mystery is not required, and is productive of suspicion and distrust. Open, fearless and above-board work is far more in consonance with the spirit of independence and free institutions.

Seventh.—The tremendous power conferred upon chief officers has been a source of wide-spread dissatisfaction. The mere dictum of an individual determines whether a strike, involving thousands of employees and millions of dollars, shall or shall not occur. He is, in this sense, an absolute monarch. From his decision there is no appeal. The unanimous vote of the organisation cannot prevail against it. Such autocratic power vested in a single person is not only dangerous to a degree that defies exaggeration, but is at war with the American idea of government, in which the one-man rule has no place. The responsibility often involved in a final decision is too great and too grave to rest upon any one man, however sturdy his integrity or unerring his judgment.

Eighth.—The subject of grievances and grievance committees has itself become a grievance that cries aloud for correction. The petty complaints that ceaselessly arise among employees, and keep them in a state of agitation and unrest, have brought odium upon organisations and weakened their power for good in directions where real grievances demand adjustment.

The very term "grievance committee" has become a reproach and a by-word. This brood of evils is in a large measure due to the personal jealousies and enmities flowing out of the inharmonious relations existing between organisations, each of which seeks supremacy without regard to the welfare of the other.

The complex grievance machinery entailing prolonged delays, the vast number of local, general and joint committees—an army in themselves—are well calculated to increase rather than diminish grievances. For every complaint that is remedied another takes its place, and thus they multiply, until railway officials lose patience and seek refuge in refusal to make further concessions.

Such petty grievances as are herein indicated ought not to exist at all, and once correct methods of organisation are inaugurated, will entirely disappear. Righteous complaints and just demands are always in order, and should receive prompt attention and be pressed to a speedy and satisfactory adjustment.

Ninth.—Organisations have become so numerous and their annual and biennial conventions occur so frequently, that the question of furnishing free transportation for delegates, their families and friends, is being seriously considered by railway officials as an abuse of privileges without a redeeming feature. This incessant demand for special trains, special cars, the recognition of credentials, and passes without limit, is compromising the character and dignity of organisations, and placing their officers and members under obligations which must, sooner or later, in view of the constant agitation for increased pay and other concessions, prove a source of embarrassment and humiliation.

Tenth.—The extraordinary fact cannot be overlooked, that while present organisations are provided with expensive striking and boycotting machinery, and while millions of dollars, wrung from their members, have been expended in support of strikes, they have with scarcely an exception been overwhelmed with defeat. The history of railroad strikes, as conducted by railway organisations, is a recital of brave but hopeless struggle, of strikers defeated, impoverished, black-listed, pursued and driven to the extremity of scabbing or starvation. Under present conditions this result is inevitable, and a century of organisation on present lines will not change it. Railway employees have contributed from their earnings untold millions in support of organisations, and are, therefore, entitled to protection instead of promises that can never be fulfilled.

It cannot be denied that the policy of present organisations has filled the land with scabs, who swarm in the highways and byways awaiting anxiously, eagerly, the opportunity to gratify their revenge by taking positions vacated by strikers. Thoughtful men have no difficulty in accounting for the failure of railroad strikes. Neither are they at a loss to suggest a remedy. Organised upon correct principles, governed by just laws and animated by unselfish purposes, the necessity for strikes and boycotts among railway employees will disappear.

Experience teaches that defective organisation leads to strikes and defeat as certainly as perfect organisation will insure peace and success.

Eleventh.—The ever increasing body of idle engineers, conductors, etc., seeking in vain for employment, is the legitimate fruit of promotion on the seniority basis. The pernicious effects of this system can scarcely be over-estimated. A lifetime of faithful service counts for nothing. When dismissal comes, ofttimes for trivial offence, the victim finds the doors of his calling everywhere barred against him. He is compelled to go to the very bottom and serve again his entire apprenticeship. The natural tendency is to weaken organised labour by creating a surplus of experienced men whose necessities make them available to corporations in recruiting their service in times of trouble. It is not strange that the victims of the seniority iniquity renounce organisation and take their place with the unorganised.

What is required is a system of promotion that recognises and rewards merit rather than seniority. Other things being equal, seniority should, of course, have preference. In filling vacancies selections should be made from the line of promotion and from the unemployed in a ratio evincing due regard to the rights of both.

The American Railway Union will include all classes of railway employees, separately organised, yet all in harmonious alliance with one great brotherhood.

There will be one supreme law for the order with provisions for all classes, one roof to shelter all, each separate and yet all united when unity of action is required. In this is seen the federation of classes which is feasible, instead of the federation of organisations, which has proved to be utterly impracticable. The reforms sought to be inaugurated and the benefits to be derived therefrom, briefly stated, are as follows:—

First.—The protection of members in all matters relating to wages and their rights as employees is the principal purpose of the organisation. Railway employees are entitled to a voice in fixing wages and determining conditions of employment.

Fair wages and proper treatment must be the return for efficient service, faithfully performed.

Such a policy insures harmonious relations and satisfactory results. The new order, while pledged to conservative methods, will protect the humblest of its members in every right he can justly claim. But while the rights of members will be sacredly guarded, no intemperate demand or unreasonable proposition will be entertained.

Corporations will not be permitted to treat the organisation better than the organisation will treat them. A high sense of honour must be the animating spirit, and even-handed justice the end sought to be attained.

Thoroughly organised in every department,' with a due regard for the right wherever found, it is confidently believed that all differences may be satisfactorily adjusted, that harmonious relations may be established and maintained, that the service may be incalculably improved, and that the necessity for strike and lockout, boycott and blacklist, alike disastrous to employer and employee, and a perpetual menace to the welfare of the public, will for ever disappear.

Second.—In every department of labour, the question of economy is forced to the front by the logic of necessity. The importance of organisation is conceded, but if it costs more than a working man is able to pay, the benefits to accrue, however great, are barred. Therefore, to bring the expenses of organisation within the reach of all, is the one thing required, a primary question which must be settled before those who stand most in need, can participate in the benefits to be derived.

The expenditures required to maintain subordinate and grand lodges, every dollar which is a tax upon labour, operate disastrously in two ways, first by repelling men who believe in organisation, and second by expelling members because of inability to meet the exactions, and in both of which the much vaunted fraternity feature, it is seen, is based entirely upon the ability to pay dues. In this it is noted that the organisations, as now conducted, are for men, as a general proposition, who have steady work at fair pay, while others less fortunate in these regards, are forced to remain outside to be the victims of uncharitable criticism.

Hence, to reduce the cost to the lowest practicable point is a demand strictly in accord with the fundamental principles of economy.

This reduction of cost, the new organisation proposes to accomplish in a way that, while preserving every feature of efficiency that can be claimed by existing organisations, will so minimise expenses that members will not be forced to seek relief, as is now the case, in the abandonment of organisation. To accomplish this reduction a number of burdens such as grand and subordinate lodges, annual and biennial conventions, innumerable grievance committees, etc., will be eliminated. As these unnecessary features will not exist, the entire brood of taxes necessary to maintain them will be unknown.

: Third.—The new organisation will have a number of departments, each of which will be designed to promote the welfare of the membership in a practical way and by practical methods. The best thought of working men has long sought to solve the problem of making labour organisations protective, not only against sickness, disability and death, but against the ills consequent upon idleness, and those which follow in its train : hence there will be established an employment department in which it is proposed to register the name of every member out of employment. The department will also be fully informed where work may be obtained. It is doubtful if a more important feature could be suggested. It evidences fraternal regard without a fee, benevolence without alloy.

Fourth.—In the establishment of a department of education, a number of important features are contemplated, as, for instance, lectures upon subjects relating to economics, such as wages, expenses, the relations of employer and employee, strikes, their moral and financial aspects, etc. In this connection a daily paper will be established, whose mission it will be to advocate measures and policies in which labour has vital interests, and also the publication of a standard monthly magazine, which will occupy a still broader field in the discussion of questions which engage the attention of the best writers and thinkers of the times.

Fifth.—There will be a department designed to promote legislation in the interest of labour, that is to say, the enactment of laws by Legislatures and by Congress, having in view well-defined obligations of employer and employees, such as safety appliances for trains, hours of labour, the payment of wages, the rights of employees to be heard in courts where they have claims to be adjudicated, and numerous others in which partisan politics will play no part, the common good being the animating purpose.

Sixth.—In the department of insurance sound business principles will be introduced, something that has not hitherto engaged the serious attention its importance merits. At present insurance entails grievous burdens without corresponding benefits ; to lessen the cost while maintaining every security and every benefit, will be the problem the department will solve. It is the purpose to have a life as well as an accident department, both to be optional with the membership.

With this declaration of its purposes and with boundless faith in its conquering mission, the American Railway Union consecrates itself to the great cause of industrial emancipation.

PART III.—WAR.

CHAPTER I.—A PROPHET OF THE SOCIAL REVOLUTION.

REV. GEO. HERRON,
*Prof. of Applied Christianity,
Grinnell, Iowa.*

SOME thirty years ago there was a small child, homeless and friendless, earning a precarious living as a printer's devil in an office in Boston. One day while the boy was busy among the compositors, a strange wild man made his appearance and asked for work. There was something about the stranger which commanded attention, and, in spite of his ragged wretchedness, inspired some awe. He stood six foot in his boots, and there was something in his face which showed that he was born to command. He was a capable compositor, and the foreman provided him with a case at which he soon settled down, and proved to be one of the best typos in the shop. But although he did his work, and did it well, he never chummed with any of his mates. At night he lodged in the garret. In his eye there was a certain awe-inspiring gloom, and in his carriage a haughty reserve which repelled the confidence of his fellow-workmen. But the little printer's devil was strongly attracted to the silent and distant man.

The attraction was mutual, and at night time, when the office was closed and the stranger had retired to his garret, he would take the boy with him. While the little waif nestled closely in the strong man's arms, the silence of the night was broken, and the quondam tramp poured into the eager ears of his boyish listener stores gathered in many fields both of life and of literature. There, by the aid of a candle, in an ill-furnished room, he taught the boy to read Shakespeare, and afterwards introduced him, strangely enough, to the mysteries of the Gnostic philosophers and inspired in the child a great passion for Greek philosophy. McCleod, for that was the man's name, was a gentleman and a scholar, and after a few months he was promoted to be foreman of the shop which he had entered as a penniless tramp only a short time before. The foreman did not cease to be friends with the printer's devil, who still continued to sit at the feet of his master and to look up to his teacher as if a new Gamaliel had been sent to open up to him all the treasures and mysteries of literature and philosophy. After a time, however, to the great distress of the boy, McCleod disappeared as mysteriously as he had come, but not until he had inspired the boy with a genuine intellectual enthusiasm. In after years, when the boy had grown up, he always said he never thought of his teacher without being reminded of Michael Angelo. Why, he did not exactly know, but between the great Italian artist and McCleod there seemed to him to be a close resemblance. He often vainly longed for his friend to return, but he never saw him nor heard from him again. The mystery seemed impenetrable, but one day the veil was strangely rent when he read in the papers of a desperate encounter which had taken place in Tennessee, at the end of which McCleod had been killed. Then it came out that this mysterious stranger, who had taught him about the Gnostics and the philosophers of ancient days, was none other than the near relative of the famous James Brothers who earned for themselves an almost heroic fame among the desperadoes of America. McCleod, who had been a bandit before he came to Boston, had found the craving for the wild life of the hills too strong for him and had returned to his old ways. He was shot dead in a mountain pass after having held a United States marshal and fifteen deputies at bay for some time.

The youth, thus strangely initiated into the wider life by one who was an outlaw and outcast, grew up with an intense sympathy for the disinherited of the world. McCleod, the quondam tramp, the real outlaw who died a bandit's death fighting against the officers of the law, had been to him his best friend and truest helper. It is not surprising therefore that the youth should not have forgotten the lesson so early and so vividly impressed upon his mind. When he grew to man's estate, he threw himself with all the energy of a passionate nature into work for the poor and the degraded. He became a Christian evangelist, and his earnest words, accentuated with intense sympathy, were potent to rouse many in his re- vivalist campaigns. After a time he began to see that mere revivalism, although excellent in its way, was hardly adequate for the needs of humanity. The bitter and cruel injustice of circumstance, the cor- rupting and brutalising environment which defaces the divine image in man, and the triumph of insolent injustice in the affairs of men, filled him with per- plexity and pain. While never leaving hold of his evangelical faith, he worked gradually and steadily into a larger conception of life, and applied himself energetically to the study of economics. As the result of his studies and of his experience, he became an earnest and impassioned assailant of the existing order of things in America, and he.is to-day the man of all other men who may be regarded as the prophet of the social revolution in the United States.

That man, whose training and preparation for his work I have just briefly glanced at, is the Rev. George D. Herron, D.D., who is now Professor of Applied Christianity at Iowa College, Grinnell, and the author of several little books which read like the utterances of the latter-day prophet. When I was in Chicago I went to Grinnell to address the students at the college where my colleague—Dr. Albert Shaw—was educated, and when there I had the pleasure of making Dr. Herron's acquaintance. Grinnell lies at the highest part of the State of Iowa, on the very ridge of the watershed. Grinnell College stands in the midst of the undulating, black, stoneless, olea-ginous soil, the detritus left in the basin of a sea which has long ago dried up. Grinnell is famous for two things. Twelve years ago a cyclone struck the town, and mowed down its houses as a mower levels the grass of the meadow, and the memory of that terrible visitation is still in the memory of the survivors. It is still more notable as being the seat and centre of the forward movement of Western Christianity. Pre-sident Gates, a large-spirited, far-seeing, courageous man, who is the principal of the college, boldly chal-lenged last winter, in the columns of the *North Western Advocate,* the attitude of the Church on Social questions. His manifesto rang like a trumpet-peal, summoning to the battle the lethargic and indifferent Churches of the North-West. Many of the best men rallied to his support, and the battle still goes on. In Professor Herron, Dr. Gates found a co-adjutor after his own heart, and the two bid fair to stamp the impress of their minds very deeply on the coming generation. Dr. Herron is not yet forty, with a physique which seems to be too delicate for the burden of the message with which his soul is laden. Like most of the men who are shaping things in the West, he is psychical, and has a realising con-sciousness of the invisible world, which sustains him not a little in the midst of his vigorous crusade against the forces of iniquity in high places in the Western Republic. When I met him he was just on the eve of starting for the East, in order to carry round the fiery cross of revolt against the sweating system in States which, owing to the lack of any legislation restraining this modern slavery, were profiting by the restrictions placed upon it in more enlightened States.

We had a good deal of talk about the outlook in America. I found him weighed down, almost over-whelmed, by the sense of coming woe. What grieved him most was what seemed to him to be the un-christian attitude of the Christian Church. Instead of being instinct with the spirit of the Nazarene, it was too often the subservient vassal of Antichrist. "In twenty-five years," he said to me in tones of deep conviction, "in twenty-five years America will see an outburst of vengeance and despair which will be far worse than the French Revolution, unless something can be done to avert it." But he looked in vain on the horizon for the agency which would be able to cope with the task. The Church, which should be the natural daysman or mediator between the opposing forces, was supine, or worse than supine. In too many cases it was bound hand and foot by the ropes of Mammon in the shape of its wealthy members, seat-holders and trustees. But if the Church could not be relied upon—nay, if the Church itself had thrown in its lot with the oppressor—what was to be done ? Dr. Herron frankly said that he did not know ; all that he could see was that it was the bounden duty of all to whom was vouchsafed a view of things as they are, and as they will be if the present forces are allowed to work themselves out, to use every means at their disposal to rouse the consciences and minds of the people to an adequate sense of the great crises of our time.

When I left Grinnell President Gates was good enough to give me a copy of Dr. Herron's little book, " The New Redemption," a call to the Church to reconstruct society according to the gospel of Christ. It is dedicated to Dr. Strong, and it is one of several little books in which the author has endeavoured to deliver the message with which he feels himself to be intrusted. Among these books there is one, " The Message of Jesus to Men of Wealth," while he was just putting through the press his latest work, entitled, " Christian Society." " The New Redemption " consists of six chapters, and I do not think that I could do better than give some extracts from the book in which in burning words he expresses the conviction which is growing in the minds of many of the younger men who in America have paid a disinterested attention to the economic conditions of modern society. The keynote of the book is struck in the first chapter, which is entitled, " The Social Revolution."

Dr. Herron takes as the text of his first discourse the

familiar passage in the Apocalypse : "I saw a new heaven and a new earth, for the first heaven and the first earth had passed away, and the sea was no more." Dr. Herron asserts that he approaches the social problem, not from the standpoint of a political economist, but from that of a Christian apostle. His object was to cross-examine some of the false principles which have bred social inequalities, and to assert the true principles which can procure social justice. Every few centuries God drops a great idea into the soul of man. It thrives on persecution and throned by crucifixion. It destroys man if he rejects it ; it saves man if he accepts it. The master idea of the world two thousand years ago was Redemption. Now—

A great idea is leading the world's thought and lifting its hopes. Everywhere are the signs of universal change. The race is in an attitude of expectancy, straitened until its new baptism is accomplished. Every nerve of society is feeling the first agonies of a great trial that is to try all that dwell upon the earth, and issue in a divine deliverance. We are in the beginnings of a revolution that will strain all existing religious and political institutions, and test the wisdom and heroism of the earth's purest and bravest souls; a revolution that will regenerate society with the judgments of infinite love. We must get ready for the chance by making straight the way of the Lord Christ into the heart of the social strife, that He may purify it with the hope of justice; by giving Him command of the revolution, that He may lead it into a larger redemption of the earth. God honours our generation by bringing upon it the sorrow and trial of seeking a road to social order, of finding a way to something like an equitable distribution of economic goods, a mutualism of the responsibilities and benefits of civilisation. The idea of brotherhood, co-operation, unity, is both destroying and recreating the world. It will not do to say the revolution is not coming, or pronounce it of the devil. Revolutions, even in their wildest forms, are the impulses of God moving in tides of fire through the life of man. To resist them is to be consumed, and to compel the remission of sins by the shedding of blood. To receive them as from God is to receive the kingdom almost without observation. The dangerous classes in every age and nation are they who, in the interest of religious or political parties, say that the wrong cannot be set right, that selfishness and injustice and inequality are natural virtues, essential to progress and the stability of civilisation.

It is evident from these opening passages that Dr. Herron attaches an entirely new sense to the familiar phrases which have been heard a thousand times in our churches. Although a Christian, he is

M

instinctively a Socialist, and declares war to the
death against a civilisation based upon competition.
To him competition is only a shade better than
cannibalism :—

> In fact, we are and have been in a state of industrial anarchy—of social
> lawlessness. Selfishness is always social disintegration—competition is not
> law, but anarchy. That competition is the life of industry is the most
> profane and foolish of social falsehoods. Cain was the author of the com-
> petitive theory ; the cross of Jesus stands as its eternal denial ; it is social
> imbecility ; it is economic waste ; it is the destruction of life ; it is the
> deformity, brutality, and atheism of civilisation ; it will be as outrageous to
> the civilisation of the future as cannibalism is to the civilisation of the
> present.

To him nothing is more absurd than the appeal of
the capitalist to law and order. The whole social
question, he maintains, is rapidly resolving itself
into a question whether or not law, as capital, can
be brought into subjection to law.

> Our so-called industrial order is the disordering of nature. It is the dis-
> organisation of human life. The social problem is the call of the state to
> become Christian. The state can save itself only by believing in the Lord
> Jesus Christ as the supreme authority in law, politics, and society. The
> state is the social organ. To meet the strain that will be put upon it by the
> revolution, the state must be redeemed from the worship of property and from
> commercial theories of government. The Sermon on the Mount is the science
> of society ; it is a treatise on political economy—it is a system of justice.
> Industrial federation lies in the nature of things. An industrial democracy
> would be the social actualisation of Christianity. It is the logic of the
> Sermon on the Mount, which consists of the natural laws by which industrial
> justice and social peace can be obtained and established.

Inequality of possession seems to him a kind of
original sin, and the search for social justice, even
when conducted by atheists, is essentially a belief in
the practicability of the principles which are the
essence of Christ's Gospel. At present he declares,
and quotes authorities for the faith that is in him,
that we have attained not social justice, but social
injustice :—

> It is hardly disputed that capital, under our modern industrial system, is
> receiving more than a just share of the fruits of labour, and the labourer is
> receiving relatively less and less of the profits of his toil. The increase of
> wealth and wages is in no sense equitable. "Thoughtful men see and
> admit," says Judge Walter Q. Gresham, "that our country is becoming less

and less democratic, and more and more plutocratic," and plutocracy he pronounces the most insidious of all forms of tyranny. "Nothing," says Dr. Theodore Dwight Woolsey, "would lead the mass of men to embrace Socialism sooner than the conviction that this enormous accumulation of capital in a few hands was to be not only an evil in fact, if not prevented, but a necessary evil beyond prevention. . . . A revolution, slow or rapid, would certainly bring about a new order of things."

It is the work of the Church to bring together in a divine unity the various human interests that are now at strife, but he has almost as much faith in the capitalists as he has in the Church for the attainment of this desirable end. He says :—

It lies within the power of the American capitalists who call themselves Christians, by taking the Sermon on the Mount and patiently working it into the foundations of industry, to be the creators of a new and divine civilisation that would surpass all our apprehensions of the Revelation of John.

Christianity has yet to become Christian, and he says :—

The social revolution, making the closing years of our century and the dawning years of the next the most crucial and formative since the crucifixion of the Son of Man, is the call and opportunity of Christendom to become Christian. The whole social problem is a question of how to manifest Christianity as the natural humanity of man; how to reveal the cross as the universal law of sacrifice by which God made and redeemed the world.

Few men have expressed more strongly and in more provocative fashion the modern revolt against millionaires than has Dr. Herron. He says :—

The priests who accompanied the pirate ships of the sixteenth century, to say mass and pray for the souls of the dead pirates, for a share of the spoil, were not a whit more superstitious or guilty of human blood, according to the light of their teaching, than Protestant leaders who flatter the ghastly philanthropy of men who have heaped their colossal fortunes upon the bodies of their brothers. Their fortunes are the proudest temples of the most defiant idolatry that has ever corrupted the worship of the living God. Their philanthropy is the greatest peril that confronts and deceives and endangers the life of the Church, and thinks to bribe the judgments of God and deceive the Holy Ghost. The industrial world is itself the supreme opportunity for modern Christian philanthropy. The mighty brother-loving tasks to which the Spirit of God calls the genius and enterprise of our age, are the conversion of manufacture and commerce into the ministers of divine righteousness— into instruments for the execution of the justice of divine love.

Dr. Herron is no pessimist, for he, like other men, has visions of a better future :—

As I look anxiously and prayerfully into the future, I see the men who work and the men who own, labour and capital, marshalling themselves upon

M 2

opposite sides of a conflict that may bring woe to all that dwell upon the earth. As the hosts anger and strengthen, I see one like unto the Son of Man moving down the gathering lines to bind all the conditions and interests of human life in the mutualism of the justice of the kingdom of God I see Him reach to clasp the hands of strife in a federation of love, which is the realisation of the freedom of God in humanity.

This federation of love, in his opinion, is inconsistent with the wages system, a theory which he expresses with an emphasis which leaves nothing to be desired. But, like seers in general, he abstains from particularising as to the precise method by which a more practical arrangement is to be discovered and put in its place :—

The buying and selling of labour in the cheapest market is based upon the arrogant and intolerable assumption that man is made for property, and not property for man. The wages system is economic slavery ; it is a profane traffic in human flesh and blood. The only safety of capital itself is in the abolition of the so-called law of wages, and the federation of money and work in the creation of property as a communion with God in the perfection of man in the freedom of Christ.

He calls aloud to the Church to put its hand to the plough.   If it does so, it will not fail of the support of its Divine Founder.

The cause of modern social agitation is not the ownership of property, but the individualism which has enthroned the mammon of selfishness in the place of the fatherhood of God as the providence of progress. The immediate business of the Church is to go in and possess the world of work, wages, and wealth, and make it divine, in the faith that everything is wrongly done that is not done in the name of Jesus Christ. . . . And in the darkest hour of mortal despair, through the fiercest storm of human passions, there will come that same Jesus who stilled the waves of His native sea, to speak the commanding word that shall hush the social strife in the peace of perfect justice. The truth of God's human fatherhood and man's divine sonship, with the brotherhood of need and service which it means, makes all ownership a ministry of God's providence and the creation of property a continuation of the redemptive energy of God in Christ.

But, he laments, the Church itself fails to recognise its law.

What will this generation do with Jesus Christ ?   He is here, and on trial in the social problem. The love of Christ is still the most revolutionary, element that can be introduced into society. It can mean nothing less than entire social reconstruction. Its application to the industrial world, its assertion as social law, may be rejected as destructive of order, and described as dangerous to the peace of the Church and State. The principles that rule the motives and successes of men are the very elements of disorder and disintegration. What we have been accustomed to call economic laws is the lawlessness of society. There is no law but love. The old foundations upon which society stands will have to be removed. Society must be reborn into a kingdom of love, and the nations eat of the tree of the healing Christ-like, that there may be a just and righteous civilisation. The axe of God is being laid at the roots of the tree of strife that has poisoned the earth with its fruit since the days of Cain. The kingdom of heaven is at hand with a new conception of redemption as social and national. The natural operations of the love of Christ as the law of life alone can procure the social justice which is the search of the Spirit of God in the people. There can be no peace to the earth until the last intrenchment of organised selfishness, the last citadel of false civilisation has gone down before the white-robed hosts of the conquering Christ. They who cry peace between justice and injustice, between love and selfishness, between truth and hypocrisy, are the prophets of the devil, however sweet their words, and not speakers for God. Will the Church believe in the love of Christ, and will society receive it as law and justice, or shall He be put to a new crucifixion? It is this question that makes our day historic with the greatest destinies since the day that awoke upon the cross of the Son of man. Not since the Nazarene gathered about Him His Galilean disciples have there been such universal moral and political changes as we now see in their beginnings. The reformation of Luther and Wickliffe was small in its issues compared to the social re-adjustments and moral revolutions that shall come forth from the supreme crisis towards which history is now moving. The old things are breaking up to pass away, with what confusion and sorrow no one can tell, and a new and divine society is preparing to come in—a society so just, so pure, so loving, as to be an eternal incarnation of Christ. The crisis is God's call upon the Church for men who will take the social ideal of Jesus, and dedicate themselves to its realisation in theology and science, in government and industry : men who believe.

But the crisis offers to the Church salvation or perdition. The work is to be done with the Church, if the Church will; if not, then without it.

Unless the Church repents of its moral sloth and blindness, and accepts its new and greatest mission with the cross it brings, its temples of material splendour will become dust beneath the eager feet of the children of the kingdom. If the Church that accepts Christ's name refuses to bear His cross of social redemption, it will justify the statements that it is not a Christian institution, and God will regenerate civilisation without the Church.

But salvation now, as always, is to be wrought out by sacrifice.

To look the present evil age squarely in the face, and decide to follow Christ through the midst of it, and teach His love as the cure of its evil, and as the law its activities must obey, is to make up one's mind to accept some form of a crucifixion at the hands of those who want not the reign of Christ or the dominion of His love. They who resolve to make the subjection of the world to the law of love the one thing they do, need to understand from the first that they bring not peace among men, but a sword. Through great tribulations will the new redemption come, bringing crowns of thorns and crosses for its prophets. The early workers upon the foundation which Jesus is laying for a divine society will accomplish the fall of this hideous, colossean materialism which we call civilisation; but they themselves will be crushed in the fall and buried beneath the ruins. They have a baptism to be baptised with that will straighten them till it is accomplished. The shadow of the cross, under which Jesus wrought His love into the hearts of men, hangs heavy upon the closing years of our century, and no man can do the work which God wants done now without walking a path that leads straight to a new Calvary.

It has never been enough that men simply believe that Christ is their Saviour. Every new revelation and larger conception of the Gospel has needed the witness of some form of martyrdom. For I frankly acknowledge and declare, no man can practise this Gospel without suffering loss and persecution through conflict with the opinions and customs of the world.

So long as the world is not under the dominion of Jesus it is impossible for the true Christian to be other than a disturber of the world's peace. The Gospel is no message of peace to the world, but a sword of judgment and conquest.

We have travelled far from the old doctrine that still lingers in some secluded nooks and corners, that the first duty of the Christian Church is to act as a kind of surpliced policeman for the maintenance of things as they are. Dr. Herron says : —

Revolution is the Christian's business, and it is the treason of the Church that cries peace where there is no peace. The social revolution is a new coming of the Kingdom of God. It is the matchless opportunity of the Church. A brotherhood of righteousness, a kingdom of social justice is bound to come; and whether it come quietly or tumultuously, through the evolution of love, or through the wrath of blind and Christless vengeance, depends upon the attitude of the Christian Church towards the Social question. There is no infidelity so terrible in its consequences as the want of effort on the part of one who calls himself a Christian to regenerate our social conditions. There is no atheism so frightful as the opinion and consent that society must remain as it is. The worst charge that can be made against a Christian is that he attempts to justify the existing social order.

Those who are at ease in Zion will, no doubt, resent this preaching of the doctrine of the Christ, but Dr. Herron tells us roughly that religious selfishness is the only sin that Christ seemed to denounce as incurable. The cross, he thinks, now as ever attracts rather than deters. There is a fascination about martyrdom, and a divine thirst for self-sacrifice in the soul of man.

Not only do we betray Christ, but we deceive and wrong the world itself, by presenting the Christian life as other than a life of cross-bearing and self-crucifixion in the service of Christ. In seeking to save its life the Church is losing that which it would save. Many of the noblest souls are drifting from the Church because it dares not appeal to their moral heroism by the power of the cross.

It is not the cross that is turning men from Christ, but the Church which bears and offers no cross. It is the uncrucified Christianity that speaks from the modern pulpit and sits in the Church's pews that is driving the passion for humanity into other channels of service than the Church. There is a great mass of moral nobility pent up in the souls of multitudes of young men who long to be led into a larger life and diviner work than the Church affords. But where are the inspired leaders who shall give this nobility its opportunity?

A divine quality of glorious womanhood, hungering in the souls of a thousand girls of the new world, that is stealing upon the Church like a thief in the night, yearns to express itself in some crusade against the refined paganism and monstrous selfishness of society.

But who will lead them under the power of divine affections into the freedom of the self-crucified life?

It is not suffering and self-denial, but the want of opportunity for these, that is the cause of the Church's failure to enlist much of the best life and bravest thought of our times in the service of Christ. Where one would turn away by the call to self-denial, two would respond with joy, if the conditions of Christian discipleship were clearly stated according to the Gospel, and the cross of Christ uplifted. For the call of the cross alone has power to summon the moral heroism of the world to action in the service of truth and right. If suffering on behalf of Christ were presented as a favour and opportunity, with the insistence that belief on His name is proclaimed as salvation, a white-robed army, greater than any man can number, would arise to march through tribulations to the victory of faith that overcometh the world.

One more extract and I have done :—

Sometimes I think I see the angels of the ascension coming back to the earth clothed with a flame of judgment to speak to the Church of our day: Why stand ye gazing up into heaven, and repeating your ancient prayers, and speaking your approved sermons, and building your steeples high? Are you, O Church of Christ, using this Gospel for your spiritual pleasure, faithless through the spiritual selfishness that deceives the very elect, or are you following Him who pleased not Himself about the things of this life, who made Himself of no reputation in the eyes of the religious castes and the socially respectable, but went about in the form of a servant, doing good to the poor and vile and ignorant? Are you intent on making life religiously and materially comfortable, making your enjoyment and convenience the measure of your creed and conduct, or are you profound and passionate with the purpose to claim and subdue this world as the heritage of Christ's sacrifice and the Kingdom of His Cross? This Christ will come again, it may be in an hour when ye think not, perhaps He may be here, to find you worshipping the Mammon of gain and forsaking the cross of your redemption. Even now is this Jesus who ascended into heaven coming again in power and glory of the Father to manifest the practicability of His love as the law of man. What else is the conflict between the employed and the unemployed classes, the combinations of the one in labour unions and the other in monopolies, but a stumbling of the world unawares into the brotherhood of Christ? What are our modern problems but the coming of Christ upon a vaster field of opportunity? What but a greater vision of Christ is lifting the eyes of the nations above commercial theories of government and materialistic notions of society? What but a preparation for new unfoldings of the truth as it is in Jesus can be the theological unrest that is shaking the bosom of the Church universal? There are hours when I seem to see the ghostly faces of the glorified dead, who have cemented the structure of Christian history with the blood of their lives, peering out of the sad splendour of the martyr-ages, to wonder at our blindness to our opportunities, and stretch forth yearning hands to seize what we pass by, eager to suffer again for the grace that is being brought to us in the larger revelation of Jesus Christ.

We are not unfamiliar in England with such doctrines, although I do not know of any teacher who combines so much of the passion of the Socialist with the faith of the Christian as Dr. Herron. It can easily be imagined what indignation is occasioned by the utterances of this latter-day prophet. In June last, at the Nebraska University, Professor Herron delivered an oration at the Commencement Exercises which occasioned no small sensation. The title of his discourse was, "A New Political Vision." In the course of his address he said :—

" The people to-day are looking for new political conditions. Civilisation is a vast undisciplined army, yet conscious of a universal change. The people are not angry, but only in sorrow and anxiety. The world is full of discontent and moving toward revolution. The race is learning that it is not an aggregation of individuals, but a union into one body. The association of men in justice is now the aim of politics. The whole trouble is due to the want of common unity of aim. We must have politics which bring universal harmony of progress."

Dr. Herron then entered into details, and set forth before the students and the governor of the state, who was also present, the evidence in support of his assertion that the existing state of things could not last. The rich, he said, were becoming richer, while the poor were becoming poorer ; the judiciary were corrupt ; the law-makers were the tools of the monopolists ; while, as for the Government control of the railways, that had been summarily settled by the railways assuming control of the Government.

After this exposition of that state of things as they are, Professor Herron went on as follows :—

"The most significant fact in society to-day is that it turns to the mind of Christ as the ideal for humanity. If this ideal could be attained it would bring unity of the masses. The living Christ is the real king of America. The Christian state will be the organized democracy. Americans are not democratic, either socially or politically. In a pure democracy the people will be their own representative. The Christian state will be the organized economy of the people. The great trouble with our system of government is the over-production of middle-men. The system of wages is a system of slavery. There can be no equality till there are no more hirelings. Our state will be the organized law of the people.

"The aim of law is the education of men in those questions which unite them in the right. At no time since the age of the Roman state has law received so much attention as to-day. Yet all know there is no justice in the courts. If there is anarchy everywhere, it had its origin in the courts. Christian organization in the state would be perfection, while anarchy would be its destruction. God sent this American nation to be an example to other nations of the earth. We have failed. We have forsaken our trust. We are a fallen nation. Except the nation repent it cannot survive. We must prepare the way for the Christian state and for the kingship of God."

As might be expected, such utterances were not allowed to go unchallenged. Governor Crounse, who followed Professor Herron, repudiated indignantly what he had said as being both unwarranted in fact and discouraging to the youth just entering upon life. Said the Governor :—

"I do not believe that this country is wholly bad and tottering on the verge of destruction. I do not agree with him that our courts are bad; that they are cesspools of corruption and the founts of anarchy. Neither do I believe that Coxey and his followers are the highest types of American citizenship. I believe our institutions are the grandest and best system of government, the best ever known or devised."

Therein spoke the American optimist. Possibly even Governor Crounse has reconsidered his opinions in the light of the lurid glare of the incendiary fires at Chicago.

CHAPTER II.—THE STRIKE AT PULLMAN.

WHEN Mr. Debs organised the American Railway Union, it was with the avowed object of preventing strikes. Accidents will occur, however, even in the best regulated families, and Mr. Debs's union found itself involved in a round dozen of disputes one after the other, in all of which, notwithstanding the intense depression of trade, he succeeded, if not in pulling off the victory, at least in securing sufficiently good terms so as to increase his prestige and establish his hold over the union. His most notable victory was gained in May, when after an eighteen days' strike on the Great Northern Railway the dispute was ended by an arbitration, which recognised the justice of 75 per cent of the claims of the Union.

The Great Northern employees, some 5000 in number, demanded a return to the wage scale which had prevailed up to August 1st of last year. This the Railway Company refused. The men went out on strike, and for eighteen days there were thousands of miles of the Great Northern Railway upon which not a wheel turned. The American Railway Union co-operated with the Knights of Labour in order to secure this tie-up. The Knights were even prepared to go further, and were threatening to call out all the men who handled freight for the Great Northern from the Pacific Coast to St. Paul. Alarmed at the threatened extension, the business men of Minneapolis and St. Paul persuaded the disputants to consent to arbitration. The arbitrators decided that 75 per cent. of the reduction made since last August must be restored. Such a victory naturally elated the Union and tended to increase the support on which Mr. Debs could count.

This strike had hardly been settled when the Pullman strike commenced, and there is no doubt but that the one struggle had a considerable effect upon the other. The movement at Pullman was on the same lines as that on the Great Northern, namely an attempt to secure the restoration of the wage scale which prevailed before the reductions of last year. So far from the American Railway Union pressing on the strike, the action of its officers was in the opposite direction. The dispute, which is destined to have so far-reaching an effect upon the labour questions of America, began in a quarrel between some painters and the Pullman managers. It is interesting to notice this, because it illustrates forcibly how great a matter a little fire kindleth. At the beginning of May the freight car builders in one shop at Pullman were ordered to make some change in the way in which they worked the paper into the sides of the freight cars. I do not profess to understand the nature of the change, but the men protested that it was equivalent to a reduction of $5 a week on their average wage. No reason was given, and they refused to work at the reduction. They waited upon the superintendent and asked for redress. He said he could do nothing. They then appealed to the General Superintendent. He said he did not care to talk with them. That was the beginning of the whole quarrel. The men, feeling that they had been arbitrarily cut in their wages and resenting the refusal to make any explanation, or even to listen to their grievances, decided

to demand a return to last year's pay. Thereupon
all question as to the paper and the freight cars
disappeared. Mr. Pullman gave way on that point
too late. The fire was in the heather.

Five local unions, and the Railway Union, composed of painters, upholsterers, tinners, car builders,
and others, held a conference, and unanimously decided to demand a restoration of their old pay. The
Vice-President of the Union, Mr. Howard, who had
just arrived from the victory over the Great Northern,
addressed the conference and strongly opposed any
precipitate action. He admitted that he could not
but blame Pullman's superintendents, who had denied
to their men the right to meet them and discuss their
grievances, but he hoped there would be no need
for either a strike or a boycott. It was in vain,
however, that Mr. Howard endeavoured to avert the
inevitable conflict. The upholsterers brought forward
as a special grievance the fact that the President
of their Union had been dismissed immediately after
his election to that office, although he was a skilled
and temperate workman. On the 7th May, Vice-
President Wicks was waited upon by forty-three
employees, representing every department of work
at Pullman, complaining of an immense number of
grievances. They complained of tyranny and abuse
on the part of the forewomen, dishonesty of managers,
favouritism, and arbitrary black-listing. They further alleged that they wanted their old wages back
again, and double pay for Sunday work. Mr. Wicks
at once said that he would investigate the complaints,
but that any return to the old wages was impossible.
They were losing $20,000 on one contract alone,
which had been entered into solely for the purpose of
keeping the works going. So far as the Company

was concerned, it would have suited them better to have shut down the works all winter. He said further that the Company had four million dollars worth of cars standing idle in their yards, which were depreciating every day. The men owed the Company $70,000 for rent, for which they were not being pressed. Some of the deputies wished to bolt the union and to go on strike there and then, but Vice-President Howard induced them to listen to reason and to wait for Mr. Wicks' promised investigation into their complaints. Mr. Wicks made his investigations and reported that there was no ground for the alleged grievance of the employees. Thereupon fifty specific grievances were brought forward in writing, while many others were stated to the stenographer. Further investigation was promised, and the question as to wages was resumed.

Mr. Pullman himself then entered the conference and addressed his workmen. He said that he would most carefully investigate all the complaints and mete out strict justice to the offenders. He did not think that his men could look him in the face and ask him for more pay in view of the facts. He had been informed only the other day that at no time in the history of the company had there been less friction at the works. He said he felt a fatherly affection for his employees, and had a lively interest in the town. He had been selling cars below cost price in order to keep his people employed. Mr. Pullman said further that he claimed to be a truthful man, but that the books of the Corporation were open to the men to substantiate his statements. He was about to take a contract for 800 cars, but he could only do so if his men would stand by him at the existing rate of wages. If he had to return to the old wages, he could only go on for four weeks longer until the present contracts were finished, as the old rate would make competition impossible for his Company.   Mr. Pullman then retired, and Vice-President Howard was left to plead for peace with the workmen.   He spoke very strongly against a strike, thinking that a strike at that moment would be a fatal error.   The men thereupon agreed to defer the strike, and to take immediate advantage of Mr. Pullman's offer to permit an investigation with regard to the contracts taken by him at a loss.   Mr. Howard assured them that he had the personal assurance of Mr. Pullman and Mr. Wicks that none of the committee or any of the complainants should suffer in any way on account of what they had said. At the close of the meeting late at night the freight-car builders declared that they would not go to work next day, but Mr. Howard, after half an hour's strenuous arguing, was able to avert a rupture.   Mr. Howard believed at that time it was possible to settle matters without a strike.

Unfortunately, everything was spoiled by what the men loudly asserted to be an act of bad faith on the part of Mr. Pullman.   When they asked to see the books, they were shown a statement which had been drawn up in the office, which they were allowed to read, but which they were not allowed to verify by any reference to the books. Further, they asserted that two members of the Grievance Committee had been dismissed, and in no cases had any of the abuses been admitted or remedied.   Thereupon on May 11th they unanimously decided to strike.   Mr. Howard having done everything he could for peace, told them that as the general officer of the American Railway Union he was merely the servant of the local unions, and that as they had commanded a strike it had become his duty to see that they won. He warned them that there must be no disorder, no gathering in knots or lounging about the streets, and no drinking. Sub-committees of three were appointed from each of the twenty-five departments of the Pullman Works to preserve good order, to prevent intimidation of other workers who wished to work, and to see that no pledges were violated. Mr. Howard, who much deplored the strike, said that if the Pullman Company had shown as much interest in their own affairs as the officials of the American Railway Union, there would have been no trouble. The company seemed to regard the complaints of their workmen as if they were of no account, and Mr. Howard went on to say :—

"I tell you that a harsh word from a superior in a shop may be a little thing to the man who says it, but it may make the man who hears it miserable for months. The letting out of any of the committeemen at just this time was particularly unfortunate, and strengthens the men in their determination to make trouble. I advised strongly against the policy of striking, but is too late now to do anything but win if we can."

When the die was cast, Mr. Wicks said that in the case of one foreman they had found the griev-ances well founded, and that if the strike had not been declared that foreman would probably have been discharged for tyranny and abuse. In nearly all of the other instances, so far as the investigation had proceeded, the complaints were so frivolous and trivial that they could not be noticed. As to the alleged dismissal of complainants, only one was paid off, and that was due to the fact that there was no more work in his shop for him to do. Two more workmen who had taken no part in the complaints had shared his fate.

Vice-President Howard intimated that, unless the strike were soon settled, the members of the American Railway Union would refuse to handle any of the Pullman rolling stock. It may be noted that Mr. Pullman emphatically denied that there was the least desire to close the works before the strike was declared. " Why should we close down ? " he asked ; " everything was going satisfactorily." Thus, on the 11th May, the great strike began. Mr. Howard stated that the men believed that a lock-out was contemplated, and this left them no option but to take matters into their own hands. The chairman of the strike committee said that nothing but despair induced by the reduction of wages below the standard which makes the life of an American workman endurable has actuated us to strike. Mr. Pullman took the matter very philosophically. He said that he did not know how long the strike would last, but that it would be a good thing financially for the stock holders of the company. His assistant manager ridiculed the idea that the Union could possibly tie up the 2000 cars which were running in various parts of the country.

For a time all went quietly. The shopkeepers, however, refused to sell goods excepting for cash. So far from showing any desire to resort to violence, one of the strike committees declared that they would swear in 2000 men to protect the works, in case they were re-opened with fresh workmen. There was no need for acting upon this heroic resolve, for the works were not re-opened for months.

On May 14, President Debs for the first time addressed the strikers. He was preceded by Vice-President Howard, who closed an earnest speech by an appeal to the men to avoid all violence and disorder, by saying, " We want the working people of this country to learn to act for themselves, and we want you to comply with the spirit which Christ our Saviour expounded while on earth, to do your duty to your fellow-men." Mr. Debs made a more militant speech, in which he sounded a key-note which has subsequently been taken up all round.

I am with you heart and soul in this fight. As a general thing I am against a strike, but when the only alternative to a strike is the sacrifice of manhood, then I prefer to strike. There are times when it becomes necessary for a man to assert his manhood. I am free to confess that I do not like the paternalism of Pullman. He is everlastingly saying: " What can we do for our poor workingmen." The interrogation is an insult to the men. The question is not, What can Mr. Pullman do for us; it is, What can we do for ourselves ?

Under this system of paternalism in vogue it is only a question of time until they own your bodies and have your souls mortgaged. It is a question that can be demonstrated to a mathematical nicety. In ten years more of this system he will own your bodies and have your souls mortgaged. Pullman's pretended philanthropy makes this a question of emancipation. His specious interest in the welfare of the " poor workingman" is in no way different from that of the slaveowner of fifty years ago. Remember that no power that can be devised will be neglected to divide you. But if you will follow Mr. Howard's advice there is no power on earth to make this strike a failure. Division means defeat and disaster.

Remember that the American Railway Union would rather be defeated honourably than triumph in disgrace. We believe in evolutionary revolution. We prefer agitation to stagnation. The same process that makes a Pullman, makes a thousand paupers. And the remedy is all in your own hands. We must change the conditions of affairs—not by force, but by the right and intelligent votes of the toiling thousands.

Two days later he spoke even more strongly :—

I believe a rich plunderer, like Pullman, is a greater felon than a poor thief, and it has become no small part of the duty of this organisation to strip the mask of hypocrisy from this pretended philanthropist and show him to the world as an oppressor of labour. One of the general officers of the company said to-day that you could not hold out against the Pullman Company more than ten days longer. If it is a fact that after working for George M. Pullman for years you appear two weeks after your work stops, ragged and hungry, it only emphasises the charge I make before this community, and Pullman stands before you a self-confessed robber. A rich man can afford to be honest; a poor man is compelled to be.

I do not believe in violent methods, but I do believe in telling the truth. The paternalism of Pullman is the same as the interest of a slaveholder in his human chattels. You are striking to avert inevitable slavery and degradation. Here is your father-in-law anxious about all his children. " You only owe me $70,000 for rent now, and I am not pressing you for payment !" Was there ever a greater public sham? All the time worried about your

N

welfare and piling up millions in one of the great monopolies of the age, by putting his hands into your pockets. I differ from the gentleman who contends that Pullman's gift of $100,000 for a monument is a matter to be considered—it is too easy to be generous with other people's money.

Do you know what this man does with his conductors and porters? Do you know that they are forced to live upon the charity of the travelling public? Mr. Debs continued: Charging exorbitant prices for his accommodations, lost to all sense of shame, he not only expects but depends upon the generosity of the people, who pay him the revenue upon which he waxes fat, to give his employees enough to live on. Only last month I went in a Pullman car over part of the western country. The conductor told me he was paid $30 a month, and had from this to board himself and support his family. The porter had $10 a month. Both were away from home two weeks at a time. That conductor asked me for money to buy him something to eat. This is the work of a great philanthropist.

"When the officials of the Pullman Company believe they are going to reduce you to subjection in a week or ten days they are making the mistake of their lives. This strike is going to be won, if it takes months, and it will be won because we are right."

Meanwhile Mr. Pullman departed for the east. Everything went on quietly at Pullman, but credit being stopped and no wages coming in, the pinch of hunger began to be felt, and they appealed to the Trade and Labour Assembly to support them. This they unanimously decided to do, and on May 28th the following appeal was issued, in which the keynote was sounded even more strongly than before :—

To the Public of Chicago :—The people of Pullman are destitute and starving. Over 5000 human beings are in dire necessity and appeal to the liberal-minded people of Chicago for help. Their unfortunate condition is not due to any fault of theirs. They have been noted for their thrift, sobriety, and industry. The fault lies in the hard times and a hard task-master. Forced for years to work on starvation wages, so that dividends could be paid on watered stock, they have at last struck against the soulless corporation which sought to fatten on the very marrow of their bones.

They struck against a slavery worse than that of the negroes of the south. These, at least, were well fed and well cared for, while the white slaves of Pullman, worked they ever so willingly, could not earn enough to clothe and feed themselves decently—hardly enough to keep body and soul together.

Now that they have struck for living wages, for a fair day's pay for a fair day's work, they find themselves penniless, with gaunt famine and despair staring them in the face.

Big-hearted, open-handed citizens of this big-hearted City of Chicago, these unfortunates turn to you appealing for aid. Help them as you would wish to be helped in the hour of affliction. Their cause is the cause of humanity. Their struggle is the struggle of honest industry against corporate greed.

At the beginning of June the first convention of

the American Railway Union was held in Chicago; 415 delegates, representing 120,000 railway men who had joined the union since August, 1893, were present; 15,000 of these men lived in and about Chicago; 15 of the local unions were in Pullman, and 36 in Chicago and the neighbourhood. The convention was notable as having been the first Railway Convention at which a woman was present. The assembly was held with closed doors, but from the brief notices in the papers we gather that Mr. Debs in his presidential speech expressed the hope that no member of the order would haul a pound of coal mined by non-union labour. He referred to the Pullman strike with great bitterness, declaring that it was a terrible illustration of corporate greed and pharisaical fraud which has now for years prevailed in this country, which has created conditions, striking to the stoutest heart terror and alarm. The convention then going into session passed a resolution that compulsory arbitration would be " undemocratic and un-American, leading to despotism and the consolidation of government which means the enslavement of the labouring masses of America." For some time it seemed doubtful whether or not the convention would recommend taking any action with regard to the Pullman strike. Vice-President Howard said that he thought it would be unwise, as the union had not the membership which it ought to have before taking so strong a step. Besides, he said it would be doubtful whether it would be effective, and it would certainly embroil the union with the railroad companies and the travelling public, and cause a revulsion of sentiment against the position which they had taken up towards Pullman. At present the universal opinion was favourable to them.

N 2

Meanwhile the company rejected the sixth proposal of arbitration which had been made since the strike began. One such proposal was made by the Civic Federation, but it met with the scantiest courtesy from the hands of the company. At last, on June 15th, an open meeting of the convention was held, in which the whole question of Pullman was taken into consideration. Before this discussion came on, however, it was reported that Mr. Wicks was willing to see a deputation of the men; but he refused to recognise any labour union. Thereupon it was determined to make a last effort to settle the question. The following conversation took place :—

" We come, Mr. Wicks," he said, " as a committee from the general convention of the American Railway Union to ask for a restoration of the pay of your employees to that received in 1893."

" It cannot be granted, gentlemen," Mr. Wicks replied.

" Will you recognise the American Railway Union in this matter? "

" No, sir."

" Do you speak for Mr. Pullman ? "

" I speak for Mr. Wicks, the second vice-president of the company."

" If the general officers of the union come to see you will you receive them ? "

" I shall always be glad to talk with the gentlemen," Mr. Wicks replied.

" Will you arbitrate the differences with the men ? " Mr. Lynch asked.

" We have nothing whatever to arbitrate," was the reply.

The subject as to whether the boycott should be declared was still regarded as an open question. Mr. Wicks stated his view of the case :—

" Our contracts with the railway companies should be better understood," Mr. Wicks said, " before any action is taken. Closing our shops is no injury to us. We made our position clear at the outset. It is to our pecuniary advantage not to take losing contracts at the present time as a matter of course. As for necessary repairs, our agreements with the railway companies, the terms of which are no secret, leave it optional with us whether we do the work ourselves or have it done by the railroads at our expense and under our inspection. We are not suffering in any way, and the reserve of 430 cars lying in the yards at Pullman have not been drawn on in any way.

" Railway companies pay us three cents a mile for the privilege of hauling our palace cars," the vice-president continued. " They are under no obligation to haul them, but they may not substitute those of any other company. If a strike be declared, we do not expect them to be used, and if any one cuts them off of course they will not be. But this question of boycotting cars is a very serious matter for the American Railway Union, and for the railroad companies. Really, the Pullman Company is not as deeply concerned as they,"

The Convention then received the report from the Pullman Committee, and as this document is the only authentic statement of the men's case, I give it here in full.

F. E. Pollans, chairman of the Pullman delegation, after a brief preliminary survey of the causes leading up to the strike, read the following statement:—

Mr. President and Brothers of the American Railway Union,—We struck at Pullman because we were without hope. We joined the American Railway Union because it gave us a glimmer of hope. Twenty thousand souls—men, women, little ones—have their eyes turned toward this convention to-day, straining eagerly through dark despondency for a glimmer of the heaven-sent message you alone can give us on this earth.

In stating to this body our grievances, it is hard to tell where to begin. You all must know that the proximate cause of our strike was the discharge of two members of our grievance committee the day after George M. Pullman himself and Thomas H. Wicks, his second vice-president, had guaranteed them absolute immunity. The more remote causes are still imminent. Five reductions in wages, in work, and in conditions of employment, swept through the shops at Pullman between May and December in 1893. The last was the most severe, amounting to nearly 30 per cent. But our rents have not fallen. We owed Pullman $70,000 when we struck May 11; we owe him twice as much to-day. He does not evict us for two reasons—one, the force of popular sentiment and public opinion; the other because he hopes to starve us out, to break through in the back of the American Railway Union, and to deduct from our miserable wages when we are forced to return to him the last dollar we owe him for the occupancy of his houses. Rents all over the city, in every quarter of its vast extent, have fallen in some cases to one-half. Residences, compared with which ours are hovels, can be had a few miles away at the price we have been contributing to make a millionaire a billionaire. What we pay $15 for in Pullman is leased for $8 in Roseland. And remember, that just as no man or woman of our 4000 toilers has ever felt the friendly pressure of George M. Pullman's hand, so no man or woman of us all has ever owned or can ever hope to own one inch of George M. Pullman's land. Why, even the very streets are his—his ground has never been platted of record, and to-day he may debar any man who has acquiring rights as his tenant from walking in his highways. And those streets! Do you know what he has named them? He says after the four great inventors in methods of transportation. And do you know what their names are? Why, "Fulton," "Stephenson," "Watt" and—"Pullman."

Water which Pullman buys from the city at 8 cents a thousand gallons he retails to us at 500 per cent. advance, and claims he is losing $400 a month on it. Gas, which sells for 75 cents per 1,000 feet in Hyde Park, just north of us, he sells for $2 25. When we went to tell him our grievances he said we were all his "children."

Pullman, both the man and the town, is an ulcer on the body politic. He owns the houses, the schoolhouses and churches of God in the town he gave his once humble name. The revenue he derives from these, the wages he pays out with one hand, the Pullman Palace Car Company, he takes back with the other, the Pullman Land Association. He is able by this to bid under any contract car shop in this country. His competitors in business, to meet this, must reduce the wages of their men. This gives him the excuse to reduce ours to conform to the market. His business rivals must in turn scale down. So must he. And thus the merry war, the dance of skeletons bathed in human tears, goes on. And it will go on, brothers, for ever, unless you, the American Railway Union, stop it, end it, crush it out.

Our town is beautiful. In all its thirteen years no word of scandal has arisen against one of our women, young or old. What city of 20,000 persons can show the like? Since our strike the arrests, which used to average four or five a day, have dwindled down to less than one a week. We are peaceable, we are orderly, and but for the beneficence of kindly-hearted people in and about Chicago we would be starving. We are not desperate to-day because we are not hungry and our wives and children are not begging for bread. But George M. Pullman, who ran away from the public opinion that has arisen against him like the genius from the battle in the "Arabian Nights," is not feeding us. He is patiently seated beside his millions waiting—for what? To see us starve. We have grown better acquainted with the American Railway Union these convention days, and as we have heard sentiments of the noblest philanthropy fall from the lips of our general officers—your officers and ours—we have learned that there is a balm for all our troubles and that the box containing it is in your hands to-day only awaiting opening to disseminate its sweet savour of hope.

George M. Pullman, you know, has cut our wages from 30 to 70 per cent. George M. Pullman, you know, has caused to be paid in the last year the regular quarterly dividend of 2 per cent. on his stock, and an extra slice of 1½ per cent., making 9½ per cent. on $30,000,000 of capital. George M. Pullman, you know, took three contracts on which he lost less than $5,000. Because he loved us? No. Because it was cheaper to lose a little money in his freight car and his coach shops than to let his workmen go. But that petty loss, more than made up by us from money we needed to clothe our wives and little ones, was his excuse for effecting a gigantic reduction of wages in every department of his great works, of cutting men and boys and girls with equal zeal, including everyone in the repair shops of the Pullman palace cars, on which such preposterous profits have been made.

George M. Pullman will tell you if you could go to him to-day that he was paying better wages than any other car shop in the land. George M. Pullman might better save his breath. We have worked too often beside graduates from other establishments not to know that work for work and skill for skill no one can compete with us at wages paid for work well done. If his wage list showed a trifle higher, our efficiency still left us heavily the loser. He does not figure on our brain and muscle. He makes his paltry computation in dollars and cents. We will make you proud of us, brothers, if you will give us the hand we need. Help us to make our country better and more wholesome. Pull us out of our slough of despond. Teach arrogant grinders of the faces of the poor that there is still a God in Israel, and, if need be, a Jehovah—a God of battles. Do this, and on that last great day you will stand, as we hope to stand, before the great white throne "like gentlemen unafraid."

Turning to more specific grievances, and giving *place aux dames*, local union No. 269, our first girls' union, is made up of young women working in the carpet department, the new linen-room, the linen-repair room, the glass-embossing department, and the laundry. Before May, 1893, the various departments were all paid at the rate of twenty-two and a half cents an hour. The cut reduced this to ten cents an hour, a scaling down of 68 per cent. Many girls providing for invalid mothers or small sisters or brothers have been able to make but six cents an hour. The Illinois statutes compel an eight-hour day for women. Listen to the reasons given by the girls themselves for their action :—

The working girls of the Pullman car shops organised recently to be protected against the abuse and tyranny of forewomen, whose delight it has been to make the girls' life one of discontent, humbling and crushing them in spirit, forcing many of them to become pliant tools and debased informers, degrading the loveliness of their sex, all of them the dupes of a merciless, soulless, grasping corporation, at once devoid of all sense of shame and humanity, and defying the laws and the presence of the Creator, and encroaching upon the rights of those who toil, weave, and spin. Our work is tedious and laborious, requiring skill, endurance, and persistency to accomplish the severally allotted tasks. In the name of justice and eternal right we appeal to this convention to exercise its power and relieve those wrongs that gnaw at the hearts of the working girls of Pullman.

The freight car shops, whose workmen were organised as No. 143 last November, present for inspection the following table of prices, showing the strides corporate selfishness can take in successive years:—

Lot 1515—						Oct. 1888.	Nov. 1893.
Car carpenter	..	..	..	..	..	$13.00	$7.00
Truck builder	..	..	..	..		90	60
Truck labour	..	..	..	..		31	0.9
Hanging brakes	..	..	..	..		1.20	65
Delivery forgings and castings	..	..	..			1.05	35
Delivery lumber	..	..	..	..		88	21
Framing	..	..	..	..		40	12
Total	..	..	..	..		$17.74	$9.01

Lot 1528—						Oct. 1888.	Nov. 1893.
Car carpenter	..	..	..	..		$17.00	$7.00
Truck builder	..	..	..	..		1.20	70
Truck labour	..	..	..	..		27 7-10	10
Hanging brakes	..	..	..	..		1.20	65
Delivery forgings and castings	..	..	..			1.10 7-10	41
Delivery lumber	..	..	..	..		1.03 7-10	38
Framing	..	..	..	..		40	12
Total	..	..	..	..		$22.22 1-10	$9.36

Wicks' patent refrigerator—						1889.	1894.
Car carpenter	..	..	..	..		$36.00	$19.50
Truck builder	..	..	..	..		90	60
Truck labour	..	..	..	..		32	10
Hanging brakes	..	..	..	..		1.20	60
Delivery forgings and castings	..	..	..			1.31	56
Delivery lumber	..	..	..	..		1.46	64
Framing	..	..	..	..		85	26
Total	..	..	..	..		$42.04	$22.26

These cuts are of 49, 57½, and 47 per cent. respectively, and it should be borne in mind that the first two are before the worst reduction of all, that of December, 1893. The figures are from the official books of the company.

The upholsterers of No. 190 present a similar table for your inspection :—

	1893.	1894.
Tufted headrests, with springs	$ 85	$ 41
Tufted headrests, without	65	41
Spring edge backs	67	48½
Spring edge seats, tufted	1.10	79
Spring edge seats, plain	90	65
Aisle ends	70	47
Wall ends	65	47
Scroll ends	1.25	70
Mann boudoir seat, tufted	3.00	1.71
Mann boudoir seat, plain	2.75	1.51
Mann boudoir back	4.00	2.85
Dining car plush seats	37	34
Dining car leather seats	43½	34
Dining car plush back	85	54
Dining car leather back	95	54
Drawing-room sofa seats	3.50	2.40
Smoking-room sofa seats	3.50	2.75
Extra long sofa seats	4.00	2.75
Round end sofa seats	2 75	2.10
Drawing-room sofa backs, plain	60	39
Drawing-room sofa backs, tufted	2.00	1.23
Smoking-room sofa backs, double	4.00	2.88
Smoking-room sofa backs, single	2.00	1.23
Sofa panels, tufted	60	42
Sofa panels, with arms	75	42
Plush panels, per car	1.02	79
Sofa rolls	1.40	90
Large ear chairs	5.75	4.00
Detroit chairs	5.50	3.60
Wicker chair, square	4.50	3 20
Wicker chair, round	4.50	2.90
Wicker chair, No. 369	3.00	1.75
Wicker chair, No. 1,036	1.00	70
Wicker sofa	10.00	5.00
Cutting carpets, dining car	2.00	90
Cutting carpets, sleeping car	2.00	1.10
Cutting carpets, Wilton	2.50	1.50
Laying carpet and oil cloth	1.25	80
Mattresses, new folding	30	20
Mattresses, double	25	15
Mattresses, smoking-room	40	22
Mattresses, old single	20	15
Mattresses, tourist	23	15
Loose cushions	25	20
Spring edge seats, day coaches	79	62
Hard edge seats, day coaches	43	35
Backs, day coaches	30	27
Day work	2.75	1.90
Day work	2.50	1.90
Day work	2.25	1.80
Day work	2.00	1.50
Day work, labourers	1.50	1 30

This union had its president, George Fingerhute, a sober, industrious and capable workman, discharged for joining the organisation just before the strike.

Local union No. 191 is made up of different elements. The labourers in it who have been cut from $1.50 to $1.30 for a ten-hour day cannot support their families, and asking a restoration of the 20 cents., which is the limit between life and starvation. The teamsters ask for $50 dollars a month, with a sixty-hour week and time and one-half for overtime. They ask the discharge of their foreman for gross abuse of his official position.

The painters of No. 196 ask for the wages of 1893, time and one-half for overtime, and double time for Sundays. The reductions are :

					1893.	1894.
Ornamental painters	..	..	..	..	$2.75	$2.30
Ornamental painters	..	..	..	..	2.50	2.30
Hard wood finishers	..	..	..	..	2.35	2.00
Hard wood finishers	..	..	..	..	2.30	1.75
Rubbers	..	..	..	..	2.20	1.50

Piece work prices have been so reduced that the men can with the utmost difficulty make their day rate. The ornamentation of a Pullman sleeper was reduced from $40 to $25.30, rubbing rough stuff from $22 to $15, and all other work in the same proportion. It must be borne in mind that the painters in Chicago have by their recent strike secured for themselves 35 cents. an hour for eight hours' work until June 15 and $32\frac{1}{2}$ cents. an hour thereafter. The men in Pullman have extraordinary skill, but are paid at the rate of 23 cents. an hour, a difference to-day of 12 cents. In other words, the Chicago brotherhood men are getting nearly 52 per cent. more than the members of the American Railway Union. If it be asked why the men do not leave Pullman it can only be answered that many of them have already, and that more will follow. But they demand justice where they are.

The tin and sheet ironworkers, who compose local union No. 207, were earning $2.75, $2.50, and $2.25 for ten hours' work a day before December, 1893. The two former—men of the most skill—were working before the strike for $1.90, and the average workmen in the last class for $1.60.

The chairman and vice-chairman of the strike committee at Pullman are both drawn from local No. 208, which, taking in as it does all the coach-builders, is the strongest union in the works. Its grievances are so many and various that they must be left to the delegate to present to the convention.

It was in the machinists' and woodworkers' departments, organised as local No. 240, that Brothers Petersen and Hasty, the latter the secretary of the union, were discharged, both of them being members of the grievance committee. They ask the wages paid by the Chicago Forge and Bolt Company for precisely the same work. The differences are startling, the Pullman men since the cut getting, for example, only $6\frac{1}{4}$ cents a hundred for three-quarter bolts, while the Chicago concern is paying $11\frac{3}{4}$ cents. The reduction in this department amounts to nearly 50 per cent. The threaders, millwrights, punch handlers, drill hands, and toolmakers ask for the wages of 1893. These last, men who make tools, are cut in some cases to $1.75 a day from $2.75 paid last December. In addition, the superintendent of this department is a bookkeeper merely. and has frequently admitted that he knows nothing whatever about machinery, or the requirements of the work.

The steamfitters of No. 249, who have suffered several reductions, ask $27\frac{1}{2}$ cents an hour for skilled mechanics and $17\frac{1}{2}$ cents an hour for helpers. In Chicago first-class men are paid $3.50 for eight hours' work, and men of inferior ability $2.75. The best workmen in Pullman therefore ask the same for ten hours that is given the Chicago steamfitters of the second class for eight hours.

Foundrymen make up No. 251. The brass moulders have been cut from 20 to 25 cents a day, and the labourers and furnace men 20 cents. The brass finishers lost from 25 to 50 cents a day. The moulders in the wheel shop were cut 5 cents a wheel, amounting to $1 and $1.20 a day, while the helpers have 50 cents a day less and the labourers 10 to 35 cents. In the last year the men in this department have only been given twenty-eight days' actual employment. The machine department men were reduced 25 cents a day. The iron foundrymen who do piecework were reduced from 40 to 75 cents for ten hours' work, the day workmen 40 cents, core makers from 20 to 80 cents, men in the chipping room 20 to 75 cents, and the yardmen 20 cents.

Local union, No. 257, the blacksmiths, suffered a cut between 30 and 50 per cent. Smiths making from $3.50 to $4 a day were scaled down to between $1.50 and $2.50, the helpers suffering accordingly.

Truck and platform men, organised as No. 262, have suffered so much from the piecework system that they demand the fairer plan of day wages. Their foreman has proved himself a petty tyrant, and his discharge is asked.

The cabinet-makers of No. 278 make broad charges of mismanagement. With but 158 men at work, the foremen and clerks remain the same as when 400 were employed. Sub-foremen, "straw bosses," showing favouritism when they are not displaying incompetency, make life in this department as difficult as the reduction in wages.

No. 279, the wood machine hands, are also opposed to piecework. They have suffered in some instances a cut of 40 per cent., and in no case has it fallen below 33⅓ per cent. Some reductions are appalling. Work on parlour cars, formerly worth $35 went down to $5, and on day coaches from $6 to $1.75.

In the street car department in No. 290 the iron machinists were cut—it is almost incredible—from 70 to 85 per cent., stripers and letterers from 40 to 70 per cent., and surface painters and finishers about 30 per cent. When complaint was made to a foreman in this shop, he told the men to quit if they didn't like it, and he would send over for some of his countrymen, who could do as much work as any six Americans. This is a sample of prices for a standard closed car:—

	1892.	1893.	1894.
Body	$41.00	$33.50	$25.00
Inside finish	39.00	27.00	22.00
Trimming	—	17.00	12.00

Hoods were cut 40 to 50 per cent., cab work 40 to 60 per cent., and wood machinists, whose foreman was so incompetent that he could not fix a price on work until it approached completion, were scaled down 70 cents. a day.

The brickmakers of No. 321 submit the following comparison of wages paid in Cook County:

	Chicago.	Country.	Pullman.
Labourers (per hour)	$ 20⅛	$ 20	$ 13½
Burners (12 hours)	2.50	2.25	2.10
Dryers (12 hours)	2.50	2.00	2.15
Car shovers (per hour)	31¼	22½	17½
Belt boys (per hour)	17½	8	13½
Hoppermen (per hour)	28⅛	20	15
Pug millers (per hour)	28⅛	20	17½
Empty car shovers (per hour)	28⅛	20	13½

	Chicago.	Country.	Pullman.
Clay diggers (per hour)	28⅛	25	20
Dust men (per hour)	18½	20	17½
Dry pan men (per hour)	28⅛	22½	15
Setters (per 1000)	20	19	15
Tossers (per 1000)	19	17	13
Walling and daubing (arch)	3.00	2.50	2.00
Loading (per 1000)	32	32	27
Steamfitters (per hour)	34⅜	25	13½
Engineers (per hour)	34⅜	30	20
Firemen (per hour)	21⅛	22½	16¾

The silver platers and brass polishers are united in local union No. 323. They, like all the rest, have suffered severe reductions and have other grievances.

Natives of Holland employed in the works in various capacities are in No. 356. Owing to their imperfect comprehension of the needs of the occasion they were the last organised of the eighteen Pullman unions. They did not go out with the others for the same reason and were locked out. Some of them are machinists, some wood carvers, and some labourers. All unite in saying that since the last reduction they could make more and live better in their own country. Piece workmen, skilled artists, some of them, were only able to make from 80 to 90 cents a day.

Now this, brother delegates, is what the Pullman system will bring us all to if this situation is not faced fairly and squarely in the American way for Americans by the American Railway Union. It is victory or death.

And so to you we confide our cause. Do not desert us as you hope not to be deserted. Be brothers in deed as well as in name, even as we are brothers in need. Teach us anew that thrilling verse and bring into use once more that

"Good old plan
That those should take who have the power,
And those should keep who can."

Every man of you, every honest heart among you, every willing hand, stands ready.

You know you can.

Will you?

Frank E. Pollans, No. 207, Chairman.
Jennie Curtis, No. 269., and eight others.

The reading of this report was followed by a statement by the vice-chairman of the strike committee. He dwelt upon the grievances of the men in the coach shops and gave in detail the reductions in wages made during his seven years' employment. The excitement was gradually getting hotter and hotter, but it was not until Jennie Curtis spoke that it boiled over. She said that the men might have been cut 30 per cent., but the girls had been cut 50 and 60 per cent. No sooner had she regained her seat than twenty delegates sprang to the floor, yelling for an immediate boycott of all the Pullman cars. Then President Debs rose. He was intensely excited and spoke as follows :—

We have won every fight, and we have had eleven. Pullman is our twelfth, and we shall win that. There is no doubt about it. I am in favour of the American Railway Union expending its last dollar and its last man in a cause so righteous. (Cheers.)

We must first appoint a committee to wait on the Pullman officials. If they refuse to settle, if they will not arbitrate, we will not move a Pullman car one inch. And after everyone is side-tracked, if the railroad companies want to go into partnership with Pullman in this fight we will inaugurate the greatest railway strike the world has ever seen. (Loud cheers.)

The crisis is approaching, and we must invite and not evade it. We have declared war on Pullman, and it is a fight to a finish. The Knights of Labour and the American Railway Union are united in a holy strife, and when we begin our battle we will never rest. The result is certain, for it means the unification of labour. (Cheering.)

Pullman is the continental monster of the times. I have some respect for a man bold enough to boast of his enslavement of labour and frank enough to admit his oppression. But Pullman posed for twenty years as the friend of the labouring man. He gave $100,000 to the Columbian Museum (a Pullman delegate exclaimed, " and cut us the next morning "), and took every penny of it out of the lives of his working men.

He must pay his people living wages. All we ask for is an honest living. Pullman for the past year has been robbing every man, woman and child in his employ.

He is a pirate on the high seas of labour, but the American Railway Union has a long arm, and it will reach in its might up to his black flag and wreck him altogether. It is our duty. (Wild cheering.)

We will brand him as infamous. What must be the logical outcome of his policy ? His men will be made slaves, and his women driven to lives of shame. Do your duty. (Cries of " We will " and cheering.)

The American Railway Union is organised for business. We have had enough patent leather organisations parading through America, fattening and feasting on labour. I would rather see us all go down in an honest fight than to live on in uselessness. (Cry of " No dry rot.") If we go down now, we go down with the most honourable record a labour organisation has ever made. But we are not going down, (Cheers and shouts of " Never.")

We will confront monopoly in its strongest fortress, and we all know what the outcome must be. We will side-track Pullman and his cars together ! We must not talk, but act, and no man who has not the courage to go to the bitterest end has a right to enlist.

You know what this man has been doing in the weeks since the strike. He has been sitting on his burrow, like a hyena, waiting for these people to lie down exhausted with starvation that he may fatten on their bones.

This is the greatest and most powerful monopoly of our time—the monumental octopus of all unscrupulous combinations.

And now I wait the bugle-call to duty.

That bugle-call was not long in coming. A weekly

assessment of 10 cents per member was ordered while the strike lasted. Every delegate present was then asked to telegraph to his local union for instructions regarding the proposed boycott. Nearly one-half of them had already been ordered to take immediate action. A committee of five was appointed to wait upon the Pullman Company to give them a last chance of averting the boycott.

The interview was brief and decisive. A committee, appointed by the general convention, waited upon the company to inform them that a boycott had been declared against the Pullman cars, which was to go into effect at noon on Tuesday, June 26, unless the Pullman Company consented to arbitrate with its men. After keeping the committee waiting for fifteen minutes in an ante-chamber, they were received by the vice-president of the company. All that he said was this : " Do you understand the position of the Pullman Company in this matter ? " " Thoroughly, sir," was the reply. " Then you know that the Pullman Company refuse to recognise the American Railway Union in this matter." " Good-bye, sir," was the only reply, and the committee filed out of the room.

Nothing more remained to be done.

Orders were issued to the General Executive Boards of the American Railway Union on the various railway systems stating that henceforth the members of the Union must have nothing whatever to do with the transportation of Pullman cars.

Mr. Pullman then issued the following manifesto in defence of the position which he had taken up :—

r In the first week of May last there were employed in the car manufacturing department at Pullman, Ill., about 3,100 persons. On 7th May a committee of the workmen had an interview by arrangement with Mr. Wicks, vice-president, at which the ¦principal subject of discussion related to wages, but minor grievances as to shop administration were also presented, and it was agreed that another meeting should be held on the 9th of May, at which all the grievances should be presented in writing. The second meeting was held. As to the complaints on all matters except wages, it was arranged that a formal and thorough investigation should be made by Mr. Wicks, to be begun the next day, and full redress was assured to the committee as to all complaints proved to be well founded.

The absolute necessity of the last reduction in wages, under the existing condition of the business of car manufacturing, had been explained to the committee, and they were insisting upon a restoration of the wage scale of the first half of 1893, when Mr. Pullman entered the room and addressed the committee, speaking in substance as follows :—

At the commencement of the very serious depression last year we were employing at Pullman 5,816 men, and paying out in wages there $305,000 a month. Negotiations with intending purchasers of railway equipment that were then pending for new work were stopped by them, orders already given by others were cancelled, and we were obliged to lay off, as you are aware, a large number of men in'every department, so that by 1st November, 1893, there were only about 2,000 men in all departments, or about one-third of the normal number. I realised the necessity for the most strenuous exertions to procure work immediately, without which there would be great embarrassment, not only to the employees and their families at Pullman, but also to those living in the immediate vicinity, including between 700 and 800 employees who had purchased homes and to whom employment was actually necessary to enable them to complete their payments.

I canvassed the matter thoroughly with the manager of the works, and instructed him to cause the men to be assured that the company would do everything in its power to meet the competition which was sure to occur because of the great number of large car manufacturers that were in the same condition, and that were exceedingly anxious to keep their men employed. I knew that if there was any work to be let, bids for it would be made upon a much lower basis than ever before. (Note that the selling prices of passenger, baggage, box, refrigerator, and street cars in the last two years have fallen by percentages, varying in the separate classes from 17 to 28, the average reduction, taking the five classes together, being 24 per cent.) The result of this discussion was a revision in piecework prices, which, in the absence of any information to the contrary, I supposed to be acceptable to the men under the circumstances. Under these conditions, and with lower prices upon all materials, I personally undertook the work of the lettings of cars, and by making lower bids than other manufacturers, I secured work enough to gradually increase our force from 2,200 up to about 4,200, the number employed, according to the April pay rolls, in all capacities at Pullman.

This result has not been accomplished merely by reduction in wages, but the company has borne its full share by eliminating from its estimates the use of capital and machinery, and in many cases going even below that and taking work at considerable loss, notably the fifty-five Long Island cars, which was the first large order of passenger cars let since the great depression, and which was sought for by practically all the leading car builders in the country. My anxiety to secure that order, so as to put as many men at work as possible, was such that I put in a bid at more than $300 per car less than the actual cost to the company. The 300 stock cars built for the North Western Road, and the 250 refrigerator cars now under construction for the same company, will result in a loss of at least $12 per car, and the twenty-five cars just built for the Lake Street Elevated Road show a loss of $79 per car. I mention these particulars so that you may understand what the company has done for the mutual interest, and to secure for the people at Pullman and vicinity the benefit of the disbursement of the large sums of money involved in these and similar contracts, which can be kept up only by the procurement of new orders for cars, for, as you know, about three-fourths of the men must depend upon contract work for employment. I can only assure you that if this company now restores the wages of the first half of 1893, as you have asked, it would be a most unfortunate thing for the men, because there is less than sixty days of contract work in sight in the shops under all orders and there is absolutely no possibility, in the present condition of affairs throughout the country, of getting any more orders for work at prices measured by the wages of May, 1893. Under such a scale the works would necessarily close down and the great majority of the employees be put in idleness, a contingency I am using my best efforts to avoid.

To further benefit the people of Pullman and vicinity we concentrated all the work that we could command at that point, by closing our Detroit shops entirely and laying off a large number of men at other repair shops, and gave to Pullman the repair of all cars that could be taken care of there.

Also, for the further benefit of our people at Pullman, we have carried on a large system of internal improvements, having expended nearly $160,000 since August last in work which, under normal conditions, would have been spread over one or two years. The policy would be to continue this class of work to as great an extent as possible, provided, of course, the Pullman men show a proper appreciation of the situation by doing whatever they can to help themselves to tide over the hard times, which are so seriously felt in every part of the country.

There has been some complaint made about rents. As to this I would say that the return to this company on the capital invested in the Pullman tenements for the last year and the year before was 3.82-100 per cent. There are hundreds of tenements in Pullman renting for from $6 to $9 per month, and the tenants are relieved from the usual expenses of exterior cleaning and the removal of garbage which is done by the company. The average amount collected from employees for gas consumed is about $2 a month. To ascertain the exact amount of water used by tenants, separate from the amount consumed by the works, we have recently put in meters by which we find that the water consumed by the tenants, if paid for at the rate of 4 cents per 1,000 gallons, in accordance with our original contract with the village of Hyde Park, would amount to about $1,000 a month, almost exactly the rate which we have charged the tenants, this company assuming the expense of pumping. At the increased rate the city is now charging us for water we are paying about $500 a month in excess of the amount charged to the tenants. The present pay rolls at Pullman amount to about $7,000 a day.

On the question of rents, while, as stated above, they make a manifestly inadequate return upon the investment, so that it is clear they are not, in fact, at an arbitrary high figure, it may be added that it would not be possible in a business sense so to deal with them. The renting of the dwellings and employment of workmen at Pullman are in no way tied together. The dwellings and apartments are offered for rent in competition with those of the immediate adjacent towns of Kensington, Roseland, and Gano. They are let alike to Pullman employees and to others in no way connected with the company, and, on the other hand, many Pullman employees rent or own their homes in those adjacent towns.

The average rental at Pullman is at the rate of $3 per room per month. There are 1,200 tenements of varying numbers of rooms, the average monthly rental of which is $10; of these there are 600 the average monthly rental of which is $8. In very many cases men with families pay a rent seemingly large for a workman, but which is in fact reduced in part and often wholly repaid by the sub-rents paid by single men as lodgers.

On 10th May, the day after the second conference above mentioned, work went on at Pullman as usual, and the only incident of note was the beginning by Mr. Wicks, assisted by Mr. Brown, the general manager of the company, of the promised formal investigation at Pullman of the shop complaints. A large meeting of employees had been held the night before at Kensington, which, as was understood by the company, accepted the necessity of the situation preventing an increase of wages, but at a meeting of the local committee held during the night of May 10, a strike was decided upon, and accordingly the next day about 2,500 of the employees quit, leaving about 600 at work, of whom very few were skilled workmen. As it was found impracticable to keep the shops in operation with a force thus diminished and disorganised, the next day those remaining were necessarily laid off, and no work has since been done in the shops.

The pay-rolls at the time amounted to about $7,000 a day, and were reduced $5,500 by the strike, so that during the period of a little more than six weeks which has elapsed the employees who quit their work have deprived themselves and their comrades of earnings of more than $200,000.

It is an element of the whole situation worthy of note, that at the beginning of the strike the Pullman Savings Bank had on deposit in its savings departments $488,000, of which about nine-tenths belonged to employees at Pullman, and that this amount has since been reduced by the sum of $32,000.

While deploring the possibility of annoyance to the public by the threats of irresponsible organisations to interrupt the orderly ministration to the comfort of travellers on railway lines aggregating 125,000 miles in length, the Pullman Company can do no more than explain its situation to the public. It has two separate branches of business, essentially distinct from each other. One is to provide sleeping cars, which are delivered by it under contract to the various railway companies, to be run by them on their lines as a part of their trains for the carriage of their passengers over the movements of which this company has no control. Contract arrangements provide for the making of all repairs to such cars by the railway companies using them—as to certain repairs absolutely, and as to all others upon the request of the Pullman Company, which ordinarily finds it most convenient to use its own manufacturing facilities to make such repairs. The other, and a distinct branch of the business of the Pullman Company, is the manufacture of sleeping cars for the above-mentioned use of railway companies and the manufacture for sale to railway companies of freight cars and ordinary passenger cars, and of street cars, and this business is almost at a standstill throughout the United States. The business of manufacturing cars for sale gives employment to about 70 per cent. of the shop employees. The manufacture of sleeping cars for use by railway companies under contract, and which, under normal conditions, gives employment to about 15 per cent. of the shop employees, cannot be resumed by the company to an important extent for a very long time, for out of the provision made for the abnormal travel last year the company now has about 400 sleeping cars in store ready for use, but for which there is no need in the existing conditions of public travel.

It is now threatened by the American Railway Union officials that railway companies using Pullman sleeping cars shall be compelled to deprive their passengers of sleeping car accommodations unless the Pullman Company will agree to submit to arbitration the question as to whether or not it shall open its manufacturing shops at Pullman and operate them under a scale of wages which would cause a daily loss to it of one-fourth the wages paid.

And thus began the great struggle, the end of which is not yet. Up to this point the strike had been conducted without the slightest disorder. The number of arrests in the town of Pullman had indeed gone down, and not a finger had been laid upon the property either of the Pullman Company or of any of the railroads using the Pullman cars. The storm, however, was about to burst.

The strike, which began with a miserable difference of opinion as to the paper used on the sides of freight cars, widened out to dimensions so vast as to throw even Mr. Pullman and the Pullman monopoly into the shade. Henceforth we hear little of Mr. Pullman beyond the fact that repeated appeals were made to him by the mayor of Chicago, supported by telegrams from no fewer than fifty other American mayors, urging him to submit the dispute to arbitration. Mr. Pullman, however, remained obdurate to the last. There was nothing to arbitrate about, he said, and he was equally resolute in his refusal to allow a question as to whether or not sufficient basis could be found for arbitration to be referred to a committee. No arbitration, no mediation, no recognition of trades unions ; Mr. Pullman must be free to do as he pleases to do with his own, and that is all that there is to it. Now, dismissing Mr. Pullman and his monopoly, let us turn to a much wider drama to which the Pullman dispute but served as the prologue.

Chapter III.—The Achilles' Heel of Civilisation.

Mr. Pullman with his thirty million dollars' worth of capital, his fleet of two thousand sleepers, and his immense interest, is but a pigmy compared with the giant who now advances to the fray. Mr. Bryce long ago pointed out that in America the railroad president comes nearer to possessing the power, the authority, and the prestige of the monarch than any other citizen of the Republic. The railroad is king in America to an extent almost inconceivable to older countries. The reason for this is that in America the railroad is a necessity of life. Without the railroad there are large communities which would simply die of starvation, and unless the railroads run regularly hundreds of thousands of American citizens would simply perish.

The American railroad system is indeed a Goliath of Gath. The railway system of the United States is in the hands of 712 independent operating companies, but, as a matter of fact, 80 of the larger concerns control over 80 per cent. of the gross receipts, leaving only 18 per cent. to be divided among the 632 smaller companies, which for practical purposes may be dismissed from account. These railway companies have constructed 170,000 miles of rail, and they have a standing army in their employ of over 800,000 men. There is no such organisation in the New World as that which is directed by the presidents and managers of the railway companies. The total capital represented by the liabilities of the railways exceeds two thousand million sterling, which in 1892 paid a dividend of practically over three per cent. In no branch of American life has competition been carried more recklessly to its utmost extreme. Now and again some experienced railway manager ventured to point out that it might be expedient to give the legislature some control over future railroad construction, but such modest suggestions are usually met with a howl of derision, it being regarded as the settled policy in the United States that railroads should be built by anybody anywhere under any conditions, no matter what the result might be, because the more competition among the railroads the better for the general public. The result can hardly be said to have justified the confidence with which this doctrine of unlimited competition was promulgated among the citizens. The cost of transportation is cheaper per passenger and per ton per mile than in any other country in the world; but, notwithstanding this, somehow or another the railroads have come to be regarded, especially in the west, as enemies rather than benefactors. The average opinion of the average man resident in America would probably be, if taken at random, for the most part socialistic, so far at least as the railways are concerned. They hate the railways. They regard them as tyrannical, unjust, partial, and generally the enemies of the human race. This may be due to ignorance and prejudice, but there is no doubt as to the widespread detestation with which the railroads are regarded by the people among whom they earn their dividends. The whole of the inter-state commerce legislation bears eloquent testimony to the conviction of the majority of the American citizens that the public is victimised by the gigantic organisation, and that, in order to secure something like ordinary justice, the government needs to be armed with very extensive powers to supervise their rates and generally to maintain justice between the big and little customers. Under the system of unregulated competition the big monopolies play into each other's hands, with the result that the little man goes to the wall at a constantly accelerating ratio. Hence the great animosity on the part of the little man towards the economic agent which gives him the *coup de grace.* Chicago, the greatest railway centre in the world, is naturally very much under the influence of western ideas on this subject. From Chicago as the centre radiate some 80,000 miles of rail, and Illinois has the largest railway mileage of any State in the Union. According to the statistics published on June 30th, 1893, there are no fewer than 70,000 men employed on the railways of the State ; of these a large number live in and about Chicago.

Illinois has a total mileage of 15,051, of which 10,315 miles are main track, 1,300 miles additional track, and 3,436 miles yard track and siding, a total increase of 373 miles over the preceding year. The state has 18·4 miles of road per 100 square miles of territory, and 36 miles of road per 10,000 inhabitants. Eighty-five per cent. of all lands in the state are within five miles of railroad ; 11·5 per cent. between five and ten miles ; 2½ per cent. between ten and fifteen miles, and 1 per cent. between fifteen and twenty miles. The total capital stock of railroads in the state is $930,557,461 ; funded debt, $1,111,749,725 ; current liabilities, $91,658,407 ; total railway capital, $2,133,965,593.

The capital stock per mile is $22,435 ; funded

debt per mile, $26,804, and current liabilities per mile, $2,209 ; total, $51,448.

Between the railway companies and their work-men there is no love lost, even less than what there is between the railways and their customers. The mere destruction of human life is enough to explain much of this bitter feeling. Every day in the rail-ways of the United States, seven employees are killed and 77 injured. The annual destruction of passengers does not average more than one per day killed and five injured. One only needs to look at Chicago on the map to understand how vitally important are all railway questions to its citizens.

This great city, with a million and a half of popula-tion, is stretched over a gridiron of rails which cross and re-cross the city, and form a complex network of tracks, every mesh of which is stained with human blood. It is not for nothing that the dismal bell of the locomotive rings incessantly as it tears its way into the heart of Chicago through the streets. In England the locomotives use the whistle, not the bell, and this solemn weird tolling of the bell is very impressing to the imagination of the visitor who hears it for the first time sounding every hour, year in, year out, summer and winter. As regularly as the sun rises these great engines slay their man in and upon the streets of Chicago. No other great city in the world has allowed its streets to be taken possession of to a similar extent, and the massacre resulting therefrom is greater than that of many battles. We in England have always one or more little wars upon our hands on our frontiers where they impinge upon the lawless tribes in Africa and Asia, but I do not think that it is too much to say that in the last five years we have had fewer soldiers killed in our wars all round the world than have been slaughtered in the streets of Chicago at the grade crossing.   The figures are : in 1889, 257 ; 1890, 294 ; 1891, 323 ; 1892, 394 ; 1893, 431.   As might be expected, the number of these railroad murders steadily increases with the growth of the population.*   In the city of Chicago there are under 2500 miles of roadway, but there are 1375 miles of railroad track within the same area.   The railroads traverse the streets at grade in 2000 places.   Under Mayor Washburne a commission was appointed to investigate the matter, and an effort was made to ascertain the obstruction to traffic caused by this system.   Mr. E. S. Dreyer, speaking at the Sunset Club, where the subject was discussed on February 1, said :—

Our terminal commission caused to be taken, by careful enumerators, a count at thirty-six of our most dangerous crossings on a certain business day, from the hour of six in the morning to seven in the evening, and their report showed that there passed during that time over the thirty-six crossings 68,375 vehicles, 9145 street cars, 221,942 street car passengers, and 119,181 pedestrians.   The gates at these crossings were lowered 3031 times, and the total time the gates were closed on the thirty-six crossings was over twelve hours, delaying 15,000 vehicles, 2320 street cars with 51,367 passengers, and 18,212 pedestrians.†

These figures, be it noted, have only regard to thirty-six of the 3000 crossings in the city.   For years past the city has protested, but protested in vain.   The railroads ride roughshod over the convenience, the rights, and the lives of the citizens.   Sisera with his 900 chariots of iron never tyrannised more ruthlessly over the Hebrews than the railroads with

* In the State of Illinois the record of accidents for the year ending June 30, 1893, shows that 802 persons were killed, 23 being passengers ; 246 employees and 533 others.   There were 3,751 persons injured ; 2,664 were employees, 399 passengers and 688 others.   The increase in the total number killed was 82, or 11·4 per cent. ; and the increase in the total number injured was 1,311, or 53·73 per cent. over the year before.

† In justice to the railways, however, it should be stated that many of the grade crossings came to Chicago long after the railroads did.   The streets were laid across the railroads long after the railroads themselves existed.

their fire chariots of steel have lorded it over the city of Chicago.

Every week in Chicago you read of grade crossing accidents, and it is very seldom that you hear of anything being done to saddle any one with the responsibility for the loss of life. The evidence before the jury is usually to the following effect: The gates were not lowered, the watchman was not in attendance, no whistle was sounded, no bell was rung. The deceased was crossing the track all unwitting of any danger, when a train dashed up with the inevitable result. In many cases the bodies are mutilated out ot all human semblance. The nightmare imagination of those gruesome artists who exult in describing the torture and mutilation of helpless victims could depict nothing more terrible than the human sacrifices which are offered up daily on the altar of the Railway Moloch by the city of Chicago. Very rarely is any one saddled with the responsibility. The railroads have taken the precaution of protecting themselves by law. By an infamous act, boodled through the Illinois Legislature by railroad influence, no jury is allowed to award more than $5000 damages against the railroads for causing the death of any citizen.

The usurpation of the streets of the city is none the less a usurpation because it was achieved by gold and not by steel. In many cases railroads have laid their tracks through the streets without even going through the formality of asking for a franchise. They have treated Chicago as a conquered territory. The strolling Tartar, who in the Middle Ages wandered absolute lord over Russia, was the prototype of the railroad corporations in the capital of the West. For the use of the streets the railroads have not paid a cent into the City Treasury. Whatever payment they made was made corruptly, and went into the pockets of the aldermen, and sometimes of the Mayor. If they paid $100 a mile for way-leave that would bring in the city a revenue of nearly $200,000. So far from doing any such thing, the railroads have imposed upon the city an expenditure which is estimated at $30,000 in the salaries of twenty-five policemen and other employees, paid by the city for the purpose of raising and lowering the gates and of warning citizens to escape slaughter. Further, they have put the city to the expense of millions in the building of viaducts over their tracks where the expenditure of life became too great even for Chicago to tolerate. In 1892 the cost of maintaining these viaducts was no less than $146,000. For the privilege, therefore, of keeping the annual total of human sacrifices down to a victim a day the city pays blood-money amounting to $176,000 a year.

But, it may be urged, the city has in its own hands the power of taxation, and it can recoup itself from the enormously valuable property within its limits. Here again we are confronted with another specimen of the way in which the citizen goes to the wall. Mr. Washburne, when Mayor of Chicago, stated publicly that the value of railway property in the city was not less than $350,000,000. It is to-day assessed at less than $19,000,000.

All this explains if it does not justify the popular sympathy with which Mr. Debs and the American Railway Union entered upon their war with the railways.

The war with the railways is a very different thing from a war with Pullman. To attack Pullman was something equivalent to a declaration of war against let us say Belgium, but the moment the war is carried across the French frontier and the French Republic enters the field, Belgium counts for nothing. So it was with the American strike. When the boycott was decided upon the battle-field was changed. It became a fight between the strongest organised representatives of both capital and labour in the United States. So far as organisation is concerned, the railroad compared to the railway union is as Goliath was to David. But Debs was as confident in his ability to bring the Philistine to earth as was David when he fitted a smooth stone from the brook into his sling.

Mr. Debs miscalculated on this vital point. Talking to a newspaper representative immediately after the die had been cast, he said :—

In Chicago it is safe to say that the Illinois Central, the Monon and the Chicago and Eastern Illinois will discontinue the use of Pullman sleepers as soon as the order is given. This last road will lose the Nashville limited train and all its southern connections. In the east Indianapolis, Detroit, Cincinnati, Toledo, and Cleveland can be relied upon to allow no Pullman cars to pass through. St. Louis, Kansas City, Milwaukee, and New Orleans are solid. So are Minneapolis, St. Paul, Denver, Omaha, Council Bluffs, Salt Lake City, and Ogden. On the Pacific slope not a single wheel can be turned if it belongs to a Pullman car. San Francisco, Sacramento, Los Angeles, San Bernardina, Portland, Tacoma, and every division terminal is thoroughly organised and ready for business.

At noon, June 26th, the boycott was declared :—

"It is war between the General Managers' Association and the American Railway Union," President Debs said yesterday of the boycott against the Pullman Palace Car Company, which goes into effect at noon to-day. "We welcome the struggle and will win, because we are right."

"I am glad the matter has become a sharply defined issue," was the comment of George M. Pullman, president of the great corporation whose interests are attacked. "The American people will learn whether thousands of millions of dollars of invested capital can be arbitrarily put aside and rendered valueless because a labour organisation has a grievance against a manufacturing concern which also owns cars used in the railway service."

Mr. Debs' first expectation that some of the railways would discontinue the use of the Pullman cars was not justified by the event. The railroads, whether they used the Pullman or the Wagner cars, decided to stand together as one man against the boycott,

At a fully represented meeting of the General Managers' Association, the following resolutions were unanimously adopted :—

WHEREAS, We learn through the public press that the American Railway Union will declare a boycott on all Pullman palace cars, and

WHEREAS, Said boycott is in relation to matters over which we have no control, and in which we have no interest whatever, and

WHEREAS, It is stated that the object and intent of the said boycott is to

PULLMAN CARS.

discommode the travelling public and embarrass the railroads, in the belief that the public and railroads affected will influence the settlement of the question as the American Railway Union desires, and

WHEREAS, It is necessary that these companies determine for themselves what cars they shall or shall not handle, and

WHEREAS, It is important that the travelling public should understand the position of the railroads in this matter ; therefore be it

Resolved. 1. That it is the sense of this meeting that the said proposed boycott, being confessedly not in the interest of any employees of said railroad companies or on account of any grievance between said railroad companies and said employees, is unjustifiable and unwarranted.

2. That the employees of the said railroad companies cannot, nor can any of them with propriety embarras said companies or discommode the travelling public because of their sympathy with the supposed wrongs of employees engaged in a wholly different class of labour.

3. That we hereby declare it to be the lawful right and duty of the said company to protest against said proposed boycott; to resist the same in the interest of their existing contract and for the benefit of the travelling public, and that we will act unitedly to that end.

Every railway system in Chicago was represented at the meeting which adopted the foregoing resolutions without a dissenting vote, not only the general managers but presidents, vice-presidents, and other general officers attested the importance of the occasion by their presence. Thus we see that the moment the boycott was declared all the railway lines, with two inconsiderable exceptions, united into an association which accepted the gauge of battle and prepared for fighting it out to the bitter end with all the energy and vigour which characterises the railway management of the United States.

The railroads had another immense advantage over Mr. Debs. Not only were they stronger financially and in possession of far greater administrative capacity than any union could hope to command, but the state of the labour market was entirely in favour of the employers against the employed. There are 800,000 railway employees in the United States. Mr. Debs did not claim to have more than 100,000 or 125,000 in his union. That is to say, there were seven men outside his union for one who was inside. Not only so, but there were more men out of work who had some knowledge of train service than all those who owed allegiance to Mr. Debs. It was calculated last year* that one-fifth of the rail-

* During 1893 nearly 13 per cent. of the entire railway mileage of the United States, representing over 12 per cent. of the entire capitalisation, has gone into the hands of receivers. During the two years 1892 and 1893 the companies for which receivers were appointed represent over 19 per cent. of

way mileage of the country passed into the hands of receivers, that there had been a decrease in a twelve-month on the lines leading out of Chicago alone of no fewer than 60,000 employees, and in the country altogether 160,000 were out of work. It therefore seemed a forlorn hope that a union of 125,000 men could hope to defeat the railway companies which had a reserve of 150,000 unemployed men to draw upon, especially as there was no dispute about wages between the employers and their men. The boycott that was ordered was a boycott of sympathy, and as such did not appeal so closely to the out-of-work non-unionist as the strike for wages or hours would have done.

So far, therefore, as could be seen at the beginning of the strike, everything was in favour of the railroads excepting one thing. The railroads, like Achilles, have their vulnerable heel, and it was a heel which is so vulnerable as to constitute the railways themselves the Achilles' heel of society. The railroad is almost as delicate a mechanism as a watch. A single sleeper displaced, one little bridge blown up, a signal box paralysed, a telegraph wire cut, can throw the whole

the mileage and nearly 16 per cent. of the capital stock and bonds of all the railways in the country.

Between January 1 and December 31 seventy-one railroads have gone into the hands of receivers. These roads represent a mileage of 22,534; funded debt, $753,917,000; capital stock, $534,035,000, and a total of bonds and capital stock of $1,287,952,000. In this last sum only outstanding bonds are counted, bonds authorised but not issued not being included.

Evidence of the unprofitableness of railway investments is shown in the fact that in eighteen years 549 roads, aggregating over 57,000 miles (one-third the present mileage), have been sold for debt, involving in loss bonds and stock aggregating $3,176,000,000. If the end of this career of disaster had been reached, there might now be hope of better results, says the Railway Age, but a host of railways are still awaiting the orders of the courts for sale, and the procession of insolvents has increased with amazing rapidity in the last few years; so that it is a painful certainty that the record of foreclosures in the coming years will be even greater than that of an equal period in the past.

organisation into confusion. Every day in the year the railroads of America carry on an average a million and a half passengers and two million tons of freight. This vast moving mass is hauled across vast expanses of country which are practically uninhabited. They pass also through villages and cities fenced off by no partition wall from the inhabitants. The railway tracks constitute 170,000 miles of spider web, the thread of which could be broken by a single sturdy tramp with a crowbar. It is this which constitutes the vulnerability of the railway. A recent writer in the *North American Review* called attention to a very remarkable fact bearing upon this point. He says :—

There is a standing order on the Central Pacific Railroad forbidding conductors of freight trains to put off tramps. Why? Simply because there are hundreds of miles of wooden snowsheds on the roads, and when the tramps are put off they set these on fire. It is cheaper to carry them on the trains.

Here we have the frank recognition of the inability of the railways to protect themselves against lawless marauders. A railway company which practically undertakes to carry tramps free because every strolling vagabond with a lucifer can with impunity block the line is not exactly the ironclad organisation with which to fight a revolt. The comparative impotence of the railways was brought out very clearly by Coxeyism, and again by the later phases of the miners' strike. By the simple process of sitting down on the railway track the strikers and Coxeyites were able to arrest the progress of a train, for, although the Americans are notoriously indifferent to human life, an engine-driver who deliberately drove his train over an unarmed man would be shot on sight. But for this liability to interruption the railways would be invulnerable tyrants. As it is their tyranny is tempered by a fear of violence which would dislocate the whole of their system. It was this weakness of theirs which, in the opinion of some observers, lay at the bottom of the victory of the American Railway Union on the Great Northern Railway. It was the first great victory which organised labour had won over the railroads, and, as such, it deserves more attention than it has received. In the opinion of a competent observer on the spot in Chicago, the Great Northern capitulated not in the least because of its regard for justice or because of its abilities to hold its own in a fair strike against the railway unions. Why then did the Great Northern give in ? The answer is given in the following paragraph :—

The Great Northern line runs for the most part through a wild and thinly settled country. The task of guarding its tracks against evil-disposed persons is practically an impossible one. From the beginning of the strike it was evident that trains could not be run without danger of violence either from the strikers or their sympathisers, and it was plain that practically the whole population along the line of the road favoured the men. Under these circumstances President Hill had to decide between tying up his road for an indefinite length of time or surrendering to the strikers. He chose the latter alternative and the American Railway Union scored a triumph.

That is to say, the American Railway Union won its greatest victory by the fear that the refusal of its demand would lead to the destruction of the property of the company. The union repudiates this indignantly. On the eve of the boycott Debs declared that his union would see to it that no violence whatever disgraced the strike, and referred to the Great

Northern strike as a proof that he meant what he said :—

> No violence of any kind would be attempted, and no destruction of property would follow the side-tracking of palace cars. During the eighteen days of the strike on the Great Northern, as we were assured upon its termination by President James J. Hill himself, said Mr. Debs, not five cents' worth of goods, equipment, or stock, had suffered damage by reason of our men's actions. Everywhere they guarded the Company's property against depredations, and that will be the case here.

After the boycott had been declared he telegraphed to the local union which had shown a disposition to interfere with the traffic by force as follows :—

> You are, under no circumstances, to interfere with trains or with any men sent to handle them. You are to stay away from the railway companies' property, and trespass in no way upon their premises. Anyone violating this order will be expelled from the American Railway Union, and be prosecuted by the organisation itself to the full extent of the law.

Nevertheless, the astute and experienced men who were defending the railroads from the attack of the union did not indulge in any delusion as to what Debs might do as a peacemaker and as a restraining influence. They were in for a strike which was likely to be protracted, and they knew perfectly well that such a strike would not be fought out without an appeal to arms. Their first step was to engage the ablest man whom they could discover in the whole range of their organisation as general-in-chief. This gentleman was found in St. Paul, and he was promptly placed in command. Mr. Egan's reputation was that of being a tireless fighter, and the moment he arrived in Chicago from St. Paul he took in hand the organisation of the campaign with all the resolution of an experienced veteran. Mr. Egan began his career in connection with the Canadian Pacific, but he had had local experience on the Chicago, St. Paul, and Kansas City Road. The executive committee of the Railway Association acted as a consultative council, but the whole direction of the strike was placed in his hands. The railway kings do not admit reporters to their conclave, and it is not known what sum was guaranteed for providing the sinews of war. But as it was recognised as a matter of life and death, corporations representing hundreds of millions of pounds were not likely to let their manager fall short of the necessary funds.

The moment Mr. Egan took command he made no secret of the plan on which he would proceed. He would fight the strike and beat it. The elements in his favour were four : first, the superior organisation of the railroads ; secondly, the number of unemployed men wanting work ; thirdly, the possibility of invoking the intervention of the Federal troops in order to secure the passage of the mails and to prevent any interference with the working of lines which were in the hands of receivers ; and fourthly, he had the general resource of every citizen threatened with loss by violence, the right to demand the presence of police, deputy marshal, and the militia, to prevent any attack upon life or property.

With Mr Egan's explanation of his plan of campaign I will end this chapter, and proceed to notice some of the leading actors who are now about to appear upon the scene :—

"We do not intend to be drawn into any controversy between Mr. Pullman and his men. The Railway Union insists that we shall not run any trains if we haul Pullman cars. For the purpose of boycotting Mr. Pullman they have ordered certain strikes. We intend to fill the places of these strikers at once and resume business.

"We ignore Mr. Pullman in this struggle. We have not sent a committee to see him, and do not intend to. There was a disposition at first among all the managers to wait a few days and give old employees a chance to go back to their places. If they don't do it, new men will be brought in. We have already opened recruiting stations in a number of cities, where employees are engaged. We guarantee to protect them from violence, and will do it. The advance brigade of imported men are due to arrive in the morning. They will be landed in the Baltimore and Ohio, the Pennsylvania and the Illinois

Central yards, and they will be protected at their work, too. These men shall not be interfered with in any way. The police will protect them, aided by our other employees.

"The authority of the United States will be invoked in a number of cases. On any lines in the hands of receivers, such as the Santa Fé, the Wisconsin Central, the Minneapolis and St. Louis, the Northern Pacific, the Union Pacific, the Erie, and others, we shall rely on United States authorities to protect our men, and we shall not hesitate to call for federal assistance should it be needed. Where we send police or our own guards to protect labourers, we will endeavour to so place them that the fewest number can protect the greatest number of workmen, such as in union yards. We are now fully equipped for this great struggle," Mr. Egan concluded, "and shall push it to a finish. Employees understand that they are still at liberty to return to their old places. Those who desire to do so may yet return, but those who stay out must understand that new men are coming to take their places and will hold them."

And with this declaration the great fight may be said to have begun.

P

PART IV.—DEFEAT.

Chapter I.—The Keepers of Law and Order.

The duty of maintaining law and order in America
falls primarily upon the sheriff when the disturbance
is confined within the State, and raises no questions
entitling the Federal Government to interfere. If the
sheriff finds that the forces of disorder are too many
for him, or if he should refuse to act, then the statute
proceeds to say that either the mayor or the coroner,
or the county judge, can advise the governor of the
position of affairs and ask for assistance. The
governor then communicates with the sheriff and
inquires from him how it is that the citizens are not
receiving the protection to which they are entitled
under the law. Should the sheriff, as frequently
happens, declare that the mob was too strong for him,
the suggestion is made that he should swear in deputy
marshals, or what we should call special constables, to
enable him to enforce the law. Any sheriff can enroll
as many deputies as he thinks necessary, and when
they are enrolled they can be armed and used as
officers of the law, just as special constables with us.
If, however, no deputies are forthcoming, or if the
maximum available force of deputies is insufficient to
overcome the forces of disorder, nothing remains but
to appeal to the governor for arms and for troops.
These troops are not regulars, but the state militia,
a force which is regarded as military principally on

account of its possession of arms and of uniforms, and the very occasional practice of military drill.

The State of Illinois, which is about as large as England, has a total of about four thousand armed men under the command of the governor. Two regiments of this army are stationed at Chicago, where they have been called upon more than once to repress disorders occasioned by industrial disputes. They were called out in 1875, when there were some riots in connection with the Relief and Aid Society. In 1877 they were called out to deal with the railway riots, and twice dispersed the mob at the point of the bayonet without firing a shot. In 1886 they were again called out to repress riots occasioned by a strike in the stock yards, and during the recent miners' strike they were repeatedly on duty ; but their presence was sufficient to establish at least an appearance of order. It will be seen from this that the pivot of authority in the American States is first the sheriff and then the governor. Upon the sheriff of the county and the governor of the State lies the whole responsibility for maintaining law and order within the limits of the State.

The situation is changed when circumstances arise which justify the intervention of the Federal Government. That intervention is only justified when disorder exists which affects interests in which the Federal authorities have a right to be heard. In the present strike the intervention of the Federal power was only possible when the strikers interfered with the free transit of the mails, or with the administration of the railroads which were in the hands of receivers, and therefore in a sense wards of the court, or if they interrupted inter-state commerce. In any one of these three cases the Federal could, and as a matter of fact did, interfere, but the due procedure had first to be gone through. The district attorney must apply to the United States Judge declaring that the local authorities are unable to keep order, and that in consequence the free transmission of the mails or inter-state commerce, or any other Federal interest, is in danger. The United States Judge for the district, which, in the case of Illinois, includes Illinois, Wisconsin and Indiana, is empowered to grant to the district attorney a general injunction prohibiting all interference with mail trains, or of trains crossing state boundaries. Having done this, the judge at any moment can call in Federal troops to uphold the injunction or enforce the law.

The difficulty of course in the case of a very widespread strike is that the Americans have hardly any troops available. The standing army of the United States is divided into eight military departments, which have less than 5000 soldiers apiece. The entire American army according to the army list consists of twenty-five regiments of infantry, ten of cavalry and five of artillery. The officers in command of the military department are bound to obey the orders of the United States Judge. The officer in command of the department of Missouri, which includes the States of Michigan, Wisconsin, Indiana, Illinois, Kansas and Arkansas equally with the Indian and Oclahama territories, is General Miles, an officer of standing and reputation, who would no doubt be capable of handling a very much larger body of men than the tiny handful that he could concentrate upon Chicago.

Surveying the scene of the outbreak of war, we find that the authorities had at their disposition a force of men amounting altogether to some 8000 men. Of these, 3000 form the police force of

Chicago, who are under the orders of Mayor Hopkins and Chief of Police Brennan. The State Militia, which could only be called out by Governor Altgeld, do not number more than 4000 men, and General Miles could not get together more than 1500 or 2000 regulars in case circumstances arose which would justify Federal interference. Of course, behind these armed and more or less disciplined men lay the vast reserve of citizens capable of being armed and enrolled as deputies or special constables. A Chicago Encyclopædia, published at the time of the Fair, said that there were about 50,000 able-bodied men trained in the use of arms

"I will say a few good words for Chicago."

GENERAL MILES' GOOD INTENTIONS FOR THE NEW YEAR.

by the secret societies of the city. Governor Altgeld in the course of the strike declared that he could if need be enroll 50,000 citizens to enforce the law. In dealing with a popular strike the difficulty always arises as to how far you can depend upon your deputies and upon your militia. In this struggle it was proved that in California there were no more hearty favourers of the strikers than the militiamen. They even went so far as to manifest their sympathy by wearing the

colours of the strikers, and still more substantially
by distributing cartridges to the very men whom
they were called upon to keep in order.   More
reliance can be placed on the Federal troops, both
because of their better discipline, and because they
are less likely to be under the influence of local
feeling.   In former days, before Homestead made the
name of Pinkertons to stink in the nostrils of civilisation, the natural resource of the threatened railways
would have been to have enlisted their own police,
or Pinkertons as they were called, but since Homestead this resource has been generally scouted, and
indeed is forbidden by law in many of the states.
The authority of the law can also be invoked against
the strikers if they are guilty of conspiracy, or of
any of the offences which can be constructively
alleged against those who are at the head of
a popular movement of this kind.   It is notable,
however, that the railroads distinctly refused to
prosecute Debs, or the other leaders.   They maintained
that the battle must be fought between labour and
capital to the end, and that any recourse to the courts
would be rather against the interests of capital than
otherwise.   It would enable Debs, said Mr. Egan, to
pose as a martyred man.   So the prosecution of Mr.
Debs was not undertaken by Mr. Egan and the rail-
oads, but by the officers of the Federal Government.

But in any state in the American Union, which is
confronted by the prospect of what may be called
incipient civil war, the first and most important
question is what kind of man have they elected for
Governor.   Now in Illinois they have a very
remarkable man as Governor, a man whom it is the
fashion to denounce and to deride, but who is in
reality an administrator of considerable originality

and of great force of character. John P. Altgeld, although of German origin, as his name implies, is as typical an American—and a western American—as I have ever met. He is not a tall man, but there

MR. JAMES SCOTT, EDITOR OF THE " CHICAGO HERALD."

was something about his face and appearance which irresistibly reminded me of Abraham Lincoln. I met him at the Auditorium Hotel immediately after breakfasting with Sam Fielden, one of the Anarchists whom he had pardoned. Governor Altgeld was elected by the Democrats in 1892 against the protest of the *Chicago Herald*, the leading Democratic paper, which is owned and to some extent influenced by Mr. John R. Walsh, who is President of the First Chicago Bank and head of the Western Union News Company, the W. H. Smith of the Mississippi Valley. The objection taken by the *Herald* was that Altgeld was a Socialist by creed and by profession, that he had written Socialist books, and that he could not be depended upon to enforce the law against law-breakers. His sympathies were declared to be with the Anarchists, and it was a slight concession to the fears of the more conservative Democrats that at the State Convention in which he was nominated, a plank was introduced into the platform of the party, stating that they demanded " protection of the life and property of American citizens at home as well as abroad." Mr. Altgeld had also written in opposition to capital punishment, and, as the Govenor of the State, it was his duty to see that the hangman did his work. He has now been two years in office, and at the last democratic State Convention which nominated Mr. Franklin McVeagh for the senatorship, a special reference was made to Governor Altgeld's administration. The manifesto declares that the Democrats of the State of Illinois " heartily commend the fearless integrity and sturdy determination which has characterised the administration of Governor Altgeld, in which great reforms have been achieved in all branches of the public service of the state, civil and military." So far as I could form an opinion during my stay in Chicago, both from the brief interview which I had with him and from the voluminous comments which his administration elicited from both parties, I should say that he had a great reserve of moral strength, considerable originality of judgment, and a very healthy disregard for the fretful fussiness of the newspapers. He is a man of strong opinions who is not afraid to express them. One of his offences in the eyes of many good people is that he is not much of a professor of religion, a fact which leads the uncharitable to denounce him as a socialistic infidel. Talking about this matter with him, he remarked dryly, that he had " not enough religion to hurt." Judging from some of his acts, it would seem that he has at least enough religion of a more or less inarticulate kind to help him to stand to his guns when he thinks that a clear issue of right and wrong is involved.

The most characteristic act of his administration was the pardoning of the three Anarchists who had been imprisoned since the Haymarket outrage for complicity in the crime. Opinion ran very high upon the subject, but if Governor Altgeld had confined himself to exercising his clemency and releasing the three men as an act of grace little would have been said. This, however, did not accord with his conception with what was right and just, so he made his message pardoning these men an elaborate vindication of their innocence, and a very pronounced attack upon the judge who condemned them. This judge was none other than the redoubtable Judge Gary, an Irishman, who in personal appearance reminded me of a miniature edition of our present Lord Chief Justice. Judge Gary is a conscientious man without interest in or knowledge of the world as it boils and bubbles around him. As he told me himself, his function was to sit apart from the multitude applying abstract principles to concrete cases which were brought before him in the courts. Governor Altgeld may have been right or wrong, but there is no doubt but that he excited much sympathy with Judge Gary by the somewhat unprecedented course which he took in criticising the justice of the sentence which he was annulling, and Judge Gary last November was re-elected by the votes of both Republicans and Democrats over all other opponents.

Of more importance, however, as indicating the line which would probably be taken by the Governor in relation to the railway strike, was the course which he had previously taken in dealing with the disorders which followed in the wake of the miners' strike. The Governor was almost badgered to death by telegrams from all parts of the State requesting arms and troops. In one case at least where he had first refused to send troops, and finally had been compelled to do so by the violent representations of the sheriff, he had the satisfaction of learning that when the troops arrived there was nothing for them to do, and that the sheriff himself had to shamefacedly ask for them to be withdrawn.

Governor Altgeld, although not a Populist, belongs to a stratum of thought which is very Populist in its tendency, and he may be counted with the other Governors, such as Governor Lewelling, of Kansas, who was at one time domiciled as a tramp in a Chicago police station, Governor Hogg, of Texas, and Governor Waite, of Colorado. All these Governors are more or less socialistic, as we should say, or, as they would say, more or less in antagonism to the exploitation of the community by the robber barons of the mines and of the railroads. Hence when Governor Altgeld was compelled to call out the State troops for the repression of disorder in the mining districts, he made it clearly to be understood that he had no intention whatever that they should be used in the interests of the employers. He caused to be read to the troops whom he had sent to La Salle the following intimation, which was a tolerably plain indication of the way in which his sympathies lay:

It is not the business of soldiers to act as custodians or guards over private property. The law authorises them simply to assist the civil authorities in preserving the peace, quelling riots, and executing the laws. Wherever troops have been or may hereafter be ordered, and when an owner of property feels it necessary to have it guarded, he must do so at his own expense, and in such a case the troops can be used only for the purpose of promptly quelling a disturbance of the peace, or suppressing a riot, or in some other way enforcing the law.

Contrast it for instance with the declaration of Governor Matthews of Indiana which was issued about the same time :—

"These men must cease their unlawful acts. If necessary every miner in Sullivan County will be arrested. The troops will remain there until there is evidence of peace. It will be difficult to wear out the state. It has gone into the contest to remain until it is over. The strikers will become tired of furnishing bail or go to jail. If the sheriff and others will not perform their duties I will proclaim martial law."

This, however, was not the only occasion on which Governor Altgeld indicated that he had very little patience with those who were clamouring for the help of the soldiers against the strikers. Sheriff Dowell, of Marion County, appealed to the Governor for troops. Mr. Altgeld told the Sheriff very plainly that he had flinched from his duty, and was endeavouring to throw the responsibility of the preservation of peace upon the soldiers. " I have ordered," continued the Governor, " the troops to Carterville in order that peace may be preserved and the law executed, but I will suggest to you that, if you have not the courage or capacity to properly discharge the duties pertaining to the office of sheriff, then you resign at once and let somebody take your place who can and will do it, for under the law troops cannot be kept long at a place where the sheriff can, by proper effort, preserve order and execute the law."

To this letter the Sheriff, not a whit daunted, replied as follows :—

"Notwithstanding your insulting telegram, you seem to have a studied method of learning nothing of strikes in Illinois, no matter how dangerous, and have little desire or capacity to control or assist in controlling them.

"I find it to be the opinion of many here, that the strike throughout the State would have been easily controlled, and the whole State at peace, without bloodshed, if you had resigned as governor, or had gotten sick and left the State in the hands of the lieutenant governor, who sympathises with and loves law and order. I am frank to say that I have at heart only the good of this county and its citizens, and, if resignations are in order, I stand ready to resign when you do. I am willing to make any sacrifice needed to benefit the citizens of Illinois."

It can be imagined then that when Governor Altgeld was confronted with the strike in Chicago, that considerable anxiety was felt by the defenders of law and order as to how far the Governor could be relied upon to use the forces at his disposal to keep the strikers from interfering with traffic.

I now come to the other great personality connected with the maintaining of order at the seat of war, namely Mr. Hopkins, the Mayor of Chicago.

The fact that the man who, the other day, was working as a lumber shover or a day labourer, should now be autocrat of the capital of the New World, is a distinct contribution to the romance of contemporary history. The Arabian Nights element is always the most interesting in the history of nations and individuals, and there is a great deal of the Arabian Nights element in the rapid rise of Mayor Hopkins.

John Patrick Hopkins was born in Buffalo. He was educated in the common school, and was the third son of a family of twelve. His father and his brothers are dead, and when quite a boy his sisters had to take to dressmaking in order to keep the family in bread and butter. As soon as he left school, which he did at a comparatively early age, he set to work to earn his living. His first place he found for himself. He started in life by heating rivets in an iron foundry. From there he went to work in the Evans elevators, and by the time he was twenty had established a good enough reputation for regularity and industry to be appointed weighmaster of the place. When he was twenty-one he came to Chicago, the city which fourteen years later was to elect him to the highest office in its gift. For four months he looked around. He fixed up his sisters in dressmaking business, and then started out to look for work for himself. He was not quite twenty-two when he went down to Pullman and asked the superintendent of the works for a job. In reply to the question of what he could do, he replied that he would do anything. Being asked if he meant what he said, he was taken at his word. The superintendent was rather pleased at his determination to try his hand at whatever turned up, and sent him to shove lumber down in the yards. There he worked as an ordinary labourer for some months until he had satisfied the management that he had good stuff in him which could be better employed elsewhere. Whatever may be said concerning the autocracy which Mr. Pullman has established in the city which bears his name, no one can deny that the autocrat and his agents have a keen eye for capacity, at least up to a certain point. Mr. Hopkins' career illustrates this. In August, 1880, he was called into the storekeeping department. The April next year he was appointed timekeeper in the store ; in the following August he became general timekeeper. Two years later he was made paymaster by Mr. Pullman.

But notwithstanding his rapid promotion and the

responsible position which he occupied as paymaster of the great industrial army which recognises Mr. Pullman as its captain-general, Mr. Hopkins was singularly independent. It used to be said of him in those days that he was the only man in Pullman who dared to call his soul his own. He was a Democrat, although Mr. Pullman was a Republican. He was young, a comparative stranger, without capital or resources of his own ; but not content with his position of salaried employé, he went into business on his own account in the Arcade. A friend of his who knew him at Pullman, and to whom I applied for some information of those early days and of the struggles by which Hopkins established his reputation, wrote me as follows :—

"This Arcade is one of the original and peculiar institutions of the little manufacturing city of Pullman, which is now, much against Mr. Pullman's will, part of the great metropolis of Chicago. It is a big, red structure with passage-ways running north and south and east and west throughout, and on either side booths and shops. In the upper stories there is a small theatre, a public library, offices and flats. In one corner of the main floor is the Pullman Savings Bank, through which the pay-roll runs and which is ready to care for the deposits of the working-men. There is no other place in the settlement where shops other than groceries and markets can be kept, and those are for the most part centred in one great market building, modelled after the same plan. It is possible for the company to dictate in these matters, as it controls every inch of the ground, and not even the streets have been dedicated as public highways. It has its own hotel, which has always lost money for the company, but which is sustained for the convenience and gratification of the officials, and especially Mr. Pullman. Even the church is the property of the company. The Catholics were indeed after a long time permitted to build on consecrated ground, but before they were given a deed it is said that a priest who had espoused the labouring men's side in a great strike had been compelled to resign. However that may be, it is sure that the reverend father without any apparent reason did fold his tent and desert his flock against their protests and despite their tears, leaving another to finish the church which he had begun.

"This was before I came to Pullman, and I speak therefore only by hearsay. But John Hopkins had been the companion of the reverend father in guilt, and his resignation had been demanded as a punishment for the crime of openly sympathising with the working men. It was forthcoming without a murmur, and after a little time spent in silence and without either suing for restoration or complaining, the young man was invited to return, and his demand for a largely increased salary was granted. It was Pullman's first surrender. But the fact was that it was not easy for any one to fill young

Hopkins' place; he knew Ole Olson in the brickyard and Ole Olson in the foundry, and he never forgot either or mistook one for the other. So much of his work was in this way personal that the conveniences for a merely mechanical system of paying were not at hand, and his successor made a sad botch of it. Besides, the absence of swagger or bitterness on the young man's part was a strong recommendation for a new trial; but, state it as you will, it was a great victory for the mayor-to-be, then little more than twenty-five years old. A similar victory was afterwards scored by a young man named Harper, who served as chief accountant, and was discharged for insubordination, and requested to return after a time to straighten out a set of books which some of the best experts in Chicago had failed to decipher. He was really a wonderful accountant, whose equal I have never known; and what because of this, and what because of a fellow-feeling for him, Mayor Hopkins has chosen him to unravel the muddle of the City Hall, a task which he seems to be performing with perspicuous ability and great despatch. But though Mr. Pullman restored both of these gentlemen to their positions without requiring an apology and with increased salaries, he did not fail to place persons with them to learn the work so as to supplant them, and each found a short shift for himself as soon as the powers felt able to dispense with his services. Perhaps this may have been apparent to John Hopkins all along, and may have had much to do with his indifference.

" Politics was the cause of war. If there was anything which Mr. Pullman could not endure, it was stiff-necked rebellion politically. Like so many American manufacturers, he had come to think protection a necessity to his business, support of it loyalty to his interest and that of his employés, and voting the wrong way in some manner a treachery unpardonable. But the imperturbable paymaster merely smiled in his usual confident and provoking way, and proceeded to do his best to carry Pullman for the Democratic ticket.

" It was not an easy thing to do. The people were accustomed to subserviency, and yet more so since the unsuccessful strike referred to in the foregoing. But Hopkins was indefatigable, and he knew Ole Olson in the brick-yards and Ole Olson at the foundry—in short he knew them all. To be sure, they worked for the Pullman Company. Doubtless largely because of their admiration for the brave fellow who had stood unabashed and victorious before the company, they did give a considerable Democratic majority in spite of the ever-increasing rumours of official vengeance. Really, by his words, his magnetic presence, and, yet more, by his example, Hopkins brought manhood and courage to the surface in men who had never given any signs of either before, and have since lapsed into the old, lack-lustre, subservient mode of life.

" This was too much, and the brilliant young paymaster had to get out without ceremony; and (whether as a fearful warning or not I cannot say) fourteen hundred others, to a man Democratic voters, were sent out too. The reason assigned was lack of work. As a Republican victory had been scored in the nation, this could hardly be ascribed to their future votes. But to an outsider it seemed as if the company by one fell blow thought to make such things impossible for the future. Not only was the leader but the flock as well, this time, driven out of the gates. As before, there was not a word of complaint from the imperturbed young paymaster, who only entered a formal protest when the rent was suddenly and greatly increased on the store-rooms occupied by himself and partner in the Arcade. Amid the sneers of the company and its satellites, he prepared to remove his business to Kensington, and for that purpose pushed, with true Chicago enterprise, the construction of a new store building.''

He established himself in "Bumtown," on the out-skirts of Pullman, which had been abandoned to saloon-keepers and disreputable houses. His advent changed everything. His store was a wonderful suc-cess. His waggons delivered goods in Pullman, for the autocracy of the company could not be stretched so far as to prevent its late paymaster from using the public thoroughfare. Mr. Hopkins is still in litigation with the company to recover the exorbitant rent exacted from him. He has also had more than one opportunity since becoming mayor of making it even with his adversaries. Not that there is any trace of bitterness in him ; no one could be more smiling, affable or debonair. But he has not lost a chance since he arrived of reminding the public of the seamy side|of the Pullman administration, whether in gas or in water, or of the district containing 100,000 population on the boundaries of Pullman which has not yet been provided with a common sewer, owing to opposition of the owners of real estate in the neighbourhood.

Mr. Hopkins was always a politician, but he was twenty-seven years old before he was appointed to an office. The position which he held was that of treasurer to the village of Hyde Park. Two years later he endeavoured to obtain the nomination to the National Democratic Convention. As usual with young aspirants, he had to fight his way to recogni-tion. He was defeated in 1888, but he made so plucky a fight against Mr. Green that his standing in the party was recognised without further hesitancy. He was placed on the committee, and in the Presi-dential campaign Pullman was delivered over to his hands by the Democrats. It was Mr. Hopkins who first startled the Republican close borough by torch-light parade through the streets, and by this and other electoral sensations he achieved a victory which startled every one. The next year he followed it up by a municipal success quite as notable, for as Chairman of the Annexation Committee he played a leading part in adding 225,000 population to Chicago. Among the towns annexed, Hyde Park was one of the most important, and the Pullman Company had the chagrin to see their estates annexed to the city of Chicago against their opposition. After this he became President of the Cook County Democracy. He took the boys down first to Springfield and then to Washington. His name was first coupled with the mayoralty in February, 1890, when, with a thousand members of County Democracy Marching Club, he went down to Des Moines to attend Governor Boies' inauguration. Hopkins, who has an extraordinary memory for names, resembling therein the Queen and Mr. Gladstone, who are said never to forget a name they have once heard, presented each member of his thousand marching Democrats, and it is said that he never made a mistake in the name of a single individual.

All this time he was building up a big business. He entered upon other work, dealing with street cleaning and street work, and he had become a very substantial citizen. All his mind was concentrated on business and politics. He took no part in society, although he belonged to several clubs. He spent most of his time in his store or at home with his mother and sisters. He dressed well and kept in well with the influential people, including President Cleveland, who last year appointed him receiver of the Chemical Bank, the duties of which responsible post he discharged with the vigour and despatch which characterise all his actions.

Q

When Carter Harrison was shot and the election was ordered to be held for the appointment of his successor, there was no intention on the part of the official gang in the County Democracy to run Hopkins. They would willingly have nominated one of themselves, but Mr. Hopkins came in and said he wished the nomination, and all opposition went down before him. He does not owe anything to the party managers, unless it may be a few grudges, which he will probably pay off in due time. He refused absolutely to make any pledges or to bind himself to any course, but insisted on having his hands free in case he were elected. With many a wry face his rivals bowed to the inevitable, and Mr. Hopkins entered for the campaign against Acting-Mayor Swift. It was hot and furious while it lasted, but so far as Mr. Hopkins was concerned the contest was not characterised by any asperity, nor did he commit himself recklessly in his election pledges. In the end he was elected by a majority of over 1200.

No sooner was the Mayor in the saddle than he began a campaign which bore the strongest resemblance to that of Mayor Pingree in Detroit. He addressed himself to the elevation of the grade crossings, ordered a list of the killed and wounded to be made up and read to the Council at their meetings. He prepared himself for a battle royal with the boodle element in the Council, which he saw would endeavour to use the attempt to elevate the tracks as a means of levying blackmail on the railways in order to embarrass him in his enterprise. Finding the city hopelessly behind in its finances, he cut his own salary ten per cent. and insisted on a general reduction all round. He surrounded himself with competent and public-spirited advisers, and began a systematic inquiry into all the abuses which have disgraced the city. Comptroller Ackerman drew up a report upon the scandalous system of assessments, which is the disgrace of Chicago, and the report was published to the dismay of all the tax-dodgers of the community. He took energetic measures against the street railways to compel them to fulfil their obligations in repairing the tracks, in paying the license-duty, and in discharging the other obligations which they owed to the city.

His first battle with the Council took place over the North-western Elevated Railway Ordinance, which the aldermen had passed, it is said, in return for 1000 dollars a vote, for making an elevated railway to the north-west. The Mayor vetoed the ordinance because it did not secure any return to the city in the shape of a percentage upon the gross receipts. His veto was sustained. The ordinance as amended provides that the city shall share in the gross profits of the railway. A committee was appointed to inquire into the unauthorised encroachments on the public domain by steam railways, with results which are not a little surprising to the public and disagreeable to the railroads. He stopped the disgraceful system of levying fees for inspection. He waged war against the system of collecting and retaining the taxes by which collectors were able to pocket scores of thousands of dollars which ought to belong to the public, and generally set on foot an investigation of the shady places of the city administration. By a ukase he peremptorily suppressed the raids for revenue upon houses of ill-fame, which have been the scandal and disgrace of Chicago for many years, and ruined at least for a time the business of the professional bailer and the justice of the peace. In dealing with the police his avowed policy has been to remove the police from politics, but the temptation to avenge himself on his adversaries was too strong to enable him to carry out that programme in its entirety. Captain Shippy disappeared, Captain Mahoney was reduced, and Inspector Ross compelled to resign. There was no attempt to justify these acts other than upon political grounds.

Mr. Hopkins' great fight, however, was waged with the boodle gas ordinance. For a whole week the victory was in dispute, nor did any one know to which side it would incline. At the Council meeting Mayor Hopkins launched one of the strongest messages which has ever been addressed to such a body. His veto was sustained, although forty-two members of the Council voted in its favour, while only twenty-two voted against it. He was saved from defeat by the defection of a certain number of Republican aldermen. The Democratic boodlers stood firm, with the result that the Mayor's next task is the ridding of the City Council of the presence of the corrupt members of his own party.

Personally Mr. Hopkins impressed me very favourably, partly, I must admit, at first on account of his resemblance to Cecil Rhodes, the Prime Minister of South Africa. Cecil Rhodes is the ablest man in the British Empire from the administrative point of view, and if Mayor Hopkins is anything like Cecil Rhodes, he will not stop far short of the presidential chair. He is, however, younger than Mr. Rhodes, and of a more nervous temperament. When he presides over a Council meeting, his fingers are continually playing with his mallet, and at times even this method of disposing of his surplus energies fails, and he gets up and walks backwards and forwards like a caged lion on the raised dais on which the mayoral chair is placed. He may get over this when he grows older, otherwise it will wear him down, for the aldermen are a tough crowd, and he has a very long row to hoe before he gets to the end of his job in Chicago. He is a demon for work, and his constitution, which has not been impaired by any excess either in drink or tobacco or other forms of dissipation, will stand a much greater strain than would ruin the strength of most of his opponents. There is a joyous *élan* about him which will stand him in good stead. He had not been elected three months before he established a reputation in Chicago which no other man possesses, and it was admitted reluctantly, even by those who are opposed to him, that if he were to stand on an independent ticket he would be elected Mayor at present by a majority of three to one. " He has a spine like a telegraph pole," exclaimed a banker, admiringly, after reading the message on the boodle ordinance. It would be difficult to describe more picturesquely the kind of backbone which is needed by a man in Mayor Hopkins' position.

Mr. Hopkins is not an orator, but if he were to take a little more trouble he would be able to excel as much on the platform as he does in administration. There is a *bonhomie* about him which is attractive to the masses, and he is quite Bismarckian in the reckless candour with which he expresses his opinions. He is not a scholar nor a student of books. He reads the newspaper, and he lives in the midst of his fellow-men.

Mayor Hopkins has continued to set an example of industrious administration, and he had so far succeeded in maintaining his hold, at least upon his own party, that he triumphed over all opposition

in securing the nomination of Franklin McVeagh
for the Senatorship. He has added to his laurels
by the stand which he took against the opening
of a race-track when the whole forces of the

MR. HARRY RUBENS,
Corporation Counsel of Chicago.

betting fraternity were arrayed against him. He
has, however, not improved his record in the matter
of the suppression of the gaming-houses. Considering
that gaming-houses are running wide open all over

Chicago, it is surprising to learn that when he was examined before the Grand Jury the mayor of the city was able to declare that he had no personal knowledge of the existence of any such institutions in the city under his jurisdiction. He has also excited against him considerable opposition owing to the vetoing of the Sunday Closing Ordnance, a law passed by the majority of the Council compelling shops to close on Sunday, not in the interests of Sabbatarianism, but in the interests of one day's rest in seven, which over three-fourths of Chicago is at present denied to the shop employees. In this, however, I suspect that we may see the hand of Mr. Rubens, his able legal adviser, who may possibly have a race bias against Sunday Closing. Mr. Hopkins, as an old employee of Pullman, was naturally intensely interested in the dispute, but so far he seems to have succeeded in preserving the impartiality expected of his position for his appeal to Mr. Pullman to consent to arbitration could hardly be regarded as a divergence from the line of strict neutrality. The only expression of opinion made by him in the course of the strike which I have been able to come across was a remark that he considered the struggle might easily be fatal to Pullman, no matter how the strike resulted for the men. The indignation excited by Mr. Pullman's obstinate refusal to consent to arbitration in any shape or form would work to the detriment of his cars all over the union. That, however, was a by-issue. The question was no longer one between Pullman and his men, but between organised capital represented by the railroads and organised labour as represented by Debs' organisation ; and while the two combatants were fighting, the Governor and the Mayor had to keep the ring.

Chapter II.—How the Conflict was Fought out.

THE story of the campaign which opened when the boycott was declared on June 26 has been told from day to day in telegrams in the newspapers. It is, therefore, unnecessary to dwell at length upon the details, but it will be more to the purpose to describe briefly the course of events.

The boycott ordered for June 26 somewhat hung fire. On some of the lines the men came out; on others they did not. On the first day of the strike comparatively few of the lines ceased working. The switchmen by leaving at midnight tied up the Central Illinois from Chicago to New Orleans. The desertion of his post by a single gateman blocked nine trains on the Central Illinois and six on Fort Wayne at Grand Crossing for three hours. The gate was not opened until 100 policemen were brought up to overawe the mob. Even then the road was blocked for another half-hour by a striker who threw himself on the line before an advancing engine and brought it to a sudden stop. On the first day of the boycott, trains running Wagner palace cars were allowed to pass freely. This was, however, but for a day. The Companies using the Wagners made common cause with the Pullman Companies, and the strikers after this made no distinction. Every railroad in the Association of Railway Managers, whether it ran Wagners or Pullmans, was attacked. By the 28th two-thirds of the lines leading to Chicago were blocked. On the 1st of July, of the twenty-two companies affected, ten stopped all attempts to run goods trains, while seven ran no trains at all. Some idea of the extent to which the strike paralysed traffic may be inferred from the fact that usually one hundred and fifty-two passenger trains come into and go out of the Dearborn station daily, but only twelve came in on June 30 and ten went out. That was the effect of the strike on the Western Indiana tracks. In the freight service of these lines only nine trains were moved. Traffic was interfered with on two-thirds of the railroads of the United States. The suburban traffic in Chicago was abandoned. Goods traffic was minimized, and every effort concentrated upon keeping up the through passenger trains.

It is impossible not to feel a certain respect for the intrepidity and resolution with which Mr. Egan and the railroad staff set themselves to break the boycott. They did not conceal from themselves the fact that they were in for a fight and a severe one ; but they prepared for it without fuss, and in the fashion of men who have been in similar crises, and who had come off victorious. They had the trump card of the unemployed up their sleeve, and they bided their time.

They began by padlocking and chaining the Pullman cars to their trains so elaborately that it took experienced trainmen with hammers and cold chisels half-an-hour to unloose them. They declared that they would run Pullmans on every train, and they kept their word. When their switchmen struck, they recruited blacklegs to fill their places, sending them to work under police protection. They had the pick of as many men as they wanted, for starving men swarm in the States, and no Unionism could deter them from earning their bread.

The strikers on their part seized and held most of the strategic centres or great railway junctions in a dozen States. They were strongest on the Pacific

MR. EVERETTE ST. JOHN,
General Manager of the Chicago, Rock Island, and Pacific Railway.

Slope and weakest in the Eastern States. At Chicago they never succeeded in entirely stopping all traffic, but they shut down the great stock-yards, and prevented the conveyance of the droves of cattle which constantly stream to the butchering establishments in Chicago. Mr. Debs and the officials of the

American Railway Union sent out energetic manifestoes denouncing all violence, but it soon became evident to the rough untutored perception of the mob that Labour would be beaten hollow unless Capital could be terrorised into submission.

The boycott had not been four days in progress before the strikers began to supplement moral suasion by violence. It was not until June 9th that any serious outrage was committed ; but when once the ice was broken, intimidation became the order of the day. On the Rock Island Railway, at Blue Island, a pointsman on strike was arrested for having opened the points so that the best locomotive on the line rolled off the track down an embankment ten feet deep. It lay on its side in the ditch, a helpless discomfited monster, carrying with it one of the Pullman cars, in which were fortunately only three passengers, none of whom was injured ; the other cars were thrown promiscuously across the line, effectually stopping all traffic.* The previous day at Hammond, Indiana, a crowd of strikers and sympathisers stopped every train by main force, cut off the Pullman cars and blocked the line. One of the trains carried 1000 passengers, who were naturally furious, but to no purpose. Elsewhere it became the rule rather than the exception to resort to violence. Here are a few

---

* The strikers stoutly deny that the engine No. 930 was derailed by any thing but an accident due to the bad construction of the locomotive. The Mediation Committee of the American Railway Union reported as follows as to the probable cause of the accident :—

We find from engineers of the road and from the son of Engineer Edgerle, who was killed by this engine last May, that she has a sprung axle, is out of line, carries a longer driving-rod on one side than the other, binds the rail on the right side and is out of square. This has always been her condition since she was manufactured, and makes her liable to jump the track at any time. We have examined the switch where the accident took place and find that the switch point has not been broken, and that the engine left the track eighteen inches before the switch was reached, conclusive proof that the switch had not been tampered with. We find also that this engine has jumped the track three times.

On the other hand, the Railroad Company as stoutly deny that the engine No. 930 was of such faulty construction as is here alleged.

items from the seat of war. On June 30th, before the boycott was a week old,—

Suburban engine No. 248, from Blue Island to Burnside, was badly stoned at Kensington by a mob of some 300 persons collected at that point. Trains 17 and 23 were stopped at the Chicago and Eastern Illinois crossing on account of towermen going out. The levers were finally handled and the trains proceeded.

A mob of strikers went to Homewood with engine 221, pulled the fire, disconnected engine 210, and returned north with engine 221, derailing it near Kensington, and leaving it blocking north-bound main track No. 4.

Engine 221 was seized by strikers and run between Chicago and Eastern Illinois crossing and Homewood, for the purpose of carrying strikers to disable all engines found between those points, and when this work had been accomplished, engine 221 was derailed and left foul of the main track without protestation, exposing other trains to danger of colliding with it.

Strikers took possession of the interlocking tower at Seventy-first Street and Seipp Avenue, removing the combination board and destroying it, and otherwise interfering and breaking the interlocking apparatus of the tower, making it necessary to close the derails and spike the switches for the main track on the South Chicago branch.

It is difficult to give in detail the general conduct of strikers on the company's premises last night. All employees in any capacity who remained at work were threatened with personal violence unless they at once discontinued work.

The railroads began to recruit special detectives. The train that left by the Illinois Central for New Orleans, on June 29, carried a carload of detectives, armed with Winchester rifles, to secure its safety. When, however, the railroads attempted to bring special detectives into Chicago there was a commotion.

A riot was imminent at ten o'clock this morning, when Illinois Central train No. 23 came in, bearing Assistant-Adjutant-General Bayle, of the State guard, a body of forty-five special detectives and the Chicago Zouaves, the latter *en route* to Little Rock, Ark. Each detective was armed with a policeman's club, a revolver, and a Winchester rifle. As soon as their presence on the train became known, the crowd set up a cry of indignation, and when the detectives stepped out of the coach they were attacked by the strikers, and three of them were beaten and disarmed. The others remained in the car all day by advice of the railroad officials, and all attempts to get food to them were frustrated by the strikers. At six o'clock in the afternoon they gladly consented to leave the city, and went on the only train sent out on the Illinois Central. All day long an enormous crowd surged about the car taunting the detectives, who wisely refrained from speech. Several strikers uncoupled the car in which they were seated, and one of their number who rushed out to interfere was quickly covered by four pistols and a double-barrel shot-gun.

There was, however, no flinching on the part of

the railroad company. The Monon Company, whose trains were stopped at Hammond, vowed vengeance. Their representative declared—

"We shall punish every man possible. The whole course of the mob at Hammond has been a series of vicious outrages. Were these crimes condoned, society would suffer. We shall fight these men to the bitter end, if it takes all the Winchesters and Gatling guns in the State or country. The law is slow, but it will triumph in the end."

Twelve hundred deputies were sworn in. The State troops were called out, and despatched to break the blockade at the various junctions. The Federal Government, meanwhile, was looking sharply after the safety of the lines which were in the hands of the receivers appointed by the United States Court, and was preparing to employ the Federal troops in enforcing the free passage of the mails.

There was, however, no disposition on the part of the strikers to abandon the struggle into which the armed forces of the State and of the Federal Government were preparing to take a part. In Colorado a small force of fifty deputy-marshals was disarmed by the crowd, and on July 2nd a mob of two thousand strikers seized and disarmed two hundred and fifty deputy-marshals who had been despatched to Blue Island to protect the cars.

The struggle, although brief, was fierce. When the train, crowded with armed representatives of the law, steamed down the line, the strikers and their sympathizers blocked the line by standing on the rails, two thousand strong. As the engine slowed up to avoid making a wholesale massacre of the crowd, the strikers saluted it with a volley of stones. On board the cars the deputies drew their revolvers and stood ready to fire at word of command. When the engine came to a standstill, knives were brandished, and amid volleys of oaths and stones the mob made a desperate and ultimately successful attempt to capture the train. The deputies beat them off with the butt end of their revolvers, but ultimately they were over-powered. One of their number was stabbed, but not seriously ; no shots were fired, and the train remained in the strikers' hands. It may be added, as a comical illustration of popular sympathy with the strikers, as well as of the fetish-like regard which Americans show to legal forms, that in the midst of this struggle a village police officer tried to arrest the engineer of the blocked train for violating the town ordinance forbidding trains to block crossings for more than five minutes ! Of him the deputy-marshals made short work by throwing the too zealous legalist from the footplate. Nothing daunted, a second police officer tried the same thing ; but in his case the deputies arrested him on a charge of attempting to interfere with the United States mails.

The immediate result of this high-handed defiance of the law was to bring the troops into the field. Governor Altgeld ordered a regiment of State militia to Blue Island, and the Federal troops at Fort Sheridan were got ready to march at a moment's notice whenever the order came from the Federal Judges, who had already served injunctions upon Mr. Debs and the strikers, an indispensable legal preliminary which cleared the way for the intervention of the Federal troops.

The boycott had not lasted a week, but it was evidently gravitating into civil war. Mr. Debs still, like the luckless Falkland, kept "ingeminating peace" and denouncing violence ; but the rank and file paid no heed to their leader. They saw that the strike was utterly hopeless unless the railroads could be terrorised into surrender, and they proceeded to terrorise them accordingly. They struck, and struck hard, at the heel of the great Achilles by blocking the lines in all directions. The official programme of the strike was that all traffic was to be brought to a standstill by the peaceful, lawful refusal of railway servants to operate the trains. The actual programme was to prevent the passage of the trains by main force. This was carried out in a variety of ways. Sometimes the strikers simply laid down or set up a child on a chair in front of the advancing train. At other times they tore up the rails, or loosened the ties, or threw a wrecked car across the line. Here and there they greased the rails so that the wheels would not bite, slipped sand into the grease boxes of the locomotive, pulled out the coupling pins, cut the tube of the air brake, and generally put a spoke into the wheel wherever and whenever they found an opportunity.

When they found Pullman cars attached to the train they stopped it, hewed off the Pullmans, and trotted them into sidings. At Riverdale they varied the programme by consuming all the viands in the dining-car and drinking all the wine. It was a species of highway robbery according to the latest improvements, carried out in the name of oppressed humanity under the aegis, although of course not with the sanction, of the American Railway Union.

When all other means failed, the strikers showered stones upon the train, adjusted the switches so as to throw them off the track, and in fact did everything, short of actually building barricades across the permanent way, that they could imagine, in order to embarrass their enemies. All this was, of course, in direct violation of law, and so far as it interfered with the free passage of the United States mails, an offence which came little short of treason to the Commonwealth. It was obvious that this could not last. Something must be done, and that promptly.

The necessity for action was not merely political, it was also economic. The blockade of the railways was threatening to reduce Chicago to a state of privation like to that of besieged Paris. We have, as a rule, but little conception of the immensity of the work that is involved in the mere victualling of a great city. When the boycott was declared, the railways on the south side alone had received for delivery in Chicago no less than 30,000 tons of ice. In the course of a week they had only been able to deliver 500 tons of this immense consignment. The remainder was dripping away under a midsummer sun. The price of ice in the city went up from 12*s.* to 40*s.* a ton, and a veritable ice famine was threatened. The strike occurred in the midst of the fine harvest. Every day in ordinary times Chicago consumes 60 car-loads of Californian fruit. When the boycott was declared not another car-load was delivered. The fruit rotted on the cars. In Illinois the tomatoes were ripening and the blackberries were ripe. Ripe fruit perishes fast, and the fruit-growers found with dismay that their crops were of no value owing to the impossibility of getting them to the market. Union County in Illinois estimated the losses of its fruit and vegetable growers at no less than £6,000 a day while the strike lasted. The supplies of fish from the Gulf of Mexico were cut off, so were the consignments of shell fish from the eastern coast.

Ice and fruit and fish, though perishable, are not absolutely indispensable. The city had bread enough in its granaries, but it was in imminent peril of running short of beef and coal. Chicago is the greatest butcher's-shop on the planet. In ordinary times a procession of 6,000 cattle wend their way with unvarying punctuality to the slaughtering houses, where they are despatched with almost automatic precision, and converted into dressed beef with amazing celerity. The railroads have always thousands of cattle to transit ; when the lines were blocked the Rock Island had 20,000 animals on its hands, the

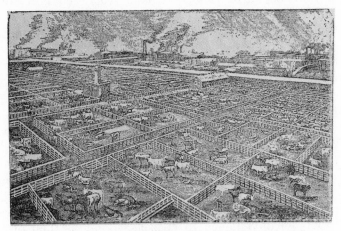

THE UNION STOCK-YARDS, CHICAGO.

North-Western 8,000, and the Burlington 6,000. All these had to be taken out of the trucks and pastured on the nearest farms. Often the unfortunate animals suffered tortures of hunger and thirst before any relief could be obtained. The Union stockyards were practically closed, and the cessation of the leading industry of the city sent 6,000 butchers and packers to join the ranks of the unemployed. Chicago has great breweries of its own, but it imports five car-loads of foreign beer per day ; that was cut

R

off, and the local breweries, deprived of ice and of coal, began to contemplate with awe the prospect of compulsory teetotalism.

But it seemed doubtful whether even water could be procured. The whole of Lake Michigan, it is true, lies at the doorsteps, but the water on the lake side is polluted with sewage, and undrinkable All the drinking-water is pumped from in-takes miles from the shore, and as the supply of coal at the pumping-stations began to run short, men wondered how life could be supported in July without water. In Chicago the average daily consumption of coal is 3,500 tons of hard, and 50,000 tons of soft. When the strike broke out there was hardly a ton of soft coal left in Chicago after the first week. Factories were closed down for want of coal, nor was there any prospect of fresh supplies being forthcoming until the strike was over. Everywhere there was the same story of privation and discomfort. The cable cars threatened to cease running owing to the exhaustion of the oil which they used for fuel. Chicago, in short, was experiencing in a time of profound peace something of the miseries of a leaguered town in time of war.

The inconvenience to citizens, so far as their own locomotion was concerned, was almost inconceivable. At the beginning of the strike the suburban traffic was discontinued. As Chicago lives in its suburbs, more even than London, some idea can be formed as to what that involves. One incidental advantage resulted in the shape of an immense increase of cycling of all kinds, which will probably be one of the few permanent benefits left by the strike. The passenger traffic was least interfered with, but many trains were blocked. Trains full of women and children were sometimes blocked for days, and in one case, at least, a whole hundred of suffering passengers were compelled to lie blistering in the midsummer sun, with scanty food and no water. The strikers refused to allow their miserable hostages this necessary of life for thirty hours at a stretch.

This was the condition of things in Chicago on July 2. All freight trains were practically stopped. The suburban traffic was very irregular. The passenger traffic was blocked on several lines. The city was suffering acute inconvenience for want of ice, food and coal. Scores of thousands were thrown out of work owing to the dead calm of industry. At certain points, notably at Hammond, in Indiana, in Blue Island, in Riverdale, at Grand Crossing, the strikers had resorted openly to actual violence and outrage. Mr. Egan, surveying the scene from the headquarters staff of the railroads, declared : " The situation is becoming critical, and in a few hours we shall be in the midst of a reign of physical violence. The emotion is growing rapidly worse and the end cannot be foreseen."

The strikers were jubilant. The reign of terror seemed as if it were about to bear the fruits of victory. But the very extent of their terrorism brought about the reaction, which, finding expression in the appearance of Federal and State troops, ultimately killed the strike. The end, however, was not to come for another fortnight, and in the course of that time much was to happen.

It must not be forgotten that the strike was from the first absolutely hopeless as a strike. The only chance of success lay in the possibility of enforcing the objects of the strike by the methods of civil war. To begin with, the American Railway Union, a mushroom thing of yesterday, never included as many members as the number of train-men actually out of work owing to the depression and the consequent reductions of staff. For 125,000 men out of 820,000 to expect to tie up all the railways when there were 160,000 trained men out of work ready to take their places was absurd. As a matter of fact, the whole of the 125,000 men never went out on strike. The strike was confined to the States of Illinois, Michigan, Indiana, Ohio, Kansas, Colorado, California, New Mexico, Arkansas, Montana, Idaho, North Dakota, Wyoming, Washington and Utah—fifteen out of forty-four States and territories, and in many of these it was very partial. The railroads, even if they had no reserve of unemployed to draw from, could have drafted all the men they needed from their staff in the States where the strike never penetrated. This might have been prevented by two means : either by creating a sufficiently strong sense of *esprit de corps* among the men that they would voluntarily refuse to assist against the strike ; or by striking terror into the breasts of the blacklegs, so as to deter them by sheer dread of murder or mutilation from taking the vacant places of the men on strike. Both were tried and neither succeeded.

The American Railway Union was from the first confronted by the opposition of two powerful and older Unions. The Brotherhood of Locomotive Engineers and the Brotherhood of Locomotive Firemen both opposed the strike and refused to take any part in it. Nor did they stand alone in this respect. Public opinion, even the public opinion of the workmen in the trade specially concerned, was not unanimous. Terrorism alone remained. But terrorism, even when using dynamite, is ineffective against the constant pressure of absolute hunger.

The strike failed because for every single man who struck there were two who were ready and eager to take their places.

Chicago was full of unemployed men, but it was thought well to bring in strangers, who would be less under the influence of local feeling. Recruiting bureaux were opened at New York and Philadelphia. Several hundred train-men were engaged and shipped to Chicago. Switchmen were promised 65 dollars a month for 10 hours' daily work, and extra pay for overtime. One of the first thousand of these imported blacklegs explained his point of view to a newspaper interviewer in terms which explain simply and clearly exactly how it was the strike failed. He said :—

"I am from Cleveland and I've been a railroader eight years. When business got slack last winter I was pulled off with several others, and I haven't worked five weeks altogether since the first of the year. I have a wife and three children depending on me, and for six months we have been living from hand to mouth. When the agent who hired me to come to Chicago asked me if I would go, I told him I would see my wife first. I went home and found her in tears at the dreary outlook. My children were actually in want of bread, and it didn't take me long to make up my mind about coming to Chicago. I am a Union man at heart, but when wife and children are in danger of starving I feel it my duty to work for them, even should I be killed in the endeavour. There are lots of men here who feel the same way."

The strikers were of course furious at the introduction of these fresh hands. Murderous threats were made, but comparatively few were executed. They were boycotted. Hotels that gave them shelter were shunned as if they had the pestilence, but beyond some ugly kicking and beating, the "scabs" were not much injured. Vice-president Howard, of the American Railway Union, swore that when the strike was won, scant mercy would be shown either to "scabs" or to the "bladder-bellied bosses."

"Before we will allow any road now tied up to resume operations they must promise to withdraw from the General Manager's Association, they must haul no more Pullman's cars, they must put every one of you back to work, and every 'scab,' that they have hired must be made to walk the plank. I want to sound a note of warning to every 'scab' right now, no matter what the colour of his hair, that we have got a combination that will drive them into the depths of the sea. When this fight is over they cannot stay on this continent."

The second week of the strike saw all these seething, fermenting elements of social strife come to a head, before the authorities were ready to deal with them. There seems to be little doubt that the police force of the city, like everyone else, were more or less in sympathy with the strikers. Trained as a force not to see whatever they do not want to see, whether it be a public gaming-house, or the offences of those who have a " pull," the police found little difficulty in winking hard at the outrages of the strikers. The Chicago *Tribune* bitterly complained of their supineness. It says :—

"Nearly 150 officers are supposed to be guarding the Illinois Central from riotous strikers; there have been riot, disorders, and violence of every sort, but the police have neither arrested any of the offenders nor stopped the lawless acts. When asked they invariably deny there has been any trouble. They denied that a freight car was burned at Burnside, Wednesday night; that the box of yard engines was cut; that a mail train and the Diamond Special were stopped last night; that engines have been cut off trains and 'killed,' or that any sort of trouble has occurred on the Illinois Central. The police, who are ostensibly guarding the place, know nothing about it."

Naturally emboldened by their impunity, the strikers and their sympathisers, who include practically every one who earns daily wages and a very great many others, showed no disposition to relax their hold upon the railroads. They had disarmed the deputy-marshals at Blue Island ; they showed on July 3rd that they were equally ready to defy the Illinois state troops. The militia ordered from Springfield to Danville had to start the train themselves and then were stopped by finding five hundred yards of the railway had been torn up by the mob. Still the local authorities hesitated to shoot. They made preparations. Springfield army rifles were piled up in the sheriff's office, and Marshal Arnold brought quantities of the new "riot gun," which seems to be not unlike the weapon which earned Mr. Forster his Buckshot soubriquet. An admiring reporter noted that the gun is loaded with six three-inch twelve-calibre cartridges which can be discharged one after the other in five seconds. Each cartridge contains twelve buckshot about the size of peas. When the cartridge is discharged the shots scatter, seventy-two of them flying in the direction of the rioters in five seconds. The gun can be emptied and reloaded several times in each minute. But the riot gun was not issued until after Independence Day.

Down in Colorado an irate marshal, baffled by the sympathy which led his deputies to lay down their arms at the summons of the strikers, declared he would hereafter hire "any kind of deputies, hoboes, horse thieves, etc., just so they are willing to fight." Detective agencies offered to get him all the men required who would fight, and the manager of one agency was started out to recruit specials.

It was evident, however, that the forces of law and of disorder could not long continue facing each other without a crisis. This was precipitated on both sides almost simultaneously. President Cleveland took the initiative on one side, the incendiaries on the other. The Federal Government, finding the mails stopped in all directions, interstate-commerce interrupted, and the lines administered by receivers representing the United States Courts interfered with, suddenly struck a decisive blow and ordered 1,300 Federal troops of all arms to Chicago, sending at the same time General Miles to take charge of the operations against the rioters.

It was on the 3rd that the 15th Regiment of Federal troops arrived at Blue Island and at once raised the blockade. Next day other companies occupied the dockyards, and took up a position at Grand Crossing. It was a strange Independence Day this year at Chicago. The city was almost in a state of siege. Besides the armed deputy marshals, and the Illinois State troops, Federal cavalry and infantry, with Gatling and Hotchkiss guns, held positions of vantage in the city, and at night the small army of horse and foot artillery encamped on the Lake Front in readiness to be launched in any direction against the rioters. Their presence in the city was not relished by the citizens. Governor Altgeld telegraphed vehement protests against the unnecessary and illegal intrusion of Federal troops into the State of Illinois. Mayor Hopkins also sneered at the soldiers. " We know nothing about the Federal troops. They were brought here for a purpose. They sit a-top of cars. We want men who will get down upon the ground to do their duty." It seems almost incredible that, with a volcano of anarchy beneath their feet, these men could have deemed it necessary to stand on constitutional pedantries and refuse to welcome the advent of a solid disciplined force of armed men upon whom they could absolutely rely to maintain order in Chicago.

The first collision between the Federal troops and the rioters took place on July 5. A Dalziel telegram reports it as follows :—

"The Michigan Central Railway attempted to-day to run a train full of live stock, consisting of seventeen trucks, from the stockyards, but it was surrounded by a crowd of 8,000 men and boys, who uncoupled the cars and captured the train. Upon the news reaching the authorities a detachment of the regular army, numbering ninety men, was ordered to the stock-yards, and they charged a mob of some 3,000 rioters. Two troops of cavalry and a battery of artillery arrived a few minutes afterwards, and the combined

forces drove the mob back. Gatling guns have been placed in positions
commanding all the streets leading to the yards. A train of empty cars
was run into the station in the forenoon to be loaded with stock, but the
men in the yard refused to load it, and the trucks are now standing empty."

From which it would seem that the fruits of victory
remained with the strikers, for they had effectively
prevented the loading of the trucks. This, however,
was not much worse than what had been going on
from the first. It needed a sterner lesson to rouse
the authorities to a sense of the dangers of the
position.

The lesson that was needed was not long in coming.
Anarchic labour, confronted by disciplined soldiery
with Gatlings, replied by the torch. On the night of
July 5th incendiaries set fire in three places to the
famous buildings of the World's Fair, and in two
hours the one splendid beautiful thing that Chicago
had ever created was reduced to a wilderness of
eighty acres of ashes and gaunt and twisted girders.
To those who have seen that fairy dream of splendour,
the Court of Honour, no violence could more rudely
symbolise the triumph of barbarism over civilisation than this destruction of the World's Fair by the
fire of the incendiary.

The Court of Honour, with its palaces surrounding
the great fountain, the slender columns of the
peristyle, and the golden dome of the Administration
Building, formed a picture the like of which the
world has not seen before. They might have been
hewn out of solid marble, those great palaces of staff,
but it would have been impossible to have produced
the delicacy of the moulding and the lightness of the
tracery in any less plastic material than that which
yielded such marvellous results in the hands of the
architects of the World's Fair.

Once only, a long time ago, I remember feeling

the same thrill produced by architectural effect. It was on my first visit to Edinburgh, when I was a boy still in my teens. Driving along Princes Street, past the museums, I saw looming up high before me the castle of the northern capital. The curious blending of the associations of Greek architecture with Scottish romance produced a somewhat similar effect to that which was produced by the architecture alone, without any historical associations or romantic traditions, at the World's Fair. The long stately lines of the great palaces, the glory of the colonnades, and the beauty of the lagoons, in which the great buildings were mirrored, when the waters were not disturbed by the gondolas, left an impression of perfect beauty and of stately symmetry I have never seen equalled in any of the most famous architectural marvels of the Old World. The Colosseum, or the ruins of the Forum, and the great mediæval cathedrals of Europe, have associations of history and of tradition which immensely re-enforce the influence of architectural genius. In the World's Fair the architecture alone produced the effect. The buildings were new from the architect's hands. It is a great tribute to the genius of the builders that the buildings which they reared could produce an instant and abiding effect equal to that which emanates from the ancient buildings round which hang the purple mist of centuries and of song.

On the night of the 31st of October the great buildings were illuminated for the last time. The fountains did not impress me as being superior to those of the Paris Exhibition, but nothing that I have ever seen in Paris, in London, in St. Petersburg, or in Rome, could equal the effect produced by the illumination of these great white palaces that autumn night. Overhead stretched a cloudless sky, in which the stars gleamed faintly. Beneath the stars the lake lay dark and sombre, but on its shores gleamed and glowed in golden radiance the ivory city, beautiful as a poet's dream, silent as a city of the dead. It was more wonderful to have seen that city in the silence and solitude, with no one near except lonely sightseers flitting like wandering ghosts across the electric-lighted squares into the dark shadows of the projecting buildings, than to have seen it even on Chicago Day, when three-quarters of a million visitors crowded into Jackson Park, filling the Fair with a human exhibit more marvellous than the Exhibition itself. If a thing of beauty is a joy for ever, then that vision of the White City by night, silent and desolate, was well worth crossing the Atlantic to see.

Mr. Graham, the Director of Works, and several of the builders who had helped in the construction of the White City, assured me, that the buildings would last for ten or fifteen years if they were preserved merely as architectural monuments. To preserve them as buildings in which exhibits might be shown would cost a great deal of money, but merely to preserve the architectural effect, which was all that I cared for, would cost next to nothing. The architectural glories of the World's Fair, the one unique thing about the great Columbian Exposition, could be preserved for the miserable sum of £5,000 a year. The smaller buildings of course would come down, but the great edifices round the Court of Honour, and those which formed the vista looking down from the Administration Building to the Art Palace, these could be preserved at a cost, so far as the architect was concerned, of £5,000 a year. It seemed monstrous that a city which had subscribed a million pounds to put up the Fair, should grudge such a bagatelle to preserve for ten or twenty years its most characteristic feature. When the facts were set forth a great deal of discussion followed, and the buildings were ultimately handed over to the South Park Commissioners, who professed an intention to preserve them.

Unfortunately, however, this intention did not include a resolution to protect them from fire. A trifling outlay and a comparatively small exercise of authority would have kept the place clear from intruders, and preserved, at least until the next century, a vision of beauty and of architectural glory the like of which cannot be seen elsewhere. But Chicago, great in executing enterprises which can be executed under the stress and strain of a strong stimulus, is not equally great in preserving and maintaining that which she has created. It is difficult to know whether most to admire the resolution and energy which created the White City, or to deplore the fatuity which led such mediocrities as the South Park Commissioners to fool away by their negligence what should have been regarded as the heirloom of the Continent, a priceless heritage which would reflect glory upon Chicago.

Time and again fires broke out during the winter, destroying one building after another, but still the Court of Honour remained. But it only lingered to supply the crowning illustration of the vandalism of anarchy. On the night of the 5th of July all the buildings round the Court of Honour were destroyed, including the administration, the manufactures, the electricity, the mining, the machinery, and the agricultural buildings, together with the terminal station. Among these—the greatest of all the buildings of

THE MACHINERY HALL (DESTROYED BY FIRE)

the Fair—the greatest building with which mortal man ever enclosed space—was that dedicated to manufactures. Mr. Washington Porter conceived the idea of transporting this immense structure of glass and iron from Jackson Park to the lake front, which was to have been a Crystal Palace for Chicago, and a Bureau of Labour for the toilers. That dream is ended now.

Incendiarism once begun is not easy to check. The whole of the next day and the day after the southern suburbs of Chicago were given over to riotous mobs who wrecked the railways, overturned cars, and made bonfires of the rolling stock. Mayor Hopkins frankly declared that the forces at his disposal were unable to answer for order in his own suburb of Kensington, and he therefore appealed to Governor Altgeld to call out the entire State force of Northern Illinois. He issued a proclamation calling upon all well-disposed citizens to abstain from congregating in crowds, as a collision between the troops and the rioters was probable. And still, after all this, after the burning of the World's Fair, and after the establishment of the reign of terror in Southern Chicago, Governor Altgeld telegraphed more urgently than ever for the withdrawal of the Federal troops !

The night of July 6 will long be remembered in Chicago. Until midnight the mobs held full control of the entire southern suburbs of Chicago, roaming through the extensive railway yards at Grand Crossing, Burnside, Kensington, Fordham, Morgan Park, and Hawthorne, and burning in repeated incendiary fires over 1,000 cars, including many Pullman coaches, as well as barns, signal-towers, and storehouses. The loss is estimated at three million dollars. Only a handful of troops and police being there, the mobs did what

HALL OF MANUFACTURES AND LIBERAL ARTS (DESTROYED BY FIRE).

they liked. The loss affects all the railways running southward from Chicago. During the contests the known casualties are two men killed and eight fatally injured. One striker shot at and killed another, being forthwith killed by a third.

The Fire Brigade, having answered sixty calls in the course of the two days, was exhausted. 5,000 Illinois troops were massed in the city. 1,200 Federal troops were also in Chicago. It was thought not improbable that martial law would have to be proclaimed, and that the President might ask the Governors of New York and Pennsylvania for 20,000 of the National Guards to restore order in Illinois. Fortunately there was no need to resort to such an extreme measure, which might have precipitated civil war.

At midnight on the 6th the work of restoring order was begun. The 1st Illinois Regiment cleared the mob out of the suburbs. The 15th occupied the railway yards and the approaches to the stock-yards. But it was not till next day that the rioters realised that they were at last face to face with men who would not hesitate to shoot. A company of the 2nd Illinois Regiment was attacked while engaged in clearing the Grand Trunk line in 47th Street of derailed cars by an immense crowd, led on by one John Burke, who overwhelmed the soldiers with a shower of stones. The lieutenant was felled with a coupling pin, and the soldiers were driven back to the cars. They fired and then charged with the bayonet, wounding twenty rioters, including Burke, who died from the effects of the wound. They were, however, unable to hold their own, and were compelled to retreat to the cars, where they were besieged. The mob meanwhile began tearing up the tracks. Reinforcements were soon at hand, and the mob fled. At Englewood, in 16th Street, and other places, there were shots fired, and charges with the bayonet.

The police estimate that 50,000 men, strikers, idlers and marauders, many of them foreigners, had for two days held undisputed control over the suburbs of Chicago. They had burnt cars, looted railway sheds, wrecked railway shops, torn up rails, and generally spread devastation through the city, entailing a loss estimated in hard cash at six million dollars. And the total amount raised by the Central Relief Association to provide for the unemployed last winter in Chicago was only 133,000 dollars.

The authorities, now thoroughly aroused, agreed to sink constitutional hairsplitting and work together. Gen. Miles with the Federal soldiers, and Gen. Wheeler with the Illinois troops, agreed with Mayor Hopkins upon a plan of operations. They established an armed camp from which reinforcements could easily be despatched in any direction, and made it known throughout the city that orders had been given to shoot, and to shoot, if need be, to kill. Gen. Miles with his regulars undertook to protect the Government buildings and the railway stations. The Mayor with the State troops and the police guarded the railway yards and dispersed the mob. The deputy-marshals with the police protected the stock-yards and the railway stations on the south. It was agreed that Gen. Miles would only charge when the Mayor asked him to do so. Altogether there were 10,000 armed men at the disposal of the authorities. Rioting ceased, incendiarism was checked. The trains began to move.

Meanwhile opinion was still fiercely divided about the merits of the strike and the right of President

s

Cleveland to interfere in the dispute. The strikers and their friends pinned white favours to their button-holes, while the admirers of the President sported as favours the Stars and Stripes—a curious latter-day imitation of the familiar badges of York and Lancaster in the Wars of the Roses.

The Chicago Trade and Labour Assembly condemned the intervention of the Federal power. The Governors of Colorado, Idaho, and Oregon supported the protests of Governor Altgeld. But President Cleveland went straight on. He took possession by his soldiers of the Northern Pacific and the Union Pacific, and operated both as post and military roads, working them as part of the military establishment. Then on Sunday night, the 8th July, President Cleveland launched his Proclamation, the effect of which was to put Chicago and the other disturbed districts under martial law. The following is the text of this famous document :—

"Whereas by reason of the unlawful obstructions, combinations, and assemblages of persons, it has become impracticable, in the judgment of the President, to enforce by the ordinary course of judicial procedure by the laws of the United States with the State of Illinois, and especially the city of Chicago, and, whereas for the purpose of enforcing the faithful execution of the laws of the States, protecting property and removing obstructions to United States mails in the State and city aforesaid, the President has employed part of the military forces of the United States.

"Now, therefore, I, Grover Cleveland, President of the United States, do hereby admonish all good citizens, and all persons who may be or may become within the city and State aforesaid against aiding, countenancing, encouraging, or taking part in such unlawful obstructions, combinations, or assemblages. I hereby warn all persons engaged in or in any way connected with the unlawful obstructions, combinations, or assemblages to disperse and retire peaceably to their respective abodes on or before 12 o'clock noon on the 9th day of July. Those who disregard this warning and persist in taking part with the riotous mob in forcibly resisting or obstructing the execution of the laws of the United States, or interfering with the functions of Government, or destroying or attempting to destroy property belonging to the United States, or under its protection, cannot be regarded otherwise than public enemies. The troops employed against such riotous mob will act with all moderation and forbearance consistent with the accomplishment of the desired end; but stern necessities confront them, and will not with certainty permit a discrimination between the guilty participants and those

...eaking of the struggle, before it culminated in ...rous defeat, Mr. Sam Gompers, president of the ...ican Federation of Labour, said :—

..e effect of the Pullman boycott and strike will be to teach capitalists, ..tes and trusts that it will be to their interest to make concessions to ..king people that they have not made heretofore. Capitalists and cor- ..s should be conciliatory, not arrogant. The isolation of employers ..ployees is not possible—the two should be on friendly terms. The ..nt brought on foot by the American Railway Union shows the rising ..the labour movement. It inaugurates the era of mutual concessions. ..rotest against the frightful conditions existing. It must act as a ..o the arrogance of the moneyed classes."

..tunately it is likely to have exactly the ..ite effect for a time. To give your opponent an ..tunity of proving that in a stand-up fight he ..vhip you as easily as Corbet whipped Mitchell, .. exactly the best way to check his "arrogance." ..e real ground for hope must be found elsewhere. ..Pullman boycott and strike is the Bull's Run of ..ur, and as it needed the disaster of Bull's ..o teach the North that they must organize and ..ce for victory, so even this cruel and crushing ..may be the saving of the industrial classes in ..United States. It is with themselves that the .. of regeneration must begin. And until they ..tute practical organization for windy blather, ..oyal obedience to their chosen chiefs for an ..t demoniac distrust of all and sundry, they will ..little progress. When reading such a manifesto ..t which Mr. Sovereign, General Master of the ..ts of Labour, addressed to that Order on the ..f this recent strike, it is difficult to resist the ..g that American trades' unionism has been dry- ..l upon the Fourth of July oratory and the .. platitudes of the conventional pulpit. Mr. ..eign's manifesto is as follows :—

..Knights of Labour have pledged their lives, their fortunes and their ..nour to the emancipation of the industrial masses from the shackles

who may be mingled with them through curiosity and without criminal intent. The only safe course, therefore, for those not actually unlawfully participating is to abide in their own homes, or not to be found in the neighbourhood of riotous assemblages. While there will be no hesitation or vacillation in the decisive treatment of the guilty, the warning is especially intended to protect the innocent. Whereof, I hereunto set my hand, and have caused the Seal of the United States to be hereto affixed.

"Done at the city of Washington, the 8th day of July, in the year of Our Lord one thousand eight hundred and ninety-four, and in the year of the Independence of the United States of America one hundred and eighteenth.

"(Signed) GROVER CLEVELAND, President.

"W. Q. GRESHAM, Secretary of State."

At the same time 1800 additional Federal troops were ordered up to Fort Sheridan to be ready in case General Miles should need reinforcements.

Fortunately there was no need for these extra batteries of artillery and troops of cavalry. The last serious fight took place at Hammond, in Indiana, which from the first had been a centre of violent opposition to the running of the trains. Hammond, although close to Chicago, is in Indiana, and the rioters took full advantage of the frontier. When the Indiana troops appeared, they retreated to Illinois; when the Illinois soldiers were to the front, they retired to Indiana. It was not till the 8th, when the Governors agreed to allow their respective forces to operate as one body irrespective of frontiers that order was restored. But here, as elsewhere, the Federal troops acted with decisive effect. On Sunday afternoon at four o'clock a mail train from Indianapolis approached Hammond, carrying on board a strong body of Federal troops. Nothing daunted, the mob attacked the train. The soldiers replied by a volley, and then followed it up with a bayonet charge. Four persons were killed and twelve wounded. The mail train got through, but it was not until heavy reinforcements of State troops had arrived, and after many affrays had taken place, that the Hammond blockade came to a close.

The Trade and Labour Assembly, when it heard of President Cleveland's proclamation, replied by unanimously voting for a general strike. But, notwithstanding the valorous resolve of the newsboys —one thousand of whom struck against selling the papers which opposed the strike—the appeal met with only half-hearted support. The railways had too obviously triumphed. Their trains were moving. The courts were moving. Mr. Debs and his colleagues were arrested and committed for trial,* and the business men hoisted flags to commemorate the defeat of Labour. There were many mutterings of discontent, and threats of a general cessation of work which could not be made good. But discipline, organization and wealth had triumphed, and Labour could only lament over the catastrophe which it had courted.

It would have been better if it had only lamented, instead of seeking to make bad worse by resorting to dynamite. The infernal machine with which an engine on the Santa Fé Railway was blown up on July 8th was an ugly incident. So also was the action of those men who threw a railway train over a bridge into the river at Sacramento, killing six of the soldiers who were on board. The struggle was singularly free from acts of exceptional ferocity. Considering that the great city lay practically at the mercy of the rioters for a week, it is marvellous how few lives were lost. To put ten thousand soldiers into the field against fifty thousand rioters, all more or less armed, and to succeed in restoring peace without killing twenty persons is an achievement of which no other country but America can boast.

* As I write the cable reports that Mr. Debs and other strike leaders have been committed to gaol in default of bail.

Chapter III.—A S

The suppression of the nothing and proves nothing, too well known before. Bu it may be it will supply stimulus to rouse the apath to action. The strike aga brings into clearer relief America is not yet anythin the lists in serious earnest. disorganised, undisciplined is doomed to writhe helpl beneath the ironshod heel time to time flounder into a and dynamite will enable it upon its adversaries, but m its reach.

Religion, save the religio not exist to bind together working classes of Americ religion in some way or othe much-abused term, sufficier trust their comrades, suf ultimate triumph of their make the daily sacrifice t obedience and punctual pa chiefs, they will remain a hopeless, helpless, blaspho whose only plan of campa sporadic violence of excite by the organised forces of tl

S
disa
Ame
"T
syndic
the we
poratio
and e
mover
tide o
It is a
check

Unf
oppo
oppo
can
is no

T
This
Lab
Run
sacri
blow
the
worl
subs
and
alme
mak
as t
Kni
eve
feeli
nurs
unre
Sov
"A
sacred

of greed and oppression with the same fortitude that actuated the revolutionary fathers more than a century ago. Then, as your general master
workman, I take the liberty to direct the officers of all local assemblies of our
order to call special meetings, discuss the Pullman boycott, and the corporations lending their influence in support of its determined policy to dominate
over the God-given rights of its employees. Notify the travelling public that
those who patronise Pullman coaches will receive no patronage from the
Knights of Labour, and order such other assistance as lies within our power
to give. Temper all your acts with mercy. In all things be peaceable and
law-abiding, but do not relax your determination to triumph in this
struggle over corporate greed. And if the exigences of the times force a
re-adjustment, let it be an unconditional surrender of corporate powers and
privileges, and an uncompromising demand for the utter elimination of
private interests in the operation of any of the means of transporting
passenger and freight, and if we are compelled to strike let it be in the spirit
of the patriots of '76."

> Strike for your altars and your fires:
> Strike for the green graves of your sires;
> Strike till greed and avarice expires,
> God and your native land.

It will take something a great deal more solid than
this flatulent flap-doodle to disturb the "Robber
Barons" in their constitution-guarded castles. In
the frontispiece I reproduce a German cartoon representing Labour, preyed upon by the vampire of
Capitalism. The worst vampire that preys upon
Labour in America is not Capitalism, but the fatal
lack of that spirit of loyal brotherhood, which is
the indispensable foundation of all effective co-operation. The workers are numerous enough to control
everything, if they cared to do so. But they care
more for party shibboleths and sectarian feuds than
for the weightier matter of the law which governs
their lives, and the lives of their children.

At the same time it is idle to cast stones at the
blind anarchist whose torch has just proved that its
deadly efficiency is quite as great in the new world
as it has ever been in the old. The existence of such
savage passions, all unrestrained, as those which led
to the night of terror of the 5th of July, is a reproach
to the community at large and a menace as well as
a reproach.

According to the latest Government statistics, the Americans possess sixty billions of wealth. Nine per cent. of the families own 71 per cent. of this, leaving but 29 per cent. to the remaining 91 per cent. of the families. The 9 per cent. is composed of two classes : rich and millionnaires. Of the latter there are 4074 families. They average three million dollars each. They constitute only three one-hundredths of 1 per cent. of the whole number of families, while they own 20 per cent. of the wealth. That is, they own nearly as much as the 11,593,887 families.

The process of accumulation goes on irresistibly. The snowball gathers as it grows. Even spendthrifts and prodigals cannot dissipate the unearned increment of their millions which multiply while they sleep. The millionnaire is developing into the billionnaire, and the end is not yet. The transformation is hidden from the multitude because the coming despot eschews the tawdry tinsel of the crown, and liberty is believed to be as safe as—well, let us say, as the populace of Rome believed the republic to be when Julius Cæsar refused the imperial purple. But everywhere the money power has the people by the throat.

The ablest men in the United States see this and deplore it. But what are they doing to mend it ? Even the modest proposal to levy a small income tax is denounced as " un-American," and the modification of the tariff seems as far off as ever. Mayor Pingree, of Detroit, sent out as his Christmas card an extract from a letter said to have been written by President Lincoln, shortly before his death, with the pertinent question : " What are you going to do about it ? " The authenticity of the letter has been disputed. But there is no doubt that, genuine or not, the sentiments imputed to Lincoln are believed by

millions to be well justified. After rejoicing that
the war with the South is nearing its close, the
letter proceeds :—

" It has indeed been a trying time for the Republic ; but I see in the near future a crisis approaching that unnerves me and causes me to tremble for
the safety of my country. As the result of the war,
corporations have been enthroned, and an era of
corruption in high places will follow ; and the money
power of the country will endeavour to prolong its
reign by working upon the prejudices of the people,
until the wealth is aggregated in a few hands, and
the Republic is destroyed. I feel at this moment
more anxiety for the safety of my country than
ever before, even in the midst of war. God grant
that my suspicions may be groundless."

" What a wonderful prophecy," adds Mayor Pingree, " and how terribly it is being fulfilled ! "

But what is to be done ? The way out—which
in England seems to lie in the progressive muni-
cipalization of all monopolies of service, and in the
assumption by the State, step by step, of all the
functions of distribution that are manifestly capable
of enlarged management—is barred in America by
the flagrant corruption that prevails in the City
Governments. Take, for instance, the nationaliza-
tion of the railways, or even of the telegraphs, as
a way of escape from such troubles as this Pullman
strike. Who is there who would recommend the
addition of such burdens to the responsibilities of
an Administration which to this day subordinates
Civil Service Reform to the Spoils system ? How
can the management of immense properties be
entrusted to venal aldermen and ward politicians ?

The remedy, of course, is the old, old specific. There

must be a revival of civic religion in America if the State is to be saved. Until the honest folk will take the trouble of governing, the rogues will have it all their own way. Thus, once again we come back to the lack of real religion as the one deadly peril which confronts us at every turn.

The task before the Americans is hard enough in itself, as we all know only too well who have to try to solve our own problems of the same kind. But in the United States the task is rendered infinitely more onerous by the fact that Americans in one respect suffer from the same curse which plagues the Irish. Ireland would never have been too troublesome if the Irish had been able to secure redress for their grievances as rapidly as the English and the Scotch. Unfortunately, owing to the remoteness of the legislature and the impossibility of compelling the House of Lords to recognise the imperative need for legislation until the time had passed when legislation could be useful, the Irish problem has become almost insoluble. The American industrial problem may go the same road for the same cause, for the Irish are not more hopelessly hampered by our House of Lords than the Americans are by their written Constitution.

As to the obstacles in the way of getting any reforms in the States, Mr. G. W. Smalley may be accepted as an unimpeachable authority. In a recent article in an English Review, Mr. Smalley says :—

" Aforetime it may have been a paradox, but it is now the mere simplicity of truth to say that America is probably the most Conservative country in the world. It is, I think, admitted by the best writers that in some very essential particulars the English Constitution is far more democratic than the American. The English machine is so contrived as to respond quickly and pretty surely to external pressure. Touch a button, and you turn out a Government. Touch another, and you modify your Constitution. In America there is no great use in touching buttons. The machine does not respond ; or does not respond till after a considerable length of time. We are ruled by a President who is in for four years, and cannot be removed except by impeachment. As a rule, the House of Representatives elected for the second half of the Presidential term has a majority of his opponents, but to that he pays no attention. He and his cabinet are independent of hostile votes in Congress. A new House of Commons in England, elected all at once on some issue of the moment, meets, or may meet, almost at once. The American House of Representatives, elected in November of one year, does not, unless specially summoned, meet till December of the year following. In the interval many things may have happened. People have time to consider whether they really want it altered, or radically altered, or not, and public opinion is brought to bear on Congress with great force; the force being always for deliberation and delay."

It would be difficult to state more accurately the actual working of the American system of government. It is based upon the principle that whenever the people make up their minds it is so certain they will be mistaken that they must be prevented by every conceivable constitutional arrangement from having their way.

After a measure gets through the House of Representatives, there is the Senate to be reckoned with, and the Senate is an extremely conservative body— a millionnaire's club it is often called. It is a plutocratic machine, but with more power than our House of Lords. The constitution of the Senate, as Mr. Smalley takes pains to point out, is absolutely opposed to the principle of representative government, which insists upon some proportion between the numbers represented and the number of representatives :—

"The checks upon ordinary legislation, including the fixed four years' term of the Executive, the Presidential veto which is frequently used (President Cleveland, during his first term, vetoed more than a hundred bills), the co-ordinate and, in all respects but one, co-equal legislative powers of the Senate and House of Representatives, the long interval between the election and the meeting of Congress, the legislative continuity of the Senate with its six years' tenure, which is never renewed all at once, but by thirds each two years, the revising jurisdiction of the Supreme Court—these and other limitations must seem to the English Radical very numerous and obstructive. To the English Conservative they may throw some light upon the strength of that Conservatism in America of which he is beginning to discover the existence. But they are as nothing to the checks upon legislation affecting the fundamental law, or, in American phrase, amendments to the Constitution."

And here again Mr. Smalley is quite right. No more careful provision has ever been made for securing the subordination of the interests of the living to the iron grasp of the dead hand than that which is laid down in the provisions for amending the American constitution. Before any amendment can be made in this ancient document, drawn up by men living on the eastern fringe of the American Continent, none of whom dreamed of legislating for the Pacific Slope or for seventy millions of people, the following procedure has to be gone through:—The proposed reform must be carried first by two-thirds majority in the House of Representatives, and then by a two-thirds majority of the Senate. When this has been done, the amendment must be sent down to each of the separate States of the Federal Union. Of these there are forty-four, and each of them has two separate legislative bodies. Mr. Smalley says :—

"These States occupy half the North American Continent; each one of them has a Constitution of its own; each has a population with distinctive traits and a strong State feeling; their legislatures are chosen under varying conditions of suffrage, meet at different periods of the year, and prescribe each their own methods of procedure. Yet three-fourths of them must concur in an amendment. If there be one less than three-fourths, the amendment fails."

But even this imposing array of checks upon the popular will does not satisfy the conservative American. Mr. Smalley says :—

"Suppose a law to have run all these gauntlets, to have passed the House and the Senate, and, if a constitutional amendment, three-fourths of the State Legislatures; suppose it to have escaped the President's veto, or been passed over it by a vote of two-thirds of both houses, it has still to take its chance of being declared unconstitutional by the Supreme Court of the United States. That is one more check, and it is also a check which cannot be got rid of, as all the others may, by eventually electing a new House, or a new Senate, or a new President. The Supreme Court is not an elective body, and I suppose that might seem to the English Radical a sufficient reason for sweeping it away. The judges are appointed for life by the President. They are responsible to no popular tribunal, not even to public opinion. They sit as a Court of pure law; the final authority from which in all America there is no appeal. Their jurisdiction, strictly defined though it be, is co-extensive with the whole Union. It is the one instance in history in which popular sovereignty, acknowledged as supreme in the long run for every other purpose and over every other authority to which it has delegated power, submits to a master whom it did not appoint, and cannot remove, and cannot escape.

"A unanimous vote of the people, the unanimous vote of House and Senate, and the approval of the President, would not make a statute law if this tribunal says it is not law."

After this clear and succinct exposition of the impediments which are placed in the way of the government of the people, by the people, through the people in the United States of America, it is possible that others may begin to discover the similarity, which impressed me so much, between the fundamental principles of the Russian Empire and the American Republic.

Great as are the physical resemblances between America and the Russian Empire, the political analogy is still closer. This, although it seems to be the most reckless of paradoxes, is nothing less than the simple fact. The fundamental characteristic of America, as it is of Russia, is the deep ingrained distrust of the popular sovereignty visible in the constitution of both countries. The Republic which professes to be based upon the principle of popular sovereignty, and whose greatest President defined its essential principle as being that of government by the people, for the people, and through the people, has, as a matter of fact, arrived at substantially the same conclusion as the Russian autocracy as to the lack of wisdom which distinguishes the popular sovereign.

English people, who expect to see the whole machinery of government changed after every general election, have ideas as to the sovereignty of the people which are entirely foreign to Americans. When an Englishman says that he believes in popular government, and when he talks about popular sovereignty, he means what he says. He means that when a majority of the legal nation has at a general election decisively expressed its opinion, no power on earth shall stand in the way of that will being done. Of popular severeignty in this sense in America there is none. The American pays no such homage to the declared will of the nation any more than if he were a Russian. The will of the nation, as declared by sweeping majorities from Maine to California, would not necessarily alter the Government, change the Ministers, or result in legislation. The assumption of the American—an assumption which is embodied in the constitution—is that the electors when consulted upon any given question, will probably return a foolish answer, therefore the constitution has been framed for the express purpose of preventing the popular sovereign having his own way. America is not governed by the sovereign will of the sovereign people expressed at the ballot-box ; it is governed by the dead hand of those who framed its constitution. The whole nation voting as one man is likely to find that its wishes are set on one side by the action of the dead hand of the framers of the constitution.

Not only so, but the whole machinery is so adjusted as to render the popular will of no effect when it has been pronounced. The President, the Senate, and the House of Representatives have each co-ordinate powers of check and counter-check. When once a President is elected, it is impossible to change the executive for four years. The Senate and the House of Representatives, two bodies originally modelled on the House of Lords and the House of Commons, differ from them materially in the fact that whereas the House of Lords is practically dead, the Senate is very much alive. All power with us is centred in the House of Commons ; only once or twice a year does the House of Lords venture to assert itself.

With that exception we are practically living under
a single-chamber constitution, and whatever the
House of Commons decides is law. But in America
the Senate has much more authority than the House
of Representatives, and if, as frequently happens,
they are of different ways of thinking, nothing
can be done. The Senate, of course, is a check
upon waves of popular emotion ; the President with
his veto is another check, and the constitution
is a third check. The sovereignty of the people in
the United States is a babe in swaddling clothes—a
sovereignty which is recognised in words, only to be
mocked at in fact. It is not even a kind of a leap-
year sovereign, for it is possible for the leap-year
sovereign, who is the President, to find himself confronted by a Congress whose one object is to render
his administration nugatory and abortive. When
you discuss this question with Americans, they always
fall back upon the argument that it is necessary to
have safeguards against sudden outbreaks of popular
folly. That is exactly what the Russians say, the
only difference being that the Russians do not take
the trouble of asking popular opinion to register itself
at the ballot-box, and the Americans do. Both,
however, agree in regarding the decision of the
ballot-box as almost certain to be an expression of
folly rather than of wisdom.

This elaborate system for the stultification of the
popular sovereignty, with which we are chiefly
familiar in the Federal constitution, is also to be found
in the constitutions of the various States to an extent
which is almost inconceivable. Take, for instance,
the constitution of the State of Illinois. What would
our labour men think, for instance, of a constitution
which, by one of its articles, rendered it absolutely

impossible to pass a Truck Act or a Mines Regulation
Act or a Factory Act? The Labour Unions of the
State of Illinois, with great pains and much agitation,
succeeded in inducing the Legislature at Springfield
to pass a law forbidding the payment of wages in
truck, a practice which has been forbidden in England
for the lifetime of this generation. No sooner did
they do this than the judges of the Supreme Court
of the State promptly ruled the Act out of existence
as unconstitutional, for the constitution of the State
of Illinois contains an article forbidding all interference with the liberty of contract. Therefore the
truck system remains in full force in Illinois until
this day. The miners of the State got an Act passed
providing that they should be paid by weight, and
not by measure. No sooner was the law passed by
the Legislature than it was sacrificed as unconstitutional. At this very moment a Factory Act, which
limits the hours of labour of women and children in
the State of Illinois to eight, is being appealed
against by the Manufacturers' Association, and it is a
foregone conclusion that it will go the way of its predecessors. These three instances will enable us to
understand somewhat of the tyranny of the dead hand
which is the ruling Tzar of the American Republic.

It is not only in the written constitution, but in
the private conversation of the educated classes, that
you find the same deeply-rooted distrust of the simple
democratic methods which prevail in the United
Kingdom. Take, for instance, the municipal governments. The Americans are living under the dominion
of the political ideas which prevailed under George
the Third. They denounce him religiously every
fourth of July, but go on living under his system all
the time. This is true enough, and it is bad enough

in all conscience. For it operates as a direct incentive to anarchy, which is the natural outcome of political and social despair.

The chief hope that lies in the future seems to be that these obstacles and evils will by their very weight rouse the American people to deal with the problem with the same heroic thoroughness and national devotion that they displayed in crushing the slave-owners' revolt. But that hope is not for to-day or even for to-morrow. As the abolitionists had to labour through an apostolate of martyrdom for many long years before the evil of slavery worked itself out with such a form of concrete devildom that the whole nation could see that it must be suppressed, so the Social Reformers of to-day will have to bear their cross in patience, until, by long years of sacrifice, they secure the redemption of their land.

APPENDIX.

"IF CHRIST CAME TO CHICAGO?"

SOME OPINIONS OF PRESS AND PULPIT.

My book "If Christ Came to Chicago?" is now in its 120th thousand. The latest edition which has just been issued in London in paper covers is published at a shilling. There are still a few copies of the first English edition in cloth at half-a-crown.

THE PULPIT.

Before quoting the criticisms which the book has received in the Press of the *Old World* and the *New*, the following pulpit utterances by well-known ministers of religion may be read with interest:—

THE REV. O. P. GIFFORD, CHICAGO.

The Rev. O. P. Gifford delivered an address before the Baptist Ministerial Association of Chicago on the subject of the book, which was afterwards published by the request of the Association. Mr. Gifford said : "W. T. Stead is a prophet and has a prophet's reward. His book is a modern interpretation of the Hebrew spirit. . . . If he had commended the commendable and not condemned the condemnable he would have been welcome; if silence had followed sight concerning things sinful he would have been praised ; but he was a prophet, not a scribe or a priest: he saw sinful people, not altars and book. If he had waited a little, he would have got used to open sin. He did not stay long enough to get used to lawlessness in high places, unrebuked sin in public places, and unmasked vice in the streets. The curse of Chicago to-day is that so many men and women have got used to seeing sin. Does Mr. Stead state the facts truly ? I have not seen them contradicted as yet. Mr. Stead makes very serious statements ; his book is a searching east wind. If he has told the truth we ought to hide our face in shame and confusion, and then take action. The truth is pitiless, let the facts be known."

THE REV. LYMAN ABBOTT, NEW YORK.

The *Outlook*, which is edited by Dr. Lyman Abbott, and which is the most influential Christian newspaper in the United States, says that the book "is graphic and true. Mr. Stead has made a study of the dark side of the most

T 2

characteristic of American cities, and has told without reserve what he has seen. There is nothing salacious or prurient in his book. It does not minister to an idle or a depraved curiosity. Its light is the light of God's judgment day shining in on the dark places of vice and sin. He is bold to audacity, and absolutely uncompromising. He hates hypocrisy and deception, and most of all that commonest form of hypocrisy, self-deception. His book is one to make men angry, because it is unsparing of the higher and more reputable forms of sin, and justly holds selfish greed in honoured forms and eminent places responsible for the vice and degradation that hides away from common sight. But we are glad that Mr. Stead has written it, and we hope that not Chicago only, but other cities as well, will read it and take its lessons to heart."

THE REV. WASHINGTON GLADDEN.

The Rev. Washington Gladden preaching upon the book at Columbus, O., said "that it was an indication of the bloody revolution that was coming quickly in this country if needed reforms were not secured in other ways. How any thinking man could read the book and still believe that America was the best governed country in the world was a mystery to him."

THE REV. W. WALSH, NEWCASTLE-ON-TYNE.

The Rev. W. Walsh, of Newcastle-on-Tyne, reviewing the book, says :— "Mr. Stead and his descent upon Chicago are irresistibly suggestive of Jonah and his apostolate in Nineveh. If journalism is Mr. Stead's profession, preaching is his vocation. He is a preacher to the age. He has to an almost unprecedented degree the preacher's gift of swift keen insight into the divinity and the devilment of human life. If this book of his is not a volume of sermons it is veritably one long preachment. For such a preacher and such a sermon the Lord's name be praised. Mr. Stead has a gospel as well as a policy, and this gospel constitutes the soul and spirit of the whole discourse. We hear a good deal about municipal reforms and municipal socialism, and what not, but it has been left to Mr. Stead to elevate all this municipal experience into the glory and grandeur of a gospel. Mr. Stead's book will do more to further the cause of public religion than all the sermons which have been preached in Christendom during the last twelve months."

THE PRESS IN AMERICA.

Mr. B. O. Flower, editor of the *Arena*, writing in that Review, says :— "'If Christ Came to Chicago' is one of the bravest, noblest of all the profoundly religious books which have appeared in the last century, and when I say religious, I use the term in its highest and truest sense. It is an earnest, passionate, and sympathetic plea for the union of all who love in the service of all who suffer. But it is more than this. It is a bold unmasking and setting forth of rapacious greed, and of that conventional immorality which is poisoning the blood of the nations. It reveals the utter heartlessness of conventionalism in religious, social, and political life. This book has grealy alarmed Plutocracy. It has frightened the plunderers of the people, as is evidenced by the savage, unjust and false attacks which have been made upon it by certain fawning spaniels of Plutocracy. The vicious spirit of conventional immorality on the one hand, and alarmed Plutocracy on the other, has represented this book as vile, coarse, and indecent. As a matter of fact, Mr. Stead's book is profoundly religious, and breathes forth from cover to cover a spirit of sturdy morality. I hope that all readers of the *Arena* will secure a copy of Mr. Stead's book, and that, after reading it, they will lend it to their friends. I believe it is one of the most valuable books which has been produced during the past thirty years. It is just the book that is needed at the present time, and will do a great deal toward helping us out of the present social quagmire."

The *Chicago Tribune* says :—" The book really belongs to a class of literature which is denominated obscene, and as such ought to be suppressed. It is all the more dangerous to public morals, for it was written with a good purpose, while actually it is a directory of sin. . . . All those who have any respect for themselves will leave the book alone as too vile a thing to be touched by the fingers of decency."

The *Chicago Dispatch*, the one paper in Chicago which stuffs its advertising columns with advertisements of houses of ill-fame, says :—" The book is flat, stale, and should be unprofitable. It is so libellous and so scurrilous that the greatest book concerns in America have refused to handle it. Who is Stead? An ex-convict, charlatan, an advertiser of filth and vice, a man whose sole claim to notoriety is the crimes he has committed against law and morality, and who holds his place in the public estimation through false pretences. Stead may be permitted to go as one would spurn a mangy dog."

The *Chicago Record*, the morning paper which has the largest circulation, says :—" From beginning to end the book bristles with startling revelations, bitter denunciations, and wholesale exposures of the city's inmost workings in all its various phases. Every existing moral, physical and spiritual condition of the people, without regard to age, sex, or condition of bank account, is subjected to a fire of criticism utterly scathing and merciless."

The *Inter-Ocean* publishes a copious analysis of the book, and laments that it is certain to give the enemies of Chicago occasion to blaspheme.

The *Chicago Herald* says :—" The book contains nothing that is novel. Much of it is a mere paraphrase of old newspaper reports relating to past events, which are disgracefully notorious in the criminal history of the city. The story of the slums is the same old story. The descriptions of poverty and vice are not peculiar to Chicago. The book required some labour. The matter was only to be procured in many out-of-the-way repulsive places from which sickening sights and suffocating stenches would drive away any but the most intrepid and the most impassable explorer. The title of this stupid yet in some respects mischievous book is shocking. Possibly it would be held as blasphemous under the common law."

The *Chicago News* says :—" Mr. Stead has grasped all the virtues and evils of our municipal and public life, and mastered not a few. It will be said that he has given the world nothing new, but that only shows that we are possessed of an indifference nothing short of criminal. There is not a person in this wonderful city possessing the average quota of observing power that does not know of the existence of every evil pointed out in Mr. Stead's book."

The *Advance* (Congregationalist) says :—" No man ever worked more assiduously than did Mr. Stead during the four months which he spent in the city. He possesses an extraordinary faculty for getting at the facts in a case. A more strikingly unselfish man it would not be easy to find. In his convictions, sympathies, and aims it must be admitted that he is intensely Christian. Surely it will be wiser to consider the facts and heed the message than it would be to stop and throw sticks and stones at the messenger."

The *Interior* (Presbyterian) keeps up the reputation of the religious press for "envy, malice, and all uncharitableness," by the following description of the black list, exposing the owners of houses of ill-fame, which no one else dared to publish:—"Mr. Stead has signalised his departure by leaving for publication a guide-book to the brothels and other places of evil resort in Chicago. It is filled with the pious nastiness and abuse of the Church and of respectable people out of which he manufactures his sensations. The very worst that can be said of Chicago is that such a man made his way into Church circles and attracted public attention."

The *Ram's Horn* (Chicago) says:—"Mr. Stead s shocking revelation is more dreadful because there is incontestable evidence of its truth. Mr. Stead's investigations have been conducted by the aid of the best detective and legal help, and denials will be met with affidavit and proof. Mr. Stead s Chicago visit has borne immediate fruit in the stimulation to heartier appreciation of the privileges and duties of Christian citizenship."

The *Religio-Philosophical Journal* (Chicago) says:—"None but an experienced and thoroughly-equipped journalist, familiar with all the modern methods of obtaining facts, could have written a book like this with regard to a great city after only a few weeks' residence in it. So far as we can judge, the information in it is accurate. Leading Chicago dailies have abused Mr. Stead for writing this book, but a more sensible course would be to thank him, and use their influence in correcting as far as possible the bad condition of things."

The *Israelite* (Chicago) says:—"The great trouble with Mr. Stead is that he is in earnest. He wants to apply practically the precepts which are enunciated every week from the Christian pulpits of the world. This does not suit the average Christian, and the same is just as true of the Jew. It is refreshing to see a man who means and tries to elevate the world. The only reward that he will receive in his own time will be abuse and ridicule, and his detractors will be largely recruited from the ranks of the ministers of the Gospel, and all because he wants people to live according to the teachings of Christ.'

The *Union Signal* (Chicago) says:—"The book is having just the effect the author intended. It is rousing the ire of the public, and especially, as is natural, of the Chicago public. For obvious reasons the book is denounced by the bum and boodle element, and for reasons not so obvious it seems to be stigmatised as pernicious by the moral and Christian element. The shame of it is not that such rottenness should be published, but that it should be possible for it to exist."

The *Altruistic Review* publishes a long character-sketch of the book, which it says haunts the memory with the perpetual question, "What would Christ think?" at every turn.

The *North Western Christian Advocate* says:—"The book is a clean cut and very plain statement of the civic and social evils of Chicago. Much that he describes is of such a hideous character that it ought to lead to the reform of the city."

The *New York World* published a sixteen-column review and summary of the book. It says:—"The book is a startling *résumé* of Chicago life—social, industrial, political, and religious. Existing evils are exposed fearlessly, and the chief abettors are named without regard to persons or consequences. Of its kind it is the most sensational book of the decade. The striking cover of this dynamite-laden book, soon to be exploded in the hardened heart of Chicago, bears the figure of Christ, with one hand raised in rebuke against a half-score of typical Chicagoans who have just risen from the gambling table, their arms laden with gold."

The *Publisher, Bookseller and Stationer* of New York says:—" There are many statements that appear to be true, but unfortunately some of them are truths which would better be left unspoken.'

The *New York Voice* says:—" We know nothing so remedial as light, and while Mr. Stead is still something of an enigma to us, we believe in the imperative necessity of this sort of work. To turn on the light, and to keep it turned on, is a civic duty of surpassing importance. For one, we thank Mr. Stead, and invite his attention to a city called New York."

The *Cincinnati Enquirer* says:—" The book gives in pointed, bristling English Chicago life. It pictures what Christ would see if He came here. He has spared neither the rich nor influential."

The *News of St. Paul* says:—" The book will cause something in the nature of a social earthquake, not only in Chicago, but throughout the country. The subjects he has treated in a way conducive to moral health, though a stinging assault upon proud hypocrisy."

The *Rochester Herald* says:—" If Editor Stead is a crank, he is unquestionably a clever one. His indictment is a terrible picture of the worst phases of life in that magnificent city. It seems to us that many who differ with him widely, who do not by any means endorse all his extravagant statements, can read his book with profit, believing in the author's sincerity."

The *St. Louis Republican* says:—" The book will do a little and temporary good, as a well-drawn caricature generally does. Mr. Stead gives us no remedy. He could not tell how to change the natures of the idle and the vicious, or how to ship them to some other clime. He performs the easy task of slandering the city by describing its faults and essential characteristics."

The *Minneapolis Journal* says:—" The book does not justify the malevolence of Editor Stead's critics. If Mr. Stead has dared to paint a vivid picture of Chicago, Chicago ought not to be angry for having her plague-spots disclosed by an English censor. Mr. Stead prints little second-hand information. He went down into the slimy, odorous depths and saw for himself. He has produced a study which cannot fail to be of service to all genuine philanthropists and reformers. What Mr. Stead says about the despotism and lawlessness of the police not only is true to the letter, but is a burning disgrace to most of our American cities, where public sentiment, if it exists against flagrant abuses, is afraid to assert itself."

The *Philadelphia Press* says:—" The book will prove to be a revelation as well as a rude shock to thousands who have forgotten God in their pursuit of gain. It is well and strongly written, and shows in every chapter its truth and the deep earnestness of its author. Many will denounce the book while marvelling at its truth, and it will be read all the same until the story of Chicago's shame passes into history."

The *Detroit Free Press* says :—" The book has been condemned on the score of the immorality it treats of, but the work is clean. It is fearless, and shows the putridity existing in all large social systems. The book is worth reading, and suggests thoughts which should result in action."

The *Cleveland Citizen* says :—" This thought-creating work is a terrible indictment of the capitalistic system. Chicago is only doing on a large scale what Cleveland is doing on a smaller scale. Probably not seven of our twenty councilmen have clean hands. There is hardly a saloon-keeper, gambler, or keeper of a house of ill-fame that is exempt from paying blackmail in one form or another. The whole social system is rotten to the core."

The *Spokane Review* (Wash.) says :—" The book will supply matter for thousands of speeches by agitators and reformers. It is a picture of Chicago printed in vivid and virile language. If it succeed in awakening greater interest in much-needed reforms, Mr. Stead will have accomplished a great work and will deserve the thanks of generations yet to come."

The *Indianapolis News* says :—" Mr. Stead's book is wonderfully comprehensive, and although he is inclined to see the worst, he has written from general observation, and his tone is indisputably fair. Probably no one will dispute his facts."

The *Washington Star* says :—" The book represents an enormous amount of original investigation, and is of greater value to the student of municipal methods than any other publication known to book readers ; the whole field seems to have been thoroughly and deeply ploughed, and it will be surprising if improvement of the crop does not soon result."

The *Colorado Gazette* says :—" The book is awful and disgusting, but it is true, and its description is not overdrawn. We acknowledge that Mr. Stead is thoroughly in earnest, that he has written from good motives, that he has been perfectly fearless, and so far as possible perfectly fair. It is a book which it is thoroughly worth while seriously-minded adult persons to read and to ponder over when they read."

The *Toronto Mail* says :—" The strength of the book lies in the truthfulness of it. Mr. Stead's statements will be in some cases denied, but there is no doubt that some of them will receive corroboration even in the city of which he writes. The police system is said to be hopelessly corrupt and inefficient, and the pestilential dirt of the city of a nature to be deeply alarmed about."

The *Toronto Week*, in a lengthy review of the book, says :—" There are not many men in England who could write as Mr. Stead has done. The justification of the book is its truthfulness. We have not found a base insinuation in a single line. We do not see how the general conscience of Christendom is to be awakened to a sense of its great responsibilities and corresponding privileges save by just such exposures."

The *Toronto Evening News* says :—" No book has appeared for five years at once so startling and so revolutionary, written in plain Anglo-Saxon so as to reveal clear-cut the naked truth."

THE PRESS IN GREAT BRITAIN.

The *World* says :—"In Mr. Stead's pitiless and extraordinarily powerful examination of Chicago life by the search-light of Christian ethics, he practically arraigns the ideals, the aims, the methods, the entire social and moral economy of that great Western Republic which vaunts itself as the pioneer of democratic liberty and progress. We recognise the extreme value as well as the amazing force of his latest and certainly most brilliant achievement. The value of his book consists in its splendidly-marshalled array of evidences of the all-pervading corruption, the licensed perjury, the municipal incompetence, the squalid tyranny that dominate this free, glorious, and outwardly prosperous citadel of a young and unfettered democracy. It is easy to forgive the author of 'If Christ Came to Chicago' his faults of taste, his calculated sensationalism, and his occasionally wild riding of a hobby that has run away with him ere this, for the sake of his marvellously vivid and minutely-finished picture of the state of society evolved from the exalted New-World theories of liberty, equality, and independence."

The *Investors' Review* says :—"We may at once say, however, that the book is well worth reading in spite of its title and in spite of the tabooed subjects it in part treats of. The title is in some respects the worst thing about it, for whatever have we to do with the purely Semitic views of social economy enunciated in their greatest perfection by Jesus Christ? Apart from this point we have no ill word to say about his vigorous attack on the social abuses in the United States. . . . The corruptions he speaks of are there, and they are a warning to those people in the United States who are clean-handed, and sane, and honourable, that they had better be up and doing if they are to save society from shipwreck, the State from disruption. To the English investor the picture here presented of two millions of people held fast in the grasp of a few dozens of scoundrels, without serious effort to release themselves—of a people neglected and despised by those who should be their leaders—is full of evil portent. If the darkness now felt is not that which precedes the better day of awakened public spirit, of revived honesty in public affairs, the immediate future of the union is a future of decay, dissolution, and despair."

The *Daily Chronicle* says :—"Mr. Stead has left his mark upon Chicago. It can be no exaggeration to say that the most prosperous city in the United States cannot continue to be quite the same, since his visit, as it was before. It cannot fail to be epoch-making in the history of the city. This little book is thoroughly characteristic of the small weaknesses and the great strength of its writer. As a fearless and faithful study of a single example of modern social, political, and industrial organisation, it is without a rival."

The *Times* says :—"In spite of its tone of dogmatic infallibility and its many lapses of taste, Mr. Stead's work is not ill-calculated to attract and interest many readers. The work consists of two parts—on the one hand, a scathing survey of the actual condition of Chicago, its municipal corruption, its unabashed worship of wealth, its misery and its vice; and, on the other, an impassioned appeal to its inhabitants to regard their municipality as the Church of the future and to 'run it,' as perhaps Mr. Stead would say himself, in the true spirit of Christian fellowship. It is written vigorously, though with too frequent a condescension to the style of 'the New Journalism,' and it is evidently based on close observation and very painstaking inquiry."

The *Daily News* says :—"The section of Mr. Stead's book, entitled 'If

Christ Came to Chicago,' which treats of ' The Brotherhood of Labour,' has acquired an additional interest since its recent publication, both because it furnishes particulars of the American trades organizations, and because it surveys the question from the very scene of the strike riots which have given so great a shock to the civilized world. One passage, indeed, wears, in the light of the terrible events of the last few days, almost a prophetic air."

The *Pall Mall Gazette* says :—" We may sum up the book as a brilliant piece of ' special ' work in a style that recalls the Amateur Casual and General Booth, bearing the marks of some highly unpleasant investigation and much patient labour. Wealth has subjugated everything in Chicago, if we are to believe Mr. Stead. What we now want to see is the other side of the shield. Mr. Stead is a master in the art of creating sensations that good may come, and of such is this book. But one rises from the hastiest perusal with the feeling that there is too much red and black in the picture. Surely, even Chicago cannot be quite so black as she is here painted."

The *Echo* says :—" Mr. W. T. Stead's book on Chicago is so many-sided that it can hardly fail to attain much popularity in England. A syndicate of aristocratic Tories might find it worth while to promote its circulation as a counterblast to Mr. Andrew Carnegie's ' Triumphant Democracy.' The Social Purity Alliance might use it as an argument against government by police. The Liberty and Property Defence League will find in it some useful warnings against unbridled democracy. Enemies of Home Rule could show from the book what might be expected if an Irish Parliament sat on College Green. Ardent Protestants might draw therefrom not a few plausible pretexts for fighting the Church of Rome at every point. Socialists of every grade will see in it new arguments against the almost omnipotent tyranny of capitalism. Meanwhile we must warn people with queasy stomachs and complacently optimist views not to touch the book at all."

England says :—" The book gives a pretty complete sketch, superficial it may be, but thorough as far as it goes, of the seamy side of Chicago. We welcome the book for the lurid light which it sheds upon the conduct of public affairs in Chicago, which no doubt fairly reflects the general standard of society all over America. Coming from the pen of so pronounced and militant a democrat, the book, which is well and graphically written, has a peculiar value."

The *National Observer* says :—" Never perhaps has the uninviting work of moral sanitary inspection been conducted with such zealous completeness. Whatever be his motives, Mr. Stead is entitled at least to the credit of having done his work fearlessly and without reserve. He went forth to see the dark side of Chicago life, and he leaves no doubt but that he has seen it, and seen it whole. Mr. Stead has performed his self-imposed task with his wonted ability and somewhat more than his wonted audacity."

The *Speaker* says :—" If, as Mr. Benjamin Kidd tells us, the most salient feature of our social evolution is the growth of altruism, then its ultimate outcome ought to be that civic religion which is preached in Mr. Stead's remarkable book. Evidently it is not easy to practise civic religion unless you mingle with a strenuous purpose a robust strain of tolerance. Mere preaching would not have helped Mr. Stead to collect the material for this book. A sense of ungodliness without an appreciation of humour would not have begotten a fellowship with a perfect jewel of electioneering ' bosses ' in the person of Farmer Jones. If Mr. Stead had done nothing but discover

Farmer Jones, he would have enriched both the wisdom and the gaiety of nations."

The *Morning Advertiser* says:—"Mr. Stead's book may be earnestly recommended to the attention of that militant democracy, to whose Balak he plays a sorry Balaam."

The *Evening News* says:—"Mr. Stead has written a remarkable book, which has all the qualities of attraction and repulsion peculiar to his work. Readers need not go to Mr. Stead's book for anything agreeable. If they want a picture of a modern Sodom and Gomorrah they will find it in glaring and unsparing colours. The chapters disgust one with American democracy. Probably censure quite as strong as Mr. Stead's could be written about certain phases of London life; but on the whole Londoners can thank God that they are not as the Chicagoans are—at least not yet. We have an incorruptible city Government to redeem us from utter condemnation."

Black and White says:—"The book is a monument of labour and research. Indeed, for a stranger in the land to have thus mastered the shady side of a great city, is a very remarkable achievement. Perhaps nobody could have written this book but Mr. Stead. He is probably the greatest journalist London has ever known."

The *Westminster Gazette* says:—"An American paper's description of it as 'an exposure of Chicago's political thievery, public corruption, vicious reports, and disreputable millionnaires' seems pretty near the mark. Although many of the abuses of which it treats are essentially American, a description of its contents will be of interest to the English reader."

The *Weekly Despatch* says:—"Mr. Stead sums up the whole situation in a word—' Be a Christ,' contending that the sacrifice of the individual citizen to the communal regeneration—the revival of civic religion for the purging away of civic abuses and civic misery and shame—is the only remedy. All this it is possible for Mr. Stead to have said of the chief city of his own land. Whoever may object to the book, few will deny that it is calculated to awaken the public conscience. That this is the writer's object those who know him best are fully assured, and that he has accomplished it few will deny."

The *Newsagent* says:—"Mr. Stead's book is interesting, more so, because the writer does not see things through other people's spectacles, and has the courage of his convictions, or his impressions, and does not mince matters. ... We agree with Mr. Stead that in his book he has 'expressed more of what seems to be the essential gospel for the present day' than in anything he has printed before. Mr. Stead certainly has the courage of his convictions, and fearlessly expresses them, and in its modified shape the book has clearly a mission."

The *Christian* says:—"With an unsparing hand the veil is lifted, and the picture that faces the reader is a truly dark and appalling one."

The *Freeman* says:—"Mr. Stead may have put things in a highly-coloured form, but if there be but a fraction of truth in the reports that come from many directions, then it is time the Churches awoke and went forth to the battle."

The *Illustrated Church News* says:—"There is a great deal in this book which is worth study by those who have to guide others."

The *Baptist* says :—"In a remarkably interesting book Mr. Stead has given to America, and indeed to the world, a stock of information which calls for the most earnest, careful, and prayerful thought on the part of everyone."

In the *Woman's Signal*, Lady Henry Somerset says:—"The picture Mr. Stead draws is a dark one, but it does not, I think, sufficiently emphasize the reason of the shadow cast over the shores of Michigan. But Mr. Stead has, perhaps, not made sufficient allowance for the fact that he visited Chicago in an exceptional year. I take it, if the history of all cities were revealed, the police of Piccadilly, even though every precaution is taken as to their selection, would not in large degree outrank those of the great new city by the western sea."

The *Christian World* says :—"It is evident that American city administration generally is in need of thorough overhauling. Englishmen, as co-trustees with America of the cause of Anglo-Saxon Christian civilisation, have not only the right but the obligation to interest themselves in this problem. It will be to them a legitimate source of satisfaction if the researches and appeals of their enterprising countryman should contribute some of the motive power needed for the carrying out of this great reform."

The *Catholic Times* says:—"No subject at first sight would seem less capable of exciting the sympathies of the average British reader; under Mr. Stead's various and graphic pen it grows into a drama of the most intense and living interest. More effective Christianity is in truth the plea which rings throughout the whole of Mr. Stead's denunciatory outburst, and in so far at least all Catholics must be in hearty accord with him."

The *Methodist Recorder* says :—"Mr. Stead has written a remarkable and, as far as America is concerned, an epoch-making book. It is no exaggeration to say that no one but Mr. Stead could have written it. To one who has lived in Chicago, who has seen these things as Mr. Stead describes them, whose business it has been to inquire into them also as a journalist, the book, as far as its relation to facts is concerned, is absolutely flawless. There is rather a holding back and softening down than any attempt at exaggeration. But, as far as one can see, Mr. Stead has not omitted a single phase of life in Chicago, either good or bad, which would serve to throw light on the question."

The *Christian Commonwealth* says :—"We do not doubt that most of Mr. Stead's graphic descriptions fall short of the real case. But when we come to consider Mr. Stead's 'Civic Church,' we cannot help asking, if Christ came to Mr. Stead, what would the great Head of the Church say to the man who has invented a church wholly unknown to the New Testament? Mr. Stead's volume contains many things that might be useful to a detective force, but we seriously question the propriety of circulating such a book for general reading."

The *British Weekly* says :—"There is much that is forcible and vivid in Mr. Stead's pages. But what really concerns us is Mr. Stead's view of Christianity and the Church of Christ. Although the author has evidently written with great self-restraint and a desire to carry as many with him as possible, his book is a condemnation of existing churches, and a plea for a new organisation of the religion based on a new creed. There must be many who, like Mr. Stead, believe that the soul can eat and drink—that the ills of the world can be cured by the devices of materialism. We believe, and we are glad to believe, that Mr. Stead's fulness of bread and shortness of work will never be possible in this world. If they are, we shall need to pray more earnestly for grace so to pass through things temporal that we finally lose not the things eternal. Mr. Stead's scheme and all like it ignore the real need of the Church and the world."

The *Darkest England Gazette* says :—" It raises a shriek ; it throws aside the curtain ; it is revelation to the general public ; it is a book to make people think, talk, blaspheme and bless. The work is that of a conscientious and enthusiastic labourer in the cause of the commonweal. No one can turn from it without feeling the exceeding loathsomeness and corruption of sin. So far, that is a distinct gain. Any book which produces that effect makes for righteousness. Then, strange as it may seem, the book which gives such prominence to Christ is painfully silent as to *His* plan of salvation for Chicago."

The *Leeds Mercury* says :—" It may be doubted if there was a more notable event in connection with last year's World's Fair, at Chicago, than the visit of Mr. W. T. Stead to that wonderful city of the West. The Chicago newspapers have retorted upon Mr. Stead, that all he has to tell was well known before, but we may be sure that it was never told before with more striking effect. They will be ready to overlook all blemishes, and to forgive all faults, if they feel that here is a powerful voice raised on behalf of the poor, the forsaken, the miserable, and the oppressed, and against corruption and dishonesty in high places, against selfishness and self-indulgence, and against indifference and unchristian conduct among professing Christians. Mr. Stead's enthusiasm may prove contagious, and bring about amendment in quarters of which he did not even dream."

The *Hull News* says :—" It would be well worth while to place this book in the hands of every man to whom our cities, towns, and rural districts have delegated authority. The money would be well spent. If any book could urge, could plead with Demos to choose out the wisest and best of his townsmen to represent him, could induce the wisest to make the sacrifice of time, energy, and money required from them who would faithfully serve the community, I believe Mr. Stead's is that book. One cannot but marvel at its faith in humanity, that wonderful faith that can remove mountains, even mountains of iniquity, and cast them far out ; devils of greed, hate, lust, gambling, can all be overcome."

The *Manchester Guardian* says :—" A lay sermon that has overflowed into four hundred and sixty pages has a somewhat formidable look, but Mr. Stead's severest critics will not deny that it is an interesting study of the relations of religion to social and civic life. The general problem of Chicago is that of all large cities. Mr. Stead, who paints Chicago in the blackest colours, is not a pessimist, but an enthusiastic believer in the possibility of perfection, or of a close approach thereto."

The *Manchester Courier* says :—" Opinions will differ as to what are the salient features of the book ; but a terrible picture of social abuses and civic degradation is given in the section entitled 'Satan's Invisible World Displayed,' which is probably unequalled in its depth of blackness. May it not be asked, however, where is the account of that indomitable energy and courage, and all those sterling qualities which have so rapidly led to the development of Chicago ? "

The *Yorkshire Post* says :—" The moral aim of Mr. Stead's reflections is unimpeachable, but his statement of unsavoury facts is at times so daringly outspoken as to transgress the limits of good taste, while the manner in which he treats sacred names and attributes verges on irreverence. . . It will no doubt have the effect of arousing the great American city from her indifference to the vice flourishing in her midst. Democracy has nothing to be proud of in Chicago."

The *Sheffield Independent* says :—" Mr. Stead gives us a series of startling, almost appalling glimpses into the inner position—social, financial, political, and religious—of that city. It goes without saying that the book being Mr. Stead's is full of moral fervour and passionate sympathy with the victims of every wrong, and a self-sacrificing devotion to the task of bringing about the better time for which we are all yearning. Our readers will never be dull while inspecting under Mr. Stead's direction, and under the stimulus of his fervent eloquence, this most conglomerate of all cosmopolitan cities."

The *Grimsby Independent* says :—" Great as has been the attack upon this book, none of its assaulters has been able to disprove, or in fact attempted to disprove, the statements made in it. The terrible degrees of wretchedness, in its multifarious forms, are here depicted with a sternness appalling. Yet many of the life stories told, in their tragedy sad and bitter, are from time to time illumined with a humanity approaching the divine, when a poor creature cast out and trod upon, blossoms out, perhaps alas only for a moment, into a beautiful and loving sister of Christ. The book is the work certainly of an enthusiast, but can be read with great profit and interest."

The *Bradford Observer* says :—" It is a book which no social reformer can afford to neglect. Mr. Stead exposes with fearless ferocity the corruption which haunts all congested masses of humanity. The pity for us is that Americans do not write similarly about social evils in England, and with the same assurance that notice will be taken of their writings."

The *Newcastle Daily Journal* has no difficulty in bearing testimony to the fact that Mr. Stead has not misapplied his journalistic tact and his individual powers of investigation into the things that lie below the surface of society.

The *Coventry Advertiser* says :—" This is an extraordinary and most interesting book. It is well worth careful perusal, and no thoughtful student of the history of the day can read it without benefit."

The *Hunts County News* says :—" The remarkable book just published by Mr. W. T. Stead will have an influence—not only upon Chicago but upon other American cities—which is to-day simply incalculable. She can no more resist the call to arise and purify herself than she could resist the fire."

The *Northern Echo* says :—" Mr. W. T. Stead's new book is written with all the bluntness and directness of purpose that characterises this whilom editor of the *Northern Echo*, whether he is dealing with a naval programme, or turning a bull's-eye lantern upon London's chief vice."

The *Brighton Daily News* says :—" The book is well worth reading for its own sake, as the expression of a very remarkable mind, and as a searching and brilliant exposure of Republican methods of government— or rather, as far as Chicago is concerned, of mis-government. The astonishing thing about it is that the American newspapers are apparently taking it with equanimity as ' the same ancient story.' If these very serious charges of Mr. Stead's are regarded lightly, as 'nothing new' in Chicago, then it is high time the great World's Fair city began to turn over a new leaf."

The *Bristol Mercury* says :—" The social state of things which he describes is very bad, and undoubtedly his charges have a very substantial basis of fact. But he is not so instructive as he might be, and we are determined to make one protest against this vague, emotional denunciation of existing evils, which attracts so much attention and does so little good. Mr. Stead mingles a singular amount of worldly wisdom, however, with his heterodox Christianity."

The *Western Daily Mercury* (Plymouth) says :—" The latest effort of the editor of the ' Review of Reviews ' is quite in keeping with those with which his name has long been associated. His mission appears to be to put before the public gaze in all its naked truth the seamy side of human nature. Mr. Stead is evidently a believer in the saying that ' out of evil good cometh,' and that if any reform is brought about in the way he desires, it can be best accomplished by revealing in a matter-of-fact way the subject to be dealt with. That the volume will be in great demand goes without saying."

The *Scotsman* says :—" He has undoubtedly brought together a mass of information—mostly gathered at first hand—which suggests mixed reflections. Black, however, as he pictures the sins and sorrows of Chicago, it is not without features for which Mr. Stead can say a good word."

The *Weekly Scotsman* says :—" Mr. Stead does his work, so far as outsiders can judge, calmly and fairly. The book is one that should be read with close attention by all interested in matters political, sociological, and philanthropic."

The *Glasgow Echo* says :—" Mr. Stead and others are to be commended for giving some consideration to this important question, which deeply affects the workers. It is to be regretted that many who are anxious to be regarded as sympathisers with the workers in their reasonable demand for a fair and righteous wage neglect to inquire as to the conditions under which the work they want executed is performed."

The *North British Daily Mail* says :—" What is needed is 'civic religion.' Whether or not Mr. Stead's book may help to meet this want some may question, but it cannot be doubted that it will, at least, greatly aid in deepening the conviction that this lack in our civic life is a most serious one."

The *Dundee Advertiser* says :—" Mr. Stead is perfectly fearless. He does not scruple to send his electric light even into the very darkest corners. Nobody is too high for him to denounce, or too humble for him to rely upon for advice and information. The bigger the injustice, the more vigorous is his attack. In Chicago he found a splendid field for the exercise of his powers."

LONDON:
PRINTED BY WILLIAM CLOWES AND SONS, LIMITED,
STAMFORD STREET AND CHARING CROSS.

DATE D